The Christlike God

John V. Taylor

The Christlike God

SCM PRESS LTD

1992

Unless otherwise stated, biblical references are from The Revised English Bible, with some Hebrew names translated literally

ISBN 0 334 00179 X

First published 1992 by
SCM Press Ltd
26–30 Tottenham Road London N1 4BZ

Phototypeset by Intype, London
Printed in Great Britain by
Mackays of Chatham, Kent

'God is Christlike, and in him is no un-Christlikeness at all.'

A. M. Ramsey

Contents

Acknowledgments

A book, like a garden, is a collection of other people's flowers, and it will be apparent in the pages that follow that I am little more than an anthologist. Gratefully do I acknowledge that, like St Paul, I am debtor to Greek and non-Greek, to town no less than gown, and if, far more than he, I deserve to be dubbed 'Spermologos' – snapper up of others' words – I have at least enjoyed a free-range pecking.

I wish to thank particularly the Alister Hardy Research Centre for access to their personal accounts of 'religious' experience; the members of the Church of England's Doctrine Commission who in 1982 wrote individual submissions on 'The Weakness of God' and encouraged me to explore my own position more thoroughly; Wycliffe Hall, Oxford, for inviting me to give the Chavasse Lectures in 1985 and Marlene Speight for reducing them to disc; the Southwark Ordinands of 1986, the 'Romess' Summer School of 1990 and the Society of Ordained Scientists in 1991 for opportunities to try out certain sections in draft; and Archbishop Michael Ramsey for agreeing so readily, shortly before his death, to my use of his famous aphorism as my title.

Beyond words, however, is my gratitude to Sister Margaret of the Society of All Saints in Oxford for the hours she has spent with the convent's word processor to produce an immaculate script and the basis for an index; and to my wife, Peggy, for sharing the proof-reading and indexing but, above all, for enduring a closetted and preoccupied husband with the kind of love which is the theme of this book.

The Cover Picture

From 1917 until his death in 1941 the Russian artist, Alexei Jawlenski, though contending against the pain of advancing paralysis, strove to abstract into form and subtle colour the elemented structures and energies of nature. Yet from every one of these 'meditations', as he called them, there appears, as one gazes, the hint of a human face, blocked out in heavy shadows, as of a broken cross. They are nothing less than icons of the inexpressible mystery that surrounds and permeates all reality, which is not any identifiable being, but the source of all being, not any person, yet making itself known to us in approaches that may only be described as personal.

The painting which has been chosen for the cover of this book was done in 1936, entitled simply 'Water'. It has grasped the flow and counter-flow, the surface and the depth, the strength in weakness and the contained force of that element. And, as in all Jawlenski's 'meditations', the face, or presence, that gives its structure to the work is, in the conventions of iconography, unmistakably Christlike.

1

When I was a Child

How we Acquire our Idea of God

1. Much talk, little thought, about God

I am amazed that so few religious people ever stop and think about God. The thought of him may often be in their minds, but they do not explore it. It does not grow, is not allowed to change. His name may be on their lips and a sense of his reality in their prayers, but giving God a thought, however devoutly or frequently, is not the same as *thinking* about him. Many people have lived for years with an unexamined stereotype of God which inspires great loyalty and provides much comfort in an uncertain world, but its changelessness is more like the fixity of an idol than the trustworthiness of a *living* God. The true God must surely be more surprising than that, since our understanding of him can never be final. A Moses, or a Zoroaster, a Plato or a Paul, are his interpreters precisely because they were free to think *new* thoughts about him when the vision was granted.

What is perhaps even stranger is that those who are not religious have just as pre-packaged an idea of God as believers. It is odd that a generation that has so little use for creeds should produce so few free-thinkers. Most people simply assume that everyone knows what the word 'God' means. They may argue as to whether he exists or not, but believers and atheists alike take it for granted that they know what they are talking about. And should anyone, especially a passionately committed Christian, dare to depict God in a manner that differs from this stock icon, the irreligious take exception no less violently than the faithful. The agreed stereotype envisages a Supreme Supernatural

Personal Being who, since he made and rules the universe, must be All-Powerful (able to do anything he chooses) and All-Seeing (including the knowledge of future events) and is therefore responsible for everything that happens. Since he is also by definition presumed to be Perfect, the evident imperfection of this world is for many people the primary reason for not believing in him. Believers and unbelievers alike, however, take it as axiomatic that this is what they are either affirming or rejecting. It is only when one of them takes time to question this conception and goes on to ask, for instance, 'Perfectly what?' or 'Is it, in fact, *power* that is required to create something out of nothing?' that they may begin to detect the flaws in their logic and discover that they do not all mean the same thing by the word 'God'.

Many believers – and I do not speak of Christians only – are inhibited from speculating freely about their God because this seems to betray a lack of trust. They resemble those wives and husbands who shrink from taking a cool, detached look at their marriage partners, and at their own feelings towards them, because that kind of appraisal smacks of disloyalty. They are sadly mistaken, of course, since a truer understanding of the other person makes the relationship more, not less, stable – unless it is inherently founded on fantasy. So, too, an enlarged and mature perception of the meaning of the word 'God', even when it entails the loss of some of our earlier ideas of Deity, is bound to purify and strengthen our response to that Being, if we sustain that response at all. It is not that we have to adapt ourselves to changes in God, as we do to changes in our human partners. Rather, as more of the truth and splendour of the divine nature dawns on our slowly awakening minds, our relationship to God shifts and expands, and so does our interpretation of all existence.

2. Thinking or loving

Thinking about God is not everything, of course. It takes you only so far. It takes you to that point where you recognize all over again that you have reached the limit of thought and must change to a different vehicle if you mean to pursue your journey. The anonymous author of the little fourteenth-century treatise, *The Cloud of Unknowing*, says emphatically about all human approach to God, 'He may well be loved, but not thought. By love he may be gotten and holden; but by thought, never.'[1]

In that case, then, why should anyone attempt the exercise of thinking the unthinkable in the first place? If it is ultimately futile as well as arrogant, would it not be wiser after all to take 'God' on trust or, at least, let the word mean what it appears to mean to everyone else? No, not wise at all, for the simple reason that it does not get you anywhere.

For it is a misunderstanding to oppose reason and 'simple faith', or thinking and loving, as alternative routes to the knowledge of God, of which one proves to be a dead end. They are not alternatives but alternating stages in a long journey. All the thinking, the questioning, the exploring, is meant to be a handmaid to the loving, the praying, the contemplation. The relationship between thinking about God and the knowledge of God is rather like that between practice-sessions with a tennis coach and the ensuing match, or between a musician's studies with a maestro and the concert tour. The arduous scrutiny of previous habits, the unlearning of faults and the mastery of a different approach prepare the way for a new quality of performance on the courts or the concert platform. Practice makes perfect, however, only if the lessons have been so absorbed that they are reproduced *without thinking*. It will not succeed if they are consciously kept in mind. So it is by thinking about God and asking ourselves what we really mean by that word that we advance to the point at which we recognize that thought can go no further and that God lies beyond its reach. Then awe and love and worship must take over from reason. Yet this is not one of those negative lessons which, once learnt, block off all further exploration with a 'No Through Way' sign. Thinking up to that point where love must take over is an experience that has to be renewed time after time, since each rediscovery of it stirs a greater wonder, awe and adoration. Every time our thinking about God brings us to a fresh realization that he is unthinkable, we can better understand that darkness of 'un-knowing' in which God invites us to approach him. Then, for the time being, thinking has done its work and must be allowed to fall away, pushed down into another cloud, 'a cloud of forgetting', as the author of *The Cloud* calls it. For he certainly understood that thinking and not thinking are mutually necessary and complementary in the spiritual life. Evelyn Underhill, who edited the first reliable publication of *The Cloud* in 1912, said in her introduction, 'It was a deep thinker as well as a great lover who wrote this: one who joined hands with the philosophers, as well as with the saints.'[2]

It is they who allow themselves to speculate about God, and to wonder about him even as they wonder at him, whose faith and love is in the long run the most impregnable. Because they have not been afraid of letting their earlier ideas of God expand in the light of experience and discovery and prayer, false concepts have fallen away. Martin Luther said, 'the trust and faith of the heart alone make both God and an idol. If your faith and your trust are right, then your God is the true God. On the other hand, if your trust is false and wrong, then you have not the true God.'[3] The openness of mind that can let the false image go and welcome a truer understanding of God is the means whereby our faith and trust can be beamed in the right direction and without it revelation becomes impossible.

3. *The challenge of other religions*

There is a further reason why a pre-packaged and unexamined idea of God is likely to let us down, especially in these days. Followers of the different great religions of the world now meet as work-mates, business associates and neighbours to a far greater extent than ever before. We have common interests as members of the same communities, as parents of fellow-pupils in the same schools and, very often, as believers in spiritual values who do not want to drift into the pervading materialism. The sudden experience of this religious pluralism can easily sweep off their feet those who have a cut-and-dried notion of God, so that they hastily grasp either at a bigotry which has no respect for other faiths, or at a neutrality which is ultimately indifferent. On the other hand, those who have the habit of thinking about their own convictions and who view their understanding of God as a continuous discovery are able not only to recognize common ground in the things to which they and the followers of another faith bear witness, but also to discern the different faces attributed in the different faiths to the concept we all call 'God', and the different values and hopes that are derived from those different faces. Hinduism has borne her patient testimony to the inclusive Oneness of God, Islam has passionately proclaimed his Sovereignty, Judaism his moral Faithfulness. 'Such differences', says a Christian thinker after six years of study in the holy city of Varanasi, 'have often led, tragically, to arid disputes, fanaticism, and mutual anathema. The remedy for this is not to abandon our convictions, as is fashionable in some Western Christian quarters today, but to expose them to the full force of what the other man says. This can lead us to make new discoveries about our own faith.'[4] Such self-discovery, clarifying the particular understanding of God to which one's own religion bears its most characteristic witness, is the task to which the pluralism of our day impels us. The different 'faces' of God which are set forth will seem in some respects to be mutually contradictory, and for a long time we may not be ready to guess how, if at all, they will be reconciled. I believe we can confidently leave that in the hands of the future if we will only persevere in the agenda for today. And for us who are Christian this is, quite simply, in reverent appreciation of the beliefs and prayers of others, to affirm that, whatever else he is, God is Christlike – humble and vulnerable in his love – and that we have found in that revelation the salvation that all peoples look for. In saying this we would be standing with St Paul who resolved that 'while I was with you I would think of nothing but Jesus Christ – Christ nailed to the cross' (I Cor. 2.2).

They who dare to start thinking about God to this extent open themselves to doubt, atheists no less than believers. That is simply another way of saying that they open themselves to truth. This entails no disloyalty for the Christian who claims to trust in the Holy Spirit, that Spirit who 'explores everything, even the depths of God's own nature' (1 Cor. 2.10). Yet if such an exploring faith is going to lead us to revise our understanding of God, what kind of revision will this require? Must we abandon a familiar image, and the words associated with it, in favour of some quite different notion, or is it enough to modify the emphasis we give to one feature or another? Or, since each of us lives in fact with several different perceptions of God – one for public worship, another for our speculative discussions, and yet another at moments of profound personal significance like the birth of a child – shall we have to integrate them all in a single comprehensive concept which will necessarily be more open-ended? The answer to these questions will not be the same for everyone, for it depends on what the word 'God' has come to mean to each individual separately. As a first step towards a more receptive, searching mind, it is no bad thing to start by asking, 'How did I actually learn the meaning of the word "God", and how have I come to give that word the meaning it has for me?' That is a more complex question than appears at first, and it may be helpful to try it out on other, more mundane, words, for we are actually tackling the question of how we learn the meaning of anything at all – how do we know what's what?

4. *The four sources of knowledge*

How, to take an elementary example, does anyone learn what a dog is? Faced by such a creature in a picture book, the baby is taught to say dog, not duck; this is the voice of *authority*. Wheeled out in his buggy, he hears the same word applied to a somewhat similar beast that trots past at eye level; thus authority is rather disconcertingly augmented by *experience*. If he has been born into a household with a dog of its own, experience comes first; the baby has known Towser as a member of the family before ever he learnt to call it a dog. Even at this early stage of comprehension the interplay of authority and experience is teaching the child a fundamental fact of language, namely, that almost all words are generalizations. They are indicators of similarity. Towser, snoring in the armchair, may bear little resemblance to the animal in the picture book, yet the child soon learns to embrace both, and even more eccentric breeds beside, within the one term, recognizing the essential doggishness the word denotes. Language depends upon likeness.

More content and colour is added to the child's concept of 'dog' by scraps of *hearsay* – Mother Hubbard's poor dog who had no bone, the saga of the faithful hound pining to death on its master's grave, and Father's wartime story of the mad dog in some Mediterranean port whose bite made sailors foam at the mouth and die. These, too, bear the stamp of authority until, with maturer *reflection*, the child begins to discriminate between legend or anecdote and the sort of information that is found in the school library, and to distinguish the chance incidentals of his own store of hearsay and experience from the universal and generally accepted meaning of the word. So learning what a dog is has consisted of an interaction between authority, experience, hearsay and reflection. A little further thought makes it clear that authority in the matter, even the authority of a scientific or legal definition, must be derived from experience, one's own or that of many others, subjected to reflection, which results in a truer and richer generalization.

This suggests that hearsay, as I have called it, is of such little account that I should omit it from my list of the sources from which we derive our knowledge of things. But that would merely idealize the process and give us a false picture of it, since in fact we draw a great deal of what we think we know from popular consensus, folk tradition and unexamined assumptions, and we get by with it well enough for most of the time. A good deal of the common stereotype of what God is, which was outlined at the beginning of this chapter, belongs to this category. To take another everyday example, when we recall how we came to know what a Red Indian is, most of us would be bound to admit that for a long time our certainties were based on nothing but hearsay. Even the word 'Indian' is itself part of the hearsay. Picture books and comics, followed by dressing-up kits, travel posters and television westerns, have established with every appearance of authority a romantic image of the past that bears no relation to the present reality. This may never matter very much for most people. But for some it may mean that they return from a visit to Canada convinced that there are no Red Indians left and quite unaware that the charming girl who was their guide in Vancouver was a pure-blooded Kwakiutl from the north-west coast. They will certainly be the poorer for retaining their inadequate stereotype, but the ones most cruelly disadvantaged by it will be the Indians themselves. And no one in Britain will make the effort to replace hearsay with authoritative information unless they are already committed in some way to the interests of those Indians.

Before I go on to examine how these four sources of knowledge – hearsay, authority, experience and reflection – apply to our knowledge of God, there are two points arising from the foregoing examples which are worth making in parenthesis, as it were. Some of those who conclude from their experience of life that there is after all no God are reacting like the visitors to Canada who fail to find the Red Indians that hearsay has led them to expect. Given a truer understanding of what is meant by the word 'God', they might recognize that they have in fact encountered him without knowing it was he. The other point relates to the nature of language itself. As has just been said, all verbs, adjectives and common nouns denote *categories* of activity, or of quality, or of things, that share a particular likeness. Rabbits, rivers and roads all *run*, and so do successful plays, because the word, ignoring their differences, points to the idea of continuous progression common to them all. A rabbit is a *rabbit*, however, not by running but only by resembling other rabbits, including even the poor performer on the cricket field; and the White Rabbit is white only by resembling all other white things. Language is constructed out of similarities, and this makes it inherently incapable as a means of talking or even thinking about God the Nonpareil. 'To whom will ye liken me and make me equal, or compare me that we may be like?' (Isa. 46.5). The very structure of thought comes to the end of itself when it is directed towards the being of God. Whatever we say of God must be unsaid in the next breath, as the Hindu mystics perceived long ago: 'This thou art, yet this thou art not.'

5. Hearsay about God

When we consider how people come to understand what is meant by the word 'God' we are bound to recognize the fact that initially they depend mainly on what they absorb as young children from their homes. If the family is committed to a particular faith, the child's understanding is mainly a matter of belonging – 'God is important to us and this is what we do.' But in a less committed household understanding, such as it is, is pieced together from hearsay. In any kind of home, however, a child's question generally takes the adult by surprise and so tends to be answered by rote rather than with a freshly considered reply that takes the child's previous understanding into account.

'Where do all the stars come from?'
'God made them.'
'Where did our Nana go from the hospital?'
'She went to be with God.'

Those questions may often, of course, be answered without mentioning God. But, since religious belief is around in some form or another, the specifically religious questions arise sooner or later.

'Can God do anything he wants?'
'Yes, of course he can.'
'Does God know baby Kevin's ill?'
'I suppose so.'

Haphazard questions and instant answers flit in and out of a child's mind and do not at that stage add up to a coherent picture. The 'problem' of God will emerge later as a necessary component of maturer reflection. I include such answers to childish questions among the material I call hearsay, not because they are untrue, but because they are usually quick, routine responses, too unqualified and unexplained to stand up to the reality of experience. Moreover, in the child's mind those answers are absorbed along with an assortment of other adult expressions commonly overheard – 'God bless!' sung out in the same tones as 'Good luck!', 'God alone knows' uttered in exasperation over something totally beyond comprehension, 'May God forgive you' made to sound like the reverse of an absolution; or 'Barukh ha-shem' (Praised be his Name) interjected into a pious Jew's report of some trivial fortuitous event; or 'Yallāh' yelped all over the Arab lands to spur a donkey or dismiss a stranger: 'Get going!' And beyond the home circle, whether they articulate and practise a religious faith or not, the child picks up further bits of the jigsaw from the sight of clergy and places of worship, scraps of well-known hymns, stories from the scriptures relayed through television, RE classes or Sunday school, awareness of religious festivals of various faiths, visits to the homes of friends who say prayers or go to public worship, rumours of hell fire from one, of miraculous healing from another, old wives' tales of punishments for sin, old sailors' tales of deliverances at sea. The generalized understanding of God that anyone puts together would seem to depend on the mere accident of what has been overheard or seen or taught out of this mélange of popular hearsay.

Many youngsters are totally confused and, sensing the adults' lack of conviction, dismiss it in time along with Santa Claus and Superman. Yet children are better equipped than is generally supposed to sort out the reliable ideas from the nonsense, if only they are allowed to reflect in their own way upon all they have picked up. This genuine scrap of conversation, for example –

'Is God always with us?'

'Yes, he's always there.'

'Even in the dark?'

'Yes, that's why we needn't be afraid.'

'Doesn't he ever go to see the Murphys?' –

exposes, not the naïvety of the child, but the literalness of the pious parent whose habit of 'talking down' has denied the child's ability to handle symbols and grasp the transcendent. The child of strict rationalist parents who asked them one day, 'Does God know we don't believe in him?' was actually showing a more detached perspective than theirs. Another small boy was asked by his mother to rub her stiff back and 'make it better'. When she murmured, 'Oh, your hands are so clever; perhaps you'll be a doctor when you grow up', he tentatively answered,

'Yes; or I might be God.' This was not arrogance but a proper perception of the hierarchy of healing. Uninhibited reflection is more likely to foster spiritual awareness than cut and dried maxims. So, although it is surprising in the face of such a hotch-potch of religious hearsay, it is not an unmixed blessing that instead of exhibiting an infinite variety of private opinions about God, we seem in our pluralistic Western societies to have settled down to a more or less uniform generalization about the Deity we either do or do not believe in.

6. Religious authority

What shapes and sustains this improbable unanimity is the authority of the several traditions which stand in the background behind all the hearsay. Popular notions on the subject of God are a mixed bag, as we have just seen, but many of them are derived, in however garbled a form, from some established heritage of orthodox teaching. The adult parrying the child's sudden questions falls back on what he or she supposes to be the right answer, thereby acknowledging, however uncertainly, the authority of the tradition: 'That's what believers believe, isn't it?' In other words, people recognize that religion is not simply an individual's ideas or an individual's conduct, nor even the uninformed folklore of a community; it is a tradition embracing a creed and a code – 'What believers believe' and 'What believers do' – with official guardians to safeguard its continuity. The different religions have come into being in different parts of the world and at various periods of history. Each is a story of human response, both obedience and disobedience, to certain fundamental insights and subsequent interpretations. I cannot do better than quote Professor John Macquarrie's words about the distinctive and sometimes contrary ideas of God which they present.

> Each tradition seizes upon certain attributes that have been important in the formation of the tradition, and in all probability will develop these in a one-sided way, to the neglect of others that have been missed . . . It is surely significant that those who hold different ideas of God nevertheless assume that they are talking about the same God. Even if one thinks that a person in another tradition has got it all wrong or has seriously distorted views about God, it is assumed to be the same God.[5]

In each case it is the authoritative tradition that gives a religion its identity. It defines it. Now, every definition has a negative as well as a positive function, since it excludes whatever lies outside the boundary of its appellation. A tame fox cannot claim to be a dog, and the term 'Red Indian' does not include every North American who puts on a feather headdress. A West African who privately worships a fetish or ancestral spirit cannot be a Muslim, though he observe all the stipulated prayers and regulations of Islam. And if I believe, as some have taught, that Jesus Christ was not crucified but, having evaded death, was exalted directly to heavenly glory, I am not a Christian, however devoutly I revere him. At the same time, of course, tradition in its positive effect gives a religion its recognizable and comprehensive form. What believers believe as a general consensus and what believers do in the main are the two indicators that distinguish them from others as a community of faith. Seen in close-up, the consensus often appears to contain so many variants and deviations that anyone might be excused for doubting whether the tradition carries any authority at all. But when we take a more distant view and see one religion set in the context of others, then its distinctive family likeness is unmistakable, and the differences between Catholic and Protestant and Orthodox Christians, or between Sunni and Shiite Muslims, are seen to be secondary to what they have in common. Hence we can say that a stable, but not completely static, tradition gives identity, but not complete uniformity, to the adherents of a religion, and, conversely, that the continuity of their corporate identity enhances the authority of its tradition.

Yes, the continuity of a religious community certainly enhances the authority of its tradition, but it does not confer it. To say that the venerable age of a religion invests its institutions with an aura of authority may be true, but it is not the whole truth. It does not explain the powerful authority of new religions. More significant is the fact that any religious community regards its faith, its forms of worship, its ethical code and social structure as an inheritance issuing from a revelation given from beyond as the start of it all, and the authority of that tradition flows from this original given-ness. The authority permeates the whole tradition and is confirmed in the thinking and the praying and the living of the believers, generation after generation. Their corporate existence is the context in relation to which any individual believer's mental or moral struggle must take place. The individual's doubts and explorations are nourished by the stability of the tradition, even while the challenge of those doubts and explorations keeps the tradition flexible and alive. This theme has been very thoroughly unfolded in two recent reports of the Doctrine Commission of the Church of England,[6] but it is important to realize that it pertains, to a greater or lesser degree, to every religion.

In more than half the great faiths of the world the authority of the tradition resides with particular force in some body of scripture. The fixed and tangible nature of a written document imbues it with a reliable objectivity that cannot be found in any 'common mind', however hallowed. So Jews give a special reverence to the Torah (the first five books of the Bible) and, with it, to the other parts of the Old Testament. For Christians the New Testament, with the Old interpreted in the light of it, are their primary authority. For Muslims the Qur'ān is the definitive and final Word of God to humanity. The Sikhs look for guidance through reading or chanting passages from the Guru Granth Sahib; the Taoists in China find inspiration from the humane precepts of the Tao Teh King, written at the same period as the return of the Jews from exile; and Hinduism has been rooted in some of the most ancient literary works in the world, the four Vedas, the *Upanishads* and *Brāhmanas* and, afterwards, the great Epics. There are differences in the degree to which these scriptures are regarded by their devotees as inspired or God-given, ranging from the Qur'ān, which Muslims believe was transmitted from Heaven verbatim in Arabic to the mind and tongue of the Prophet Muhammad, to the sacred writings of Asia, whose authors thought of themselves as sages rather than prophets, and of God as both too transcendent and too all-pervasive to communicate himself as from one mind to another.

7. Scripture and tradition

Yet even those religions that invest all ultimate authority in an inspired scripture acknowledge the role of the believing community and its living tradition in interpreting and applying the holy writ. So there has usually been some amount of disagreement between the purists, who assign a very subordinate and inessential place to subsequent interpretations of scripture, and the developmentalists who are eager to make the original revelation applicable to the thought and conditions of their own time. This was the bone of contention between the Sadducees and the

Pharisees at the time of Jesus. The former were rigidly conservative in their adherence to the strict letter of the Torah, resisting every attempt by the jurists to interpret its regulations in more practicable terms and rejecting every speculative innovation, such as belief in the resurrection of the dead, which was not clearly stated in the Books of Moses. Ironically, such loyalty to the text became so archaic as to have no relevance as a guide for living, and left the Sadducees open to all the attractions of the Hellenistic world. The Pharisees, on the other hand, tried to bring about the reality of a holy people, living in accordance with the Torah, by specifying exactly what action would constitute obedience in every possible circumstance. So their jurists built up over the years a body of opinions and precepts as an oral tradition or *halakhah*, supported by explanatory comments or *midrashim* on particular passages, all of which was to be venerated equally with the scriptures. After the defeat of the two great insurrections and the destruction of the Jewish state, the Pharisees codified the tradition in the form of the *Mishnah*, and this was combined with further commentaries to form the *Talmud* in the fifth century. Thereafter the task of interpretation was continued to the present day, for Judaism regards itself as a community of living interpretation, and the meaning of 'Torah' is expanded to embrace 'the sum total of Jewish teaching'.[7]

No Christians could ever totally deny their dependence on a tradition of interpreting the Jewish scriptures in the light of the Apostles' experience of Jesus Christ. Indeed, his own teaching, as recounted in the Gospels, was in many respects a rabbi's interpretation of the Torah, albeit with an orientation peculiarly his own. The special regard that most branches of the church have had for the writings of the early Fathers is a somewhat less formalized equivalent to the place of the *Talmud* in Judaism. Yet the same argument has raged, especially since the fifteenth century, over the degree of authority that should be ascribed to the tradition, an argument in which both sides have laid claim to the operation of the Holy Spirit. In a recent attempt to reconcile the opposing views, the issue was set out in these terms:

> Tradition has been viewed in different ways. One approach is primarily concerned never to go beyond the bounds of Scripture. Under the guidance of the Spirit, undiscovered riches and truths are sought in the Scriptures in order to illuminate the faith according to the needs

> of each generation . . . Another approach, while different, does not necessarily contradict the former. In the conviction that the Holy Spirit is seeking to guide the Church into the fullness of truth, it draws upon everything in human experience and thought which will give to the content of the revelation its fullest expression and widest application. It is primarily concerned with the growth of the seed of God's Word from age to age.[8]

No such argument exists, or could exist, among Muslims. Islam is inherently fundamentalist inasmuch as its revelation – what has been given from heaven – is the actual text of the self-explanatory, all-commanding Qur'ān. Even so, there is a supplementary body of tradition, the *Ḥadith* – that is, scrupulously attested incidents and comments from the life of the Prophet, providing a model of conformity to the Qur'ān, with guidance over matters not touched upon by the Qur'ān itself. Among the Sunni Muslims there has also been a strictly controlled sounding of the consensus of the faithful which carries some authority. All these elements have contributed to the *Sharī'ah*, the divinely willed law of Islam. In many respects the *Ḥadith* traditions about Muhammad are for Islam equivalent to the Gospel accounts of Jesus Christ but, as Bishop Kenneth Cragg has observed, 'truth-through-personality' is in Islam 'a secondary, ancillary vehicle of revelation' compared to truth in words, whereas in Christianity it is 'crucial and definitive'.[9]

The guidance of sacred scriptures, therefore, has always to be sought by asking, not only, 'What do they say?' but also, 'What does it mean?' So, to a greater or smaller degree, their authority resides in the interplay between the given text and the shared thinking about it within the believing community, past and present. Interpretation, however, has passed through strange fashions in the course of its history, so that Muslims, and all others of a puritan frame of mind, have reason to view it with caution. In a few instances we even find St Paul treating Jewish scriptures in a way far removed from the 'simple sense' enjoined by the Protestant reformers, as, for example, in his Epistle to the Galatians where he takes the story of Abraham's two wives as an allegory. In later centuries both Jewish and Christian schools of theology carried this allegorizing style of interpreting their scriptures to extravagant lengths. For one thing, it enabled them to explain away some of the Bible stories which, in their literal sense, were condemned by their pagan adversaries as morally offensive or absurd. Such a method of interpreting scripture has enjoyed a long history and is not without its exponents in these days, especially among preachers with a taste for psychological archetypes and symbols. There have been other schools of interpretation that have taken more politically slanted liberties with the plain meaning of scripture. This was popular in the sixteenth and seventeenth centuries, that great period of religious diatribes, and has returned to fashion in our own time. Yet the general orientation of thought in these days towards the scientific approach to knowledge predisposes most people to feel that such a treatment of scripture is too subjective to offer the authority they are looking for and to prefer a more analytical and historical interpretation. The sort of questions they expect the interpreter of scripture to try to answer are: What kind of statement is this, and in what circumstances was it made in this form? What was it intended to mean then, and what significance does it carry now? Those seemingly simple questions are far more complex than they appear. Nevertheless they are the questions that the believing communities of both Jews and Christians feel compelled to put to their scriptures in these days, and this is the style of interpretation that will serve their respective traditions at this moment in their history.

8. Progressive interpretation

The point I am making is that holy writ retains its authority for a community of faith only inasmuch as that community is free to put its most pressing questions to the scriptures and find the meaning that they hold for that community at that point in time. This is not to say that the believing community imposes its own interpretation upon those scriptures, since its approach to scripture must always be made in faith, and faith has empty hands and an open mind. But neither is there one correct interpretation for all times, else there would be no more need for seeking or for faith. A very old fable tells how Moses re-appeared to sit at the back of a lecture hall where the renowned second-century rabbi, Akiba, used to expound the Torah, and was dismayed to find he could understand no part of what was being taught. But his mind was set at rest when, in reply to the student who asked, 'How do you know this?', he heard Akiba say that it was a teaching given to Moses at Sinai![10] Whatever is 'once for all delivered unto the saints' remains living and authoritative only by being freshly understood under every new condition of social and religious change.

But the process of interpretation is not found only outside, and subsequent to, the scriptures; it is visibly at work within the Bible itself. What are the New Testament epistles but interpretations of the meaning of Jesus Christ? Each of the Gospels is a telling of his story, not only with a particular readership in mind, but from a particular theological position. Moreover the New Testament as a whole is spattered with quotations from the Jewish scriptures, witnessing to the mounting excitement with which the members of the new Christian movement were discovering fresh meanings in familiar texts, sometimes, we have to admit, by means of fairly far-fetched interpretation! A great deal of the Jewish Bible is a chronicle of history, but it is history interpreted. Any reader can see that the Book of Judges records the struggles of different tribes against neighbouring peoples who were competing for the land during the disturbed time of the Hebrew settlement, and that these are set down into a pattern that points this simple moral: each time the nation adopted the gods of its pagan neighbours it was subjected to invasion and oppression, but whenever they turned back to their own true God he raised up a deliverer for them. The later history of the two divided kingdoms is interpreted from a similar theological view, with successive kings who were either 'a Good Thing' or a disaster. To recognize this is not to belittle the work of those who put the annals together in this way. Their reflective assessment of the story is a great advance upon the boastful chronicles of the great kingdoms round about them. The Hebrew prophets were supremely interpreters of the moral significance of the events of their day, but frequently their gift of perception was turned upon some personal and mundane experience – the sight of an almond in early bloom or a basket of rotten figs, the conception of a child or the breakdown of a marriage – and they saw significance in it like a revelation. That 'seeing' is the perennial gift of the Holy Spirit 'who spake by the prophets'.

There in a word we have it. What speaks with authority in the Bible is neither philosophical argument nor ethical precept but experience, and the subsequent reflection whereby its significance is perceived. The theology and the morality are derived from that, but the *revelation* lies in the experience and in the reflection upon it. That is where the undeniable sense of a given-ness is to be found. This is the same basic fact that emerged from our earlier examination of how we learn what a dog or anything else is. Authority in the matter is derived from experience (one's own and that of many others) subjected to reflection (p. 6).

9. Four revelation experiences

The Bible, of course, like life itself, is so crammed with fortuitous incidents, of which the significance is sometimes quite obscure, that at first it must seem singularly unhelpful to be told that the truth about God has been revealed in the experiences recounted in its pages and in the later reflections upon them which are also found therein. Yet only a little familiarity with the Bible is needed to discover that it is rather like a symphony in which, among an enormous sequence of variations, repetitions and innovations, a few dominant themes emerge and are explored with an ever richer unfolding. In the Old and New Testaments four experiences are paramount – the Exodus, the Davidic Kingdom, the Babylonian Exile, and the event of Jesus Christ. It is hard to think of any element in the Bible that is not derived from reflection on one or other of those four revelation experiences. So far as the Jewish scriptures are concerned, this becomes very evident when one looks for the national experiences that are most frequently referred to in the Psalms.

However small-scale and obscure the actual escape of a few tribes from the Pharaoh's labour camps may have been, as many Old Testament commentators suggest, it was for those slaves such a momentous deliverance that the folk-memory of their experience and of the part played in it by Moses became the property and the determinative revelation of the whole emergent Israelite nation. This was the ever-remembered experience that defined their identity and that of their God, 'the Holy One of Israel'. Their major communal festivals, though rooted in the agricultural cycle, were essentially a celebration of the Exodus, the wilderness wanderings and the Law-giving at Sinai. Many of the social ordinances of the Torah were related back to the demands of that experience: 'Remember that you too were slaves, were aliens, in Egypt' (Ex. 23.9; Lev.19.33–4; 25.35–8; Deut. 15.12–15; 24.17–22). In time they came to re-tell the stories of the Patriarchs and even of the Creation of the world in the light of their reflection upon this experience of the Exodus, and their prophets harked back to it for the promise it held out to the Jews in exile (Isa. 42.16–19; 51.10,11; Ezek. 20.34–38).

The second revelation experience was the reign of David, the shepherd king, that brief moment of national glory and unity. From nostalgic reflection on that memory sprang the theology of the idealized kingdom, the holy city and its shrine, the spiritual centre for all nations. The tradition of a divinely promised perpetuity to David's line kindled later eschatological hopes of a reign of peace under another anointed king, the Messiah or Christ, while psalms that may have started as triumph songs for the victorious return of an earthly king lent themselves to a more religious use as proclamations of the ultimate reign of God. The school of writers who compiled the two books of Chronicles and the books of Ezra and Nehemiah in their final form were strongly influenced by the theological significance, as they saw it, of the Davidic monarchy, and their way of treating the history of the kingdom of Judah is an interesting example of the process of reflection upon the memory of a crucial experience.

The third of these seminal experiences was the destruction of that kingdom of Judah early in the sixth century BC and the Babylonian Exile. This must have affected the Jewish nation as a reversal of the other two experiences and a negation of all that had flowed from their reflections upon them. The Exile spelt dispersal, statelessness, victimization and the start of an age-long struggle for the survival of their identity. For although the return to the Land, when it came, was heralded as a second Exodus, in the event it was only partial and spasmodic. The diaspora remained as a fact, not only in Mesopotamia and Egypt, but in Jewish consciousness. From it grew the Jews' dependence upon the written scriptures and the synagogue services, their characteristic ideal of personal piety, the humane and cultured ethics of the wisdom literature and the cryptic imagery of apocalypse. Of the three great theme-experiences of their history, the Exile is perhaps the one that is etched most deeply into the corporate memory of the Jewish people because it has been so often re-enacted in later centuries, up to the Holocaust of our own day. It is also, without doubt, the great biblical theme with which Christians have been least able to identify themselves, even during the periods of their fiercest persecution. How many Christian hymns, for instance, have made use of the imagery of the Exile? This testifies to the buoyancy we derive from our faith in the resurrection of Jesus, but also, less happily, to a facile triumphalism which has disqualified us from entering into either the spiritual insights of Judaism or the Passion of God.

There remains, then, for Christians, the fourth and supreme experience to which the Bible bears witness, namely the life, death and resurrection of Jesus. Like the Exodus, the reign of David and the Exile, this was, for those who experienced it, a revelation of the true nature of God which had not been disclosed or fully apprehended before. 'From many aspects and in many ways God spoke in the past to our fathers through the prophets and in these last days he has spoken to us in a Son' (Heb. 1.1,2). 'God, who said, "Let light shine out of darkness", has shone in our hearts to give the light of the revelation of the glory of God in the face of Jesus Christ' (II Cor. 4.7). In their reflection upon their experience of him the disciples of Jesus gathered up many of the earlier ideas and images associated with the Exodus and the Davidic kingdom, and the whole New Testament is in fact a body of interpretations of the experience of Jesus Christ arising from their reflection upon it.

10. *Authority discerned and authority conferred*

So in summary at this point we can say that what is authoritative for humanity's knowledge of God is the revelation communicated to a believing community through certain given experiences and its continuing reflection upon them. Leaving on one side the comparison of the different revelatory experiences in different religions (since I am not here considering which concept of God is the more true, but how we arrive at our concepts), there remains an undeniable 'circularity' in this method of identifying the point of authority. The believing community derives its knowledge of God from certain special experiences, yet it is the community itself that decides *which* those experiences are. The believers, or people of insight among them, ruminate further on those experiences and then make their ruminations the touchstone for judging truth from falsehood. The church takes it upon itself to define the canon of its scriptures, yet submits its exploration of doctrine and ethics to the ultimate authority of that selection of scriptures. The more crudely one states this 'to-and-fro', the more clearly one sees that this is actually how authority 'works' in all walks of life.

There is a formal authority which is conferred, and there is an inherent authority which is discerned. The former is official and objective, the latter is personal and subjective. If we describe someone as a recognized authority on Middle Eastern affairs or someone else as the acknowledged authority on the paintings of Thomas Gainsborough, we are saying that a combination of painstaking study, exceptional opportunity and a natural flair has won such general esteem that anyone else seeking information on either of those subjects would be stupid to ignore the wisdom of such an expert. Nonetheless, however high their reputation, it would not of itself entitle either of them to countermand other people's decisions or stop them making a mistake. But if the one were to be made a Deputy Under Secretary or even a Head of Department in the Foreign Office, or the other appointed to the Directorship of the Tate Gallery, they would begin to exercise an executive, and not merely a moral, authority. The former could initiate the change towards a more amicable relationship with a foreign power; the latter could forbid the purchase of a picture he believed to be a fake. St Francis of Assisi would never accept the office of Minister General over his Friars when it had been created, yet the whole Order recognized intuitively the power of his inward authority, just as the people had sensed the authority of Jesus long before. Francis himself understood the influence he could wield and, even when his cherished ideals for the Brotherhood were being threatened, he refrained from using it to override the official authorities of the Order, so that he might keep intact the powerlessness of poverty to which he was committed.

There is, then, a statutory authority, and there is an intrinsic authority such as may be met in a person, a work of art, a new insight or a personal experience, and which, once perceived, evokes an unconditional 'Yes!' That is the kind of authority possessed by the revelatory experiences recounted in the Bible and by the understanding of God and of humanity that was derived from them through later reflection. And when the Jewish, and later the Christian, church defined the canon of their scriptures, they conferred on them a statutory authority whereby they became the touchstone for the discernment of truth and error.

But the establishment of a touchstone or criterion implies an expectation of new insights and continuing speculation still to come which will need testing. The given-ness of the revelation and the authority accorded to scripture are not meant to make the Holy Spirit redundant or terminate the life-giving flow of experience and reflection. For experience and reflection, which were the vehicle of the revelation recorded in the scriptures, are still the only means whereby anyone can say 'I know what you are talking about' when God is mentioned. It is of the utmost importance that we should lay hold of this fact for, until we do, religion is likely to remain increasingly theoretical to those who have it and a closed book to those who do not.

2

What we have Heard, What we have Seen

The Nature of Revelation Experience

1. Experience under suspicion

There are very few subjects that are still taboo as topics of general conversation, and 'God' is certainly not one of them. Yet while people chat far more freely about religious belief than they did thirty years ago, almost all their talk refers either to hearsay, 'Did you read . . . ?' and 'I've been told . . .', or to authority, 'The Bible says . . .' and 'Catholics believe . . .' By this and other means the speakers distance themselves from the subject. God is turned into an arguable concept that has been either upheld or disputed by philosophers, defined more or less satisfactorily by theologians, and left out of account, necessarily, by scientists. Listening to this talk, or reading the textbooks of dogmatic theology, anyone might conclude that experience plays as little part in our knowledge of God as it does in our knowledge of dinosaurs. In the course of a typical discussion as to why God did not intervene to prevent a recent disaster or whether religious education should be included in the school curriculum, the participants are not expected to mention their own prayers or recall some miraculous deliverance in their own experience, and, should someone do so, the conversation founders as though the rules of the game have been broken.

Books about belief in God usually pay their respects to religious experience as a phenomenon that has to be taken into account, and then quickly proceed to qualify this admission with warnings against subjectivism and inconclusiveness, as though the two checks of past tradition and on-going reflection were not there to correct those very liabilities. An example of this guarded treatment appeared in the Report of the Doctrine Commission of the Church of England, *We Believe in God*, in 1987.

> Those who believe in God seldom rely on rational thought alone. They testify to a variety of 'religious experiences', from a general sense of the holy or numinous on the one hand to a sensation of being directly addressed by a transcendent being on the other. Such experiences are notoriously hard to evaluate . . . Moreover, not only is such experience open to the charge of being subjective, it also appears to be unequal, if not haphazard, in its distribution. Many profound believers claim to be ignorant of it; many powerful experiences fail to result in a solid faith . . . Such experience is often ambiguous, and cannot stand on its own as an argument for the existence of God. But it is right to take account of it as one of the factors which cause people to return to the sources of their religious traditions . . . [1]

In other words, experience must be cautiously recognized as a powerful stimulus recalling people to the paths of trustworthy tradition, but not in itself a reliable ground for faith. Those who affirm this view – and I was one who subscribed to that report of the Doctrine Commission – seem strangely unaware that it contradicts the testimony of the Jewish and Christian scriptures in which, as we have seen, experience and event are the primary vehicle of God's self-revelation. Loftily conceding that such experience is 'one of the factors which cause people to return to the sources of their religious traditions', we ignore the plain fact that many of the most effectual religious experiences have served to distance people from their traditions rather than drawing them back, and we forget that the true source of the tradition was originally experience itself. The downgrading of experience in the theology of recent centuries has been largely due to the fact that our thinking about God, unlike that of the Bible, has been plagued by the question of his existence. In that particular debate, of course, another person's experience, if it appears to be uncorroborated, is open to too many explanations to carry much weight. On the principle that 'fifty million Frenchmen can't be wrong', the prayers, the hymns, the shrines of humanity are still a powerful testimony, but not a proof that the Object of this worship *is* anywhere beyond the devotions of all these people. By its very nature it is doubtful whether the self-existent reality of God can be either proved or disproved. Within the terms of the argument, and for so long as the argument persists, he must remain either the great Probability or the great Improbable, yet never on that account a matter of indifference, since the stakes are so high whichever option one backs.

But it needs to be said loud and clear that there are other questions about God besides this which call for discussion. Indeed, 'What do we mean by "God"?' must logically precede 'Does he exist?', and in any consideration of that prior question experience, and reflection upon it, is surely paramount. For, in answering the question, 'What do we mean by "God"?' logic demands that, rather than putting experience aside as 'unequal, if not haphazard, in its distribution' and 'often ambiguous', we should take note of the fact that people's encounters with transcendence *are* for the most part sporadic and arbitrary, not subject to human bidding, and when they happen they are usually open to more than one construction. On further reflection those facts might suggest that this transcendence, whatever it may be, appears to behave more like the subject and initiator of the encounter than its passive object, and that an impression of ambiguity is exactly what we should expect in a supposed encounter with a dimension of being that cannot be contained within the categories of human thought; it may be the ambiguity of 'This Thou art, yet this Thou art not.'

2. The Beyond in the midst

A much more uncritical but equally negative treatment of religious experience is that which attends exclusively to narrowly defined instances of conversion, miraculous deliverance, psychic phenomena or mystical states of mind entirely distinct from those of ordinary life. The most grievous consequence of this is that large numbers of people live in the conviction that God belongs to the realm of the supernatural, the occult or the paranormal and, since this has never been their world, religion is not for them. What they are rejecting is actually a false image of God. He is not to be thought of as a supernatural being among other lesser beings, nor as the supreme power among other forces. Strictly speaking, God cannot be perceived as an entity in himself any more than the ocean can be comprehended by a fish, for in him we and all things live and move and have our being.

> The Christian God is not an object in the universe and is not, therefore, a possible competitor for space in it. So it would not be true to say that we sometimes experience God 'neat', as it were, and sometimes at second hand . . . All our experience is experience of the world – of things, of persons. Experience of God is to learn to see these things and those persons in a certain context – a context for which we can never find adequate description and which must never be reduced to being one item among others.[2]

This truth, however, must not be pushed so far as to deny all validity or significance to experiences which, at least to the recipients, are 'special' and revelatory. Experiences of God are experiences of the ordinary seen in the context of an otherness which enfolds them all and lies within them all. If this dimension of otherness within everything is universal, dynamic and all-pervading, as believers affirm, and if human consciousness is capable, as it appears to be, of sensing the impact of that reality in some way or other, it would be more natural to assume that some encounter with it is an experience that most people have known, though they may not have associated it with any thoughts of religion. The secularization of the human outlook may have banished the supernatural from the day-to-day conversation and calculations of millions of people, but that is no reason for supposing that the beyondness at the heart of things discloses itself any less widely or frequently.

What needs to be taken into account is a far more general range of experience than the strictly psychic and paranormal, or the visionary faculty of a William Blake who, at four years old, saw God 'put his head at the window'. Such phenomena may have to be considered as part of the total picture, but much more significant is the essential normality of those occasions when people of all ages and backgrounds are made powerfully aware of a dimension of being, a vitality, an otherness within things, which transcends the mere objectivity of whatever it is that has caught their attention. The very form of words we thoughtlessly choose to use betray our recognition of a significant distinction between two types of perception. We say 'it caught my attention', not 'I gave my attention to it'. If we say 'I hit upon an idea the other day' we have chosen to emphasize our own mental creativity; but if we say 'An idea struck me the other day', the emphasis is subtly different. By making the idea the subject of the sentence we are conveying our real experience of being, in some sense, at the receiving end, the object of something other that was acting upon us, making itself known. Afterwards, we may wish to deny that aspect of the experience which our choice of words has correctly laid bare, but in fact we have truthfully described one of those moments when what is there is no longer something we are observing, thinking about or enjoying, but has taken the initiative, as it were, in making its impact upon us. 'It came to me', we say, rather than 'I came upon it'.

What people encounter at these times is not some additional entity over and above the other objects, nor even a definable property of those objects, such as their beauty or strangeness; it is the inwardness or inherent reality of the objects themselves, shining out with an intensity not previously perceived. This is what an artist is able to discern in the physical forms and substances of the world and to impart to the material in which he or she is working. Barbara Hepworth put her finger on it when she wrote, 'Vitality is not a physical, organic attribute of sculpture: it is a spiritual inner life. Power is not man power or physical capacity: it is an inner force and energy.'[3] At such moments the recipient of the experience is compelled to recognize that there is more to things than meets the eye or any of our other senses. Something that is universal shines through one particular phenomenon, timelessness hovers within some fleeting instant, and inexpressible significance surrounds a commonplace event. An otherness is revealed which is nonetheless essentially inherent in the object itself. George Herbert's simile of looking either at or through a pane of glass comes to mind; but Edith Sitwell more exactly captures the essence of it in her poem, *How many heavens?*, of which these few lines convey the gist.

The flame of the first blade
Is an angel piercing through the earth to sing
'God is everything!
The grass within the grass, the angel in the angel, flame
Within the flame, and He is the green shade that came
To be the heart of shade'.[4]

Barbara Hepworth's reference to 'vitality' and 'power' is reminiscent of the concept of *mana*, that Polynesian term for the much more widespread idea of a spiritual force emanating from certain individuals or inanimate objects. In his great book, *The Idea of the Holy*, Rudolph Otto used the word 'numinous' to describe such encounters with immanent power. It is a significant word, being derived from the Latin verb *nuo*, 'I nod' in recognition or command, and speaks of that sense of a personal communication, of being noticed and addressed, which accompanies the experience. It corresponds to Martin Buber's description of the quality of relationship that people find they have at certain moments with the physical world around them: 'You say *Thou* to it and give yourself to it, it says *Thou* to you and gives itself to you'.[5] Because of Otto's frequent use of the word 'awe', subsequent writers have wrongly limited his idea of the numinous to the primitive dread evoked by thunder and other uncomprehended powers of nature, and have thereby made it seem an improbable reaction for contemporary men and women. But, as anyone with a reasonably long experience of counselling can testify, certain moments of overwhelming creaturely abasement are far from unusual in these times, though modernity makes people more reluctant to acknowledge them even to themselves than they were in the past. A purely aesthetic experience may turn suddenly into a surprisingly religious sense of guilt and contrition.

> A friend persuaded me to go to Ely Cathedral to hear a performance of Bach's B minor Mass. I had heard the work, indeed I knew Bach's choral works pretty well . . . The music thrilled me, until we got to the great Sanctus. I find this experience difficult to define. It was primarily a warning – I was frightened. I was trembling from head to foot and wanted to cry. Actually I think I did. I heard no 'voice' except the music; I saw nothing; but the warning was very definite. I was not able to interpret this experience satisfactorily until I read some months later Rudolph Otto's *Das Heilige*. Here I found it: the 'Numinous'. I was before the Judgement Seat. I was being weighed in the balance and found wanting.[6]

Properly understood, however, Otto was not confining his instances to feelings of awe and dread, but was talking about a wide range of experiences that might excite intense delight, wonder, reassurance, fear or release, or all of these together. He would certainly have wished to assert that humanity has not outgrown the numinous.

A more recent historian of religion, Professor Ninian Smart, has proposed that a distinction should be drawn between numinous and mystical experiences. The numinous, he argues, is experienced as something exterior to the self, an 'Other' that stands over against the self in an I-Thou relationship; whereas a truly mystical state is turned inwards to the depth of the soul, there to find the essential oneness of the true self with the universal Self, the Absolute that is beyond all thought and imagination.[7] But this opposition of exteriority to interiority rests too heavily on the practice of mysticism as a deliberate pursuit, and applies more to the inferences drawn from experiences of intense perception than to the experiences themselves, which are involuntary and cannot be so neatly classified. A disclosure of one's true self below the pretensions of the surface ego is the same revelation as a perception of the vibrant reality of things within their everyday appearance. It comes by way of seeing new significance in the ordinary, and it brings a momentary intuition of the greater, unimaginable reality beyond that inmost self or that mysterious outer world, enfolding both in an ultimate unity.

Martin Buber maintained that these occasions of special awareness come and go with no consistency – as the Doctrine Commission Report, already mentioned, pointed out. They can neither be bidden nor induced, and even the strength of association cannot ensure that they will be repeated when the place of their previous occurrence is visited again or the circumstances reproduced. From primitive times until our own days priests and artists alike have claimed that when the *form* is faithfully re-presented the *power* will be there; and honest devotees have known that it is not so. Moreover the experiences of intense perception vary greatly in the impact they make and the significance that is given to them. Often they are not associated with religion, being essentially aesthetic, while at other times the experience lifts a person to a plane of consciousness far surpassing the usual expectations of religion. Because of the strangeness and surprise, those who have had the more ecstatic or revelatory types of experience, whether aesthetic or religious, tend to treat them as extremely personal and private, not trusting the possible reactions of other people; and so a great deal is never reported. Even so, references to the phenomenon crop up in autobiographies, television interviews and articles, in personal conversation or in submissions to research units, and the recurrent similarities, even to the use of the same phrases, cannot lightly be dismissed. Most of those who recall an experience of the more mystical type insist that it cannot be compared with normal modes of perception. 'Love and artistic and literary delights in all their intensity are firmly distinguishable from that experience that I had as a child. They are fine ecstasies, but they are of a different order.'[8] I am bound to respect that conviction. Nevertheless I am impressed by the many points of similarity between the obviously numinous glimpses of transcendence and the more familiar aesthetic experiences, and prefer to regard the difference between them as one of degree only. It is important that religious experiences should not be regarded as a different kind of experience, for such distinctions can be misleading. Certain levels of aesthetic perception are certainly no less transcendental than mystical or numinous experience. In both areas, the religious and the aesthetic, there are varying levels of perception: those of lesser intensity may be only a vestibule on this side of the threshold of that other dimension, yet even they offer some insight into the nature of that 'otherness' that is common to them all.

3. The impact of beauty

The philosopher Ludwig Wittgenstein was frequently irritated by the inane lack of meaning with which the word 'beauty' is bandied about, and demanded to know what a beautiful pair of eyes had in common with a beautiful Gothic church.[9] This notorious imprecision of the word no doubt betrays our slipshod use of it, but it may also point to the fact that there is something ultimately mysterious in our human perception of beauty and the kind of truth that it conveys. How is it that a certain quality in the interplay of light and atmosphere, the line of the hills and trees or the curve of a wave, should strike anyone with such a powerful flood of delight and inconsolable longing? By what alchemy does the texture and shape of chiselled stone or the pattern of line and colour in a painting take you out of yourself into a stillness and clarity that is beyond time and space? Some have tried to account for it by suggesting that there is a concord between the rhythm or pattern of the object perceived and that of our bodily movements or our language. Aesthetic analysis has identified some mathematical rules of structural balance and harmonious interplay of parts which reinforce the unity of the whole and partly explain why this is more satisfying than that. Such are, for example, the principle of the 'Golden Section' which declares that the most beautiful division of a whole into unequal parts is that in which the ratio of the smaller to the greater is the same as that between the greater and the whole, or the rule of colour harmonies that each primary colour is best complemented by the secondary derived from the other two primaries – blue by orange, yellow by violet, red by green. But none of these observations elucidates the nature of beauty. Listening to great music is for many people the most spiritual experience they know, inasmuch as they recognize in it an evocation of that perfection – call it what you will – which at the depth of their being they most desire and can neither attain nor even put into words. The sounds are no more than vibrations in the air that relate to each other in strict mathematical variations; and the musicians can explain the technical devices by means of which the composer has built his structure and the effect of his progression from key to key. But these are only the vocabulary and grammar of music. They reveal what a marvellously made object is being displayed, but they cannot account for its power to move us or interpret the meaning it conveys.

Beauty is not a specifiable property like size or colour or texture, and what is regarded as beautiful varies greatly, both as between one person and another and between one period or culture and another. Since, then, the quality of beauty cannot be ascribed intrinsically to the objects themselves, the obvious alternative is to conclude with the philosopher David Hume that 'beauty in things exists in the mind which contemplates them'.[10] Behaviourist schools of psychology are naturally inclined to favour this view, emphasizing the extent to which all human responses are conditioned by previous associations and present social pressures. The logic seems flawless, yet people can accept it only by resolutely contradicting the witness of their own experiences. For at those times when the beauty of natural forms or artistic creation bears most powerfully upon them, they know beyond doubt that what is happening is more than an act of subjective evaluation on their part. Their perception of what is there is impinging upon them, it is not being generated from within their own minds. It comes upon them as an external impact which is quite distinct from the response they may make to it. Writers in the past have told how violently they reacted to their first encounter with the music of Stravinsky, or in the nineteenth century with the paintings of Cézanne, or in the eighteenth with the wildness of the Alps, only to be drawn back by the very power they had perceived and rejected and find it beautiful beyond their imagining. The impact it made upon them was the same as at the first; it was the impact of beauty, power or truth, and only their response had changed. When music speaks wordlessly like an illumination, people know they are receiving, not imposing, its meaning. They relate to it as a 'Thou', not an 'It'. The music comes out to meet and address them as an 'other', and nothing can persuade them that they are looking merely at their own feelings reflected in a mirror of sound.

Though most people may not have given much attention to the strangeness of these ordinary occurrences and, indeed, are wiser not to do so, this mystery is at work in every concert hall and art gallery and whenever a landscape or some fellow being surprises them with glory. Pondering such common experiences, one is brought to a significant inference. If this force of beauty, power or truth, which bears upon us through and from within things, can neither be reduced to a state of mind in ourselves nor understood as an intrinsic attribute of the object of our attention, it must be accounted for in some other way. The matter is not explained by producing the composer, the artist, or even the Creator, as a neat answer to the question at this point, for the simple reason that the first two at least chose to set down those particular combinations of sound, form or colour because, having seen them in the mind's eye or heard them in imagination, they themselves had recognized the significance and beauty that was there. Their innovations of tonality and orchestration, of structure and material, are the vehicle they have devised for conveying a fresh perception of beauty, power and truth which they have perceived. The beauty, power and truth is not the product of the techniques employed, though it is inseparable from them.

It is typical of our age's idolatry of technology that many musical and art critics think they have described the essence of a new work when all they have written is an analysis of how the composer or the artist has achieved it. Meanwhile the creators of the works will often say, in effect: 'There are members of the public too uninstructed to know what we have *done*, but they hear and see what we are *saying* and it is for them that we work.' So Rembrandt and Beethoven were not magicians producing wonders for our delectation, but visionaries who had first *seen*

or *heard* through the imagination new forms of beauty that astonished them, and then strove to share them. The distinction between the beauty or significance that the artists have perceived and the works of art they have produced is repeatedly demonstrated in the insatiable sense of failure and craving to attain which appears to haunt the greatest of them even when they win universal acclaim. There are plenty of practitioners who are content to serve their craft and accept the esteem of their public or their dealers as a satisfying criterion of success; but those who truly merit the name of artist know that what they have created falls short of the truth and perfection they have seen, and they distrust the applause that tells them otherwise.

4. The infinite in the finite

So the question still stands: Whence the beauty and truth, and of what does it consist? We are driven back, I think, to the sound-waves and lines and pigments, to the light upon the landscape. That is all there is. And, as we shall see in chapter five, this is also an essential stipulation for our understanding of God's immanent presence in the world. Yet music which is nothing else but ordered vibrations is also infinitely more. The fold in the hills or the curve of the wave are only fragments of the earth's substance, yet they are also something eternal. These are two perceptions of the same thing, the one overtaken by the other, and this is the nature of every human being's relationship with external reality. William Blake said: 'If the doors of perception were cleansed everything would appear to man as it is, infinite. For man has closed himself up, till he sees all things thro' narrow chinks of his cavern.'[11] Seeing the ordinary phenomena of the external world in such a way that some inner splendour and universal significance – what Blake calls their infinitude – shines out, is no process of philosophizing about them, but entirely intuitive. Such moments of perception are given unsought and unexpected; yet the evidence of their occurrence is so widespread that any account of our human existence and of the reality that surrounds us which ignores them is blinkered and inadequate. The following incident, recalled by a woman of forty-four, is remarkably similar to many other such accounts that have been gathered and analysed in recent years, and even the very early age at which the experience is alleged to have taken place is by no means unusual.

My first remembered experience of the numinous occurred when I was barely three. I recall walking down a little cul-de-sac lane behind our house in Shropshire. The sun was shining, and as I walked along the dusty lane, I became acutely aware of the things around me. I noticed a group of dandelions on my left at the base of the stone wall. Most of them were in full bloom, their golden heads irradiated by the sun, and suddenly I was overcome by an extraordinary feeling of wonder and joy. It was as if I was part of the flowers and stones and dusty earth. I could feel the dandelions pulsating in the sunlight, and experienced a timeless unity with all life. It is quite impossible to express this in words or to recall its intensity. All I know now is that I knew something profound and eternal then.[12]

Such testimonies as that are remarkably reminiscent of what more articulate writers and poets have described. In familiar lines Wordsworth looked back to his own childhood vision of the world.

There was a time when meadow, grove and stream,
  The earth and every common sight,
    To me did seem
  Apparelled in celestial light,
The glory and the freshness of a dream.[13]

And, about a century and a quarter earlier, Thomas Traherne captured the same experience in his unforgettable prose.

The Corn was Orient and Immortal Wheat, which never should be reaped, nor was ever sown. I thought it had stood from everlasting to everlasting. The Dust and Stones of the Street were as Precious as GOLD . . . And yong Men Glittering and Sparkling Angels and Maids strange Seraphick Pieces of Light and Beauty . . . Eternity was Manifest in the Light and the Day and som thing infinit Behind evry thing appeared: which talked with my Expectation and moved my Desire.[14]

In a radio talk broadcast by the BBC Home Service on 17 February 1961 the poet, Ruth Pitter, recalled 'at no more than fourteen years old, seeing that altered landscape, looking at the very grass in the fields with stupefaction, because it had apparently changed its nature and "put on immortality", to quote St Paul'. She considered it significant that such seeing should be experienced in childhood, since it cannot in that case be explained as a compensating reaction to the disillusionments of ugly reality. But she was emphatic that these glimpses continued into adulthood and had, in fact, been the foundation of her kind of poetry.

> I was sitting in front of a cottage door, one day in spring long ago, a few bushes and flowers around me, a bird gathering nesting material, the trees of the forest at a little distance. A poor place – nothing glamorous about it, except that it was spring in the country. Suddenly everything assumed a different aspect – no, its true aspect. For a moment, it seemed to me, the truth appeared in its overwhelming splendour. The secret was out, the explanation given. Something that had seemed like total freedom, total power, total bliss, a good with no bad as its opposite – an absolute that had no opposite – this thing, so unlike our feeble nature, had suddenly cut across one's life, and vanished.[15]

Such experiences as these are often categorized as 'nature mysticism', but this is an inaccurate description. As an example of genuine nature mysticism Richard Jefferies comes readily to mind. From his boyhood in the late 1850s this countryman-naturalist had known moments of ecstatic communion with the energy, grandeur and beauty of the physical world. But in his case he was not content with sporadic visitations of the experience, and in the twelve short chapters of his personal apologia, *The Story of My Heart*,[16] he told of his passionate search for an expansion of his 'soul-life' by regular renewal of the same vivid awareness. On this basis he developed what can only be called a religious practice of prayer that was simply intense aspiration after 'something infinitely higher than deity'. It is such deliberate pursuit of a philosophy and a spiritual regimen that distinguishes the so-called nature mystic from the innumerable individuals who have known some brief, unsought encounter with infinite reality shining through a transient natural object. The unsought given-ness of these moments of revelation is typified in the experience of a youngster aged twelve at the time, walking alone at the end of the summer holidays in the Peak District.

> It was getting towards evening, and I had climbed over a wall and was standing on a piece of rough ground covered with heather and bracken and brambles, looking for blackberries, when suddenly I stood quite still and began to think deeply, as an indescribable peace – which I have since tried to describe as 'a diamond moment of reality' – came flowing into (or indeed waking up within) me; and I realized that all around me everything was lit with a kind of inner shining beauty; the rocks, the bracken, the bramble bushes, the view, the sky, even the blackberries – and also myself. And in that moment, sweeping in on that tide of light, there came also knowledge. The knowledge that though disaster was moving slowly and seemingly unavoidably towards me (and this I had known subconsciously for some time) yet in the end 'All would be well'.[17]

The sudden perception in things of more than meets the eye is not limited to natural objects or works of art that immediately strike the observer as beautiful. Just as the beauty of a new work of music or painting may elude us at first encounter, so the grace and truth of some superficially unlovely thing may reveal itself only when it comes out to meet us as a 'Thou' rather than an 'It'. The actor and author, P. J. Kavanagh, speaking in an interview for Border Television in 1984, told of a series of visionary moments given to him during the months following the death of his first wife.

> They didn't only happen in the countryside, they happened in London too. I remember looking at an advertisement hoarding where the paper had peeled off. I stopped in front of it and I just thought that the colours, the faded colours, were so incredibly beautiful and patient; as if it were willing to wait forever for someone to notice it. There was something about the impersonal non-hostility of the world and the beauty of it, the vibrating beauty of it.[18]

5. *Transfigurations*

The gift of discerning beauty and significance in unexpected objects is an important element, of course, in any artist's originality, and accounts for a great deal of the difficulty that more habit-bound minds have in trying to appreciate new work. The constructivist sculptures of Naum Gabo, for example, baffled many people when they first appeared, not only because of his use of metal and thread, but because his abstract shapes were inspired by his perception of beauty in unusual places. He wrote in 1942:

> Where do I get my forms from? I find them everywhere around me, where and when I want to see them. I find them, if I put my mind to it, in a torn piece of cloud carried away by the wind. I can find them in the naked stones on hills and roads. I see them in the green thicket of leaves and trees. I may discern them in a steamy trail of smoke from a passing train or on the surface of a shabby wall. Their apparition may be sudden, it may come and vanish in a second, but when they are over they leave me with the image of eternity's duration.[19]

It is worthy of note that so often those who have seen ordinary or even drab objects in an extraordinary way do not say merely that they have recognized them as beautiful; they talk of eternity, the infinite, or the true reality. What they see is objectively no more than anyone else would have seen, but they see it with a cleansed perception as a vehicle of something infinitely more that announces itself while remaining invisible and unknowable. For some years I have thought of these experiences as 'transfigurations', having in mind particularly a poem by Edwin Muir which reads very much like the poet's own testimony to such a moment of vision towards the physical world. Though he calls it *The Transfiguration*, Muir does not attempt, as the Gospels do, to give a description of the glorified Christ. Apart from the phrase, 'he with us', Christ is not mentioned, except as a memory ('for he had said') and a future hope ('But he will come again, it's said'). Yet he is present, though inherently indescribable, and it is the 'virtue' of his inexpressible radiance that brings about the secondary transfiguration that the disciples perceive and put into words in this extract.

> So from the ground we felt the virtue branch
> Through all our veins till we were whole, our wrists
> As fresh and pure as water from the well,
> Our hands made new to handle holy things,
> The source of all our being rinsed and cleansed

Till earth and light and water entering there
Gave back to us the clear unfallen world.
We would have thrown our clothes away for lightness,
But that even they, though sour and travel stained,
Seemed, like our flesh, made of immortal substance,
And the soiled flax and wool lay light upon us
Like friendly wonders, flower and flock entwined
As in a morning field. Was it a vision?
Or did we see that day the unseeable
One glory of the everlasting world
Perpetually at work, though never seen
Since Eden locked the gate that's everywhere
And nowhere?[20]

The omission of the transfigured Christ from the poem, though he is the presence from which the physical world receives its transformation, is specially perceptive. Muir appears to acknowledge that none of the glimpses of eternal reality or 'Thou-ness' in things which are experienced through this mode of perception are visions of God himself. They reveal this world, one might say, ablaze with his glory, but they cannot empower human eyes to look upon that tropical Sun that is the source of the illumination, and if we turn our eyes in its direction all we can perceive is darkness. These moments of cleansed vision may hint at the ultimate meaning of existence *sub specie aeternitatis* but they do not reveal the Eternal; they disclose the simple coherence of all beings in an embracing unity, but Being itself in its oneness cannot be shown. This is the ultimate paradox of spiritual reality. It does not exist in the way all *things* exist, for it is totally 'other', transcending existence; yet it permeates existence, being immanent within everything. There is more to things than meets the eye, yet that 'more', which adds so vastly to their significance, adds no measurable extra or extension to them. By being simply what they are and no more, things act as clues or symbols, pointing to what is beyond themselves – call it beauty or spirit, infinity or God – which we can never grasp or measure or bring under control. Whatever it is, it certainly makes its presence felt, yet leaves no trace as evidence, for it is not subject to the necessities or mathematics of spatial, temporal existence. It is in the world, yet not of the world, and can be recognized only in and through the world it upholds and pervades. So it is not surprising that of all the many accounts of such experiences that I have read, very few attempt to place God within whatever it is that was perceived. The majority use more reticent and impersonal terms, and, if the name of God is mentioned at all, it is almost an afterthought, as in this very early memory.

> I was three years old. I crouched down, as children do, very close to the ground. A black slug moved across the path, slowly, silently, leaving a shiny trail, and I sat back on my haunches to watch it. My cotton print dress circled the ground around me. Overhead the sky was blue, the sun shone . . . a tune was in my head and I hummed it . . . There was a movement among the trees. Not the movement made by someone passing through but an overall rustle of attention as in a crowd before the arrival of royalty. Each leaf was aware, expectant. Each blade of grass alert. God was everywhere. I felt secure; held; at one with everything around me.[21]

Subsequent reflection on such transfigurations as that creates a personal value-system and attitude to life, and the corporate reflection of many minds on many past experiences within a particular tradition creates the scriptures and creeds, the prayers and precepts of a religious system. Those who are rooted in the definitions of any such system are prone to feel the inadequacy of the vague terms in which the basic experience of transcendence is so often described. To speak of 'something beyond' of 'infinity', of 'reality' sounds like short change for the Lord God. Those, on the other hand, who have a vivid memory of being taken unawares by the awesome and enchanting mystery know that only in such indeterminate phrases can they do justice to the immensity and unknowableness of what the experience has brought near, and they shrink from any name that would domesticate it or diminish it within the commonplace assumptions implied by the word 'God'. They are right, of course. It has always been the way of prophets and mystics to speak of the bright glory but to keep silent about what it is that shines, and to say of each encounter with it: 'These are but the fringes of his power and how faint the whisper that we hear of him!' (Job 26.14).

6. The impact of meaning

The interpretation of any experience is an attempt to give it a meaning, usually by fitting it into an already existing framework of explanation. That is what the Old Testament prophets and chroniclers were chiefly concerned to do with the events of their own time, and the framework of explanation was already determined by previous reflection upon the few definitive experiences of their people's history. Even to dismiss what another person considers to have been an experience of transcendent reality as nothing but a psychological reflex is to give a certain meaning to human existence by fitting it into a given framework of explanation. But there are some experiences, of the kind that have just been described, which convey a self-authenticating sense of their own meaning. It impinges in quite a different way from the normal processes of reflection. Instead of being fitted into an accepted framework of explanations and interpreted thereby, these transfigurations challenge the previous framework, compelling those who have been through them to revise their understanding of the nature of things. They are revelations, if only to the extent that they convince the recipient once and for all that reality has other dimensions than she or he supposed.

In what sense can anyone talk about the 'meaning' of a piece of music when it is not attached to words like a song or an opera? People try to describe music in the terms of some other system of perception: it ripples or dances, or sobs or soars. But such language runs the risk of turning the music into a drama or a landscape of their own fancy. They are imposing their own meaning upon the music. Yet the music does carry its own meaning to those who can hear it, a meaning which even the composer never dreamed of putting into words. It must be in this sense that people can call music a universal language. As was said in an earlier section of this chapter, those who have the technical knowledge can analyse the modulations of key, subtleties of orchestration or inversions of phrase by which a composer has achieved his results, but these are only the vocabulary of music, and concert-goers listen not simply to the pleasures of a tune but to what it is saying. For music speaks about suspense and fulfilment, conflict, endurance and resolution; it speaks of grief and delight, of permanence and transience; it speaks of questions and answers and unanswered questions, and sometimes of a pattern and a unity embracing all. Music makes an affirmation about the nature of existence, the way things are, but says it wordlessly, and we receive the meaning directly through involvement, not by translating it into speech.

Dr C. E. M. Joad, while still a rationalist agnostic, tried to analyse his own experience of listening to the music of the great composers, which he had only gradually learnt to appreciate.

> The point upon which I wish to insist is that the musical experience is not adequately described as merely a succession of feelings; it is also a kind of knowledge, and the knowledge that it conveys comes to one with the assurance of conviction. Nevertheless it is knowledge that cannot be substantiated, demonstrated, or even communicated to those who do not share it.[22]

Scientists and mathematicians have sometimes recorded a no less convincing flash of comprehension at the end of a long struggle to resolve a problem; artists of all kinds have described days on which it seemed that nothing could go wrong, as though their work was being inspired and guided by a mind surer than their own; players and concert-goers alike cherish memories of particular performances when the very essence of the music was unveiled as though it had of its own volition taken control. These are all examples of seeing the connection, recognizing the coherence of things, with a heightened degree of intensity. Yet 'seeing the connection' is the mundane basis of all science, all art and, indeed, all thought. The coherence of everything is, on the one hand, so ordinary that we take it for granted, and, on the other hand, so remarkable as to overwhelm us at certain moments like an astonishing discovery.

> I had become increasingly worried by the apparently inevitable conclusion that if God did not exist it seemed impossible to provide any rational basis for those values which I wanted to adopt. Increasingly life seemed to be meaningless. Why, if there is no God, should anything exist in the first place? Indeed, how could anything exist? Why not just nothing? At this point in my reasoning it was as if suddenly a door had been opened in the mind and I glimpsed something which it is difficult to find language to describe. I have had no other experience with which to compare it. For a moment all time seemed to stand still. It was as if I was looking down into a great hall; but unlike an earthly hall it defies description. It was like an intuition

> of infinity and pure reason. I had caught sight of the truth, which the human faculties in their frailty are unable to grasp. There were the answers to the mysteries of human life and of the existence of the universe; and if I could not understand those mysteries at least I could know that there is something beyond, and I could have faith in the existence of God. Then the door closed quietly, and the vision slipped away like a dream. It took me a moment to catch my breath and to remember where I was. I had no doubts about the significance of what I had experienced, and I felt elated. My interest in the material world, however, was not noticeably diminished, and I continued with my meal and my cabbage, boiled as only the English know how.[23]

That philosophy student's encounter with the mystery of Being itself has, of course, been experienced by other more famous philosophers. It is a case of the truth of things that 'comes out to meet you', in Buber's phrase. Seeing the connection is the basis of 'the unitive vision', as it is called. The writer of the following account was a young man of nineteen at the time of his experience.

> Everything seemed pointless, including myself. I was oblivious to my surroundings and walked automatically as if in a trance. Then I heard a sound behind me, and when I turned round I saw four buzzards directly overhead. I felt as if they had called to let me know they were there. From the moment that I turned I felt all the fatigue drop away. As I watched the birds spiralling in the blue sky I felt identified with them, and yet at the same time I was intensely aware of my own identity, as though I were the centre of the universe and at the same time the centre was everywhere . . . I felt as if a filter had been taken from my senses and I was seeing the concrete world as it really is, and the purpose and meaning of it all.[24]

That sense of personal identification with the underlying unity of all things seems to be an almost constant element in these unexpected intuitions of the meaning of existence. It is often accompanied by an awareness that the normal categories of good and evil have been transcended and rendered irrelevant by the all-inclusive unity of 'a good with no bad as its opposite'. Phrases such as 'extreme simplicity' or 'an embracing harmony' are commonly used even of experiences that are essentially aesthetic. That this ultimate one-ness is neither deduced by logic nor learned from hearsay is evident from the fact that children have known the same flashes of insight.

> When I was about eleven years old I spent part of a summer holiday in the Wye Valley. Waking up very early one bright morning before any of the household was about, I left my bed and went to kneel on the window-seat to look out over the curve which the river took just below the house . . . The scene was very beautiful, and quite suddenly I felt myself on the verge of a great revelation. It was as if I had stumbled unwittingly on a place where I was not expected, and was about to be initiated into some wonderful mystery, something of indescribable significance. Then, just as suddenly the feeling faded. But for the brief seconds while it lasted I had known that in some strange way I, the essential 'me', was a part of the trees, of the sunshine and the river, that we all belonged to some great unity. I was left filled with exhilaration and exultation of spirit. This is one of the most memorable experiences of my life, of a quite different quality and greater intensity than the sudden lift of the spirit one may often feel when confronted with beauty in nature.[25]

In that example the typically mystical experience of all-embracing unity is combined with the more numinous sense of confrontation by a transfigured and transfiguring 'Other'. The distinction between the two types is valid, but more often than not they are found together in the same experience, as in the case of a young mother.

> The baby was put into my arms to suckle: as he attached himself to my breast and pulled on my nipple, my womb contracted strongly and I was flooded by a love of such intensity that it was all-consuming; it enveloped myself, my child, and then seemed to extend beyond to the whole of creation. I literally felt no longer an individual but attached, a part of a large living whole . . . I felt in harmony with the workings of the cosmos, and it was indescribably beautiful. Over all this I felt I was within the radius of a 'presence', of something so great, so awesome, that I myself, small consciousness that I was, could only wonder but not fully comprehend.[26]

7. The impact of rescue

It will not have escaped the reader's notice that several of the personal anecdotes quoted already in this chapter betray the existence of a state of anxiety or foreboding prior to the experience: 'Disaster was moving unavoidably towards me.' 'Everything seemed pointless.' 'Life seemed to be meaningless; why not just nothing?' This factor may appear to endorse the common assumption that those who are subject to such 'visionary' states of mind are neurotic or even psychotic. That facile conclusion, however, is contradicted by analysis both in Britain and the USA which has shown that people reporting experiences of this sort are likely to be well-balanced, socially aware, and healthily objective in their perception of themselves and of whatever need for reassurance they may have had at the time. Their capacity to acknowledge and face whatever it was that threatened them may, indeed, have been precisely the factor that rendered them receptive to the revelatory experience. The experience itself often consists of a recognition of radical inadequacy followed almost instantaneously by a sense of rescue, or at least the gift of basic trust.

A trivial personal incident may help to identify more exactly what I am talking about. After the second full day of chairing a working party in the cathedral precinct at Chester I had stayed up late to write letters. At about half past one I walked across Abbey Yard to post them. As I approached the old gateway and saw the deep velvet sky through the lamplit stone of the arch, my shoulders dropped in such a sudden and profound relaxation as to stop me in my tracks. How could I have been so desperately tense up to that moment without realizing it? And why had I now been instantly and totally released? The ancient stones, the night sky beyond, had symbolized a permanence infinitely greater than my personal transience which, in a moment shorter than it takes to tell, I recognized as the source of my anxiety. Beyond all logic it was the equivalent of: 'It is I, don't be afraid.'

I have often watched the flow of tourists into a great cathedral and have noticed how many of them stand, momentarily stunned by the scale of the interior and the changed quality of the light, and soon exhibit the physical signs of the same profound release of tension. One after another, unless they are bored out of their wits, they slowly inhale and their faces relax in a smile of deep content. Those who respond in this way detach themselves from their companions as if to enter a more private realm. I have seen some of them walk to one of the nave piers to press the palms of their hands against the rough masonry. I have known another man do the same to the trunk of a great tree at a moment of extreme desolation, and I know what is happening for them. For just as the mystery of the world's beauty or of life's significance constantly surrounds us, yet only now and then bears fully upon our conscious minds, so too the enveloping mystery of our fragile finitude lies in wait unregarded until its moment of devastating disclosure. Sooner or later almost everyone is momentarily confronted by the radical human inability to be in control, the truth that in the midst of life we are in death; and in the same package, as it were, as that dreadful falling apart, comes reassurance.

> One evening I wanted to write a letter but was unable to because I was in such a state of grief and misery. I did not know what to do with myself . . . It must sound extraordinary, but I wrung my hands and said aloud: 'I can't go on, what am I to do, I can't bear it.' Suddenly I realized I wasn't alone and that now I must pray. I said, 'Oh Lord, please help me. I can't go on like this and I don't know what to do.' I stood with my eyes shut. Gradually I was filled with a warm glow inside which increased until I felt I was held in a miraculous light. Time meant nothing, though I do not think it lasted more than half to one minute. Then slowly it left me and when I opened my eyes I was quite calm and composed.[27]

If that account reads like a religious cliché it is because the experience is a commonplace of the human condition, whether it is expressed in the language of piety or not. It is pointless for rationality to remind us that very often the victim of such moments of panic is exaggerating the disaster and so overstates the rescue. For the truth is that, in whatever circumstances one reaches the end of one's tether and control breaks down, one is encountering symbolically the end of existence and the disintegration of the ordered universe, and by the same token, the gift of reassurance is a cosmic statement. This truth was memorably expressed in Peter Berger's small book, *A Rumour of Angels*, over twenty years ago.

> A child wakes in the night, perhaps from a bad dream, and finds

> himself surrounded by darkness, alone, beset by nameless threats. At such a moment the contours of trusted reality are blurred or invisible, and in the terror of incipient chaos the child cries out for his mother. It is hardly an exaggeration to say that, at this moment, the mother is being invoked as a high priestess of protective order. It is she (and, in many cases, she alone) who has the power to banish the chaos and restore the benign shape of the world. And, of course, any good mother will do just that . . . She will speak or sing to the child, and the content of their communication will invariably be the same – 'Don't be afraid – everything is in order, everything is all right.'[28]

Peter Berger asks: Is the mother lying to the child? All living creatures, as part of their survival kit, have an in-built mechanism of fear which is triggered whenever life is imperilled. They react to pain or the threat of pain, but they do not go in fear of death. They do not know about death. Only the human species is burdened with the awareness of life's brevity, fragility, and inevitable end. Often we cannot recall when our own death first insinuated itself into our consciousness. But we learn how health, sanity and existence itself hang on the flimsiest threads and infinitesimal adjustments of chemistry, and how this miracle of individual survival is but a microcosm of the gigantic chanciness of this universe which escaped by the merest fraction the fate of becoming from the start incapable of ever, anywhere, producing life. With all the wonder and gratitude that this knowledge should inspire, it still amounts to no guarantee since we found out, almost too late, that the one life-bearing planet we know of has a highly vulnerable atmosphere and eco-system. So is the mother lying to the child? We cope with the unanswered question by busying ourselves with more immediate eventualities over which we are still in control. But this only buries it deeper within ourselves, whence it may arise in nightmare whenever some loss, failure or disruption seems to mimic the ultimate dread. Some other person's death, maybe, or a theft, the rejection of a cherished scheme, the loss of a job, the breakdown of a relationship, a change of home, throws us suddenly face to face with the darkness and dissolution and nothingness that awaits us and our world. And in that instant, as personal experience so frequently testifies, a sense of total risk is replaced by a gift of basic trust. The part of the maternal priestess is taken over by the Other whom she merely represented. In the television interview already mentioned,

P. J. Kavanagh described such an experience of reassurance after he had learnt in the hospital in Java that his wife, Sally, was dying.

> I went out of the room for a moment and sat under a tree. It wasn't a visual experience but it's best described in visual terms. It was as though streams of connections of light were going from cloud to cloud. Everything seemed connected. It wasn't an aural experience either, but if you can imagine choirs of angels, the music of the spheres, they were present. And what was really surprising about it was that there seemed enormous vats of consolation. Everything was all right, absolutely everything was all right . . . The extraordinary thing was that there was nothing in that tremendous, unbelievable demonstration of warmth, of warmth in creation, that would remit the pain, no forgetting of the sort of tunnel one was going to walk down afterwards. The pain was included in the consolation. So it wasn't any form of opting out or avoidance. Nevertheless it was like an enormous promise.[29]

Kavanagh showed in this interview that he understood how easily his personal suffering might have focussed his attention upon the comfort he was deriving from such opening up of this other dimension in his perception of reality, rather than upon the reality, whatever it was, that was disclosing itself to him in the series of experiences that followed. But in fact the reverse happened. 'So much of the core of the experience', he said, 'seems to me not to have to do with myself: that the trouble is myself. And what the experiences had in common was the sudden release from self.'[30]

That seems to be the key to such experiences of radical reassurance, and it explains why they are true experiences of rescue, even when there is no remission of the pain nor escape from the catastrophe. 'The trouble is myself.' The human person, who already transcends all other living creatures in knowing his or her own mortality and being outraged by it, can go beyond and transcend that human self by trusting not its own autonomy but the ultimate goodness of the otherness that lies beyond. True maturity consists in the surrender of our will-to-control and in the self-abandonment of basic trust. This is the paradox of human nature and we shall return to it in later chapters. The German Roman Catholic Karl Rahner has said: 'In the fact that a human being experiences his finiteness radically he reaches beyond this finiteness and experiences himself as a transcendent being, a spirit.'[31] Of course it is not only the realization of our mortality that can open us up to receive the mysterious reassurance that is like a rescue. The crushing weight of a too great responsibility, the arctic chill of ultimate aloneness, the impossibility of communicating fully with even the closest friends, the surprise of loving and being loved unconditionally – any of these may bring us to the end of the tether. The common factor in them all is an irretrievable loss of control and a necessary abandonment to other forces. Nothing but the unresisting acceptance of our existential finitude and powerlessness can set us free from the anxiety and enable us to find our self-transcendence in trustful self-abandonment to a reality beyond ourselves. It is when wind and waves and darkness have taken over, when there is nothing but the abyss beneath our feet, that the Lord approaches.

8. God takes the stage

In the same series of television interviews, Dr Sheila Cassidy re-told the story of her interrogation under torture at the hands of secret police in Chile in 1975. Though her account includes no transfigured perception of the physical world, it bears out Kavanagh's testimony to the kind of reassurance that neither eliminates the suffering nor functions as a mental technique of escape. Using a medical image that came naturally to her as a doctor, she said:

> If you could imagine a situation where somebody you knew was actually a bystander at something horrible happening to you, not intervening, knowing they were there but not achieving any comfort from the fact that that person was there. I've no idea why God wasn't intervening. History shows that God doesn't intervene in a lot of things. There's nothing special about me! . . . The curious thing is that all that time that it was happening I knew that God loved me. Don't ask me how . . . it was a very curious clinical thing like God being present in an operating theatre.[32]

Many people reading these words will sense an indefinable change of key in comparison with all the other experiences of transcendence previously recounted in this chapter, except possibly the one on page 44 above. Some will recognize the more familiar language of encounter with a personal God and will feel at home with it, others will be less at ease and faintly unsympathetic. The difference between the two reactions, however, cannot be simply correlated with the lack or possession of religious faith. What constitutes the change of key is more subtle than that and calls for further exploration.

Amid all the varieties of this experience of 'otherness in the ordinary' it is impossible to ignore the innumerable people who have been convinced at one time or another that God *has* intervened to rescue them in some way. The Mediterranean coasts are ringed with small chapels containing the votive offerings of past sailors and fishermen who believed they had been saved from disaster at sea. Thousands of the villagers of South India owe their particular devotion to this or that god, including in many cases Jesus Christ, to a miraculous healing that followed a prayer and an offering at a particular shrine or church. In all walks of life men and women recall instances of special providence directing their choice in what proved to be a vital decision. Many claim that these were the experiences that gave them their certainty of God and their understanding of his true nature. And conversion itself, especially when it brings about a dramatic change of moral or mental disposition, is usually felt to be the supreme example of divine initiative and rescue. Moreover, we have already seen that three, at least, of the four crucial events of the biblical revelation belong to this category of deliverance. No assessment of religious experience is complete which has not taken account of the 'mighty acts of God'. The God of the Bible is indubitably a Saviour-God.

Then why the uneasiness? Much of it stems from the contentious cluster of moral, philosophical and theological questions concerning God's relationship with the universe which are raised by the idea of divine intervention, and these will be considered in the later chapter on Providence. Here and now my concern is still to explore the role of human experience in giving content to the word 'God'. The typical accounts that have been quoted throughout this chapter, *by their very imprecision*, break open the commonplace stereotype that the name 'God' conveys and make room for the more immense, indefinable Reality that has never left itself without some witness, and however ignorantly worshipped, however religiously domesticated, still impinges upon human awareness as the *mysterium tremendum fascinans*, the Infinite, the

Eternal, the Other (Acts 14.15–17; 17–23). The staggering claim of the Christian faith, which this book seeks to examine, is that that unknown, that impenetrable silence, that everlasting source of all existence, is Love; but the meaning of that statement is lost when we diminish in our thinking that which we are calling love. It is the subtle danger-signals of that diminishment which prompt the uneasiness and make us sense the change of key.

Miracles, by their very rarity, draw attention, and argument, to the rescue and away from the rescuer. This is just what Jesus himself evidently feared, and the Old Testament is much concerned with the problem of a people that dwelt more upon the story of its deliverance than upon the character of the Deliverer. Moreover, the danger of extolling the acts of God and telling of his interventions is that, by bringing the Eternal on to the scene, as it were, we 'place' him here or there and turn him into one of the characters in the story. Sheila Cassidy is too sound a Catholic not to be well aware that the divine love supporting her through her horrible ordeal filled the room and held the whole suffering, violent world in its embrace; yet her image of someone standing by, which her immediate need demanded as the truth for that moment, tends in the telling to reduce God's universal presence to something localized, an additional person side by side with the others. It is almost inevitable that this should happen in anyone's account of miraculous help or deliverance because the experience is so specific and personal. The same tendency can be seen at work in the Old Testament, and also in the deliberate efforts to correct it at a later stage. On the strength of their extraordinary liberation from slavery the Hebrew clans assumed that the unnameable I AM was their own tribal deity whose presence could be localized and whose favour was partisan. It took the prophets of the eighth and seventh centuries to remind them that their Saviour-God was the universal and only deliverer of all nations (Amos 9.7; Isa.19.19–25).

Paradoxically it might almost be said that the more believers expect their God to intervene on their behalf, the more they belittle him even to the point of absurdity. George Müller, the nineteenth-century philanthropist, who for sixty-eight years maintained his schools, orphanage and scripture distribution with no fund-raising apparatus whatever, has been held up as a signal example of evangelical faith. Yet the unkindly superior comment of William James contains more than a little truth:

'His God was, as he often said, his business partner. He seems to have been for Müller little more than a sort of supernatural clergyman interested in the congregation . . . but unpossessed of any of those vaster and wilder and more ideal attributes with which the human imagination elsewhere has invested him.'[33] That kind of familiarity with God, which seems almost to be 'experiencing him "neat" ', is what many people cannot reconcile with their own most convincing moments of illumination which have pointed directly to the undergirding Reality, but never disclosed that Reality itself. For they have intuitively been given the truth which early Jewish rabbis were affirming when they referred to God as *ha-Makom*, the Place, or, as we might say, the Context in which all things come to pass, but which can never itself be perceived.[34] God is the mind within which the drama is unfolding, but which can never itself appear on the stage.

Yet no sooner is that said than it must be retracted by any Christian. It is another case of 'This Thou art and yet this Thou art not'. For belief in the incarnation of the Word implies that all that is communicable of the mind of God *did* enter the drama as one of the characters. It implies that the vaster, wilder reality of the Infinite Source, precisely because it *is* love, initiated its own diminishment to the scale required for both self-revelation and rescue. All the more reason, therefore, that those who have experienced the impact of rescue in any form should exercise the same modesty in their claims as those who have known the impact of beauty, of meaning or of re-assurance, and say with them: 'We have seen creatures and persons and events in this world lit up by the glory of God, but the unapproachable light to which those things have pointed we have neither seen nor can see' (I Tim. 6.16).

9. *The impact of humanity*

There are, no doubt, more types of experience whereby the otherness of things comes out to address the human person with unsought intimations of God. The great apologist, C. S. Lewis, would certainly have included the impact of moral demand, the undeniable 'I ought' that impinges upon every individual to a greater or lesser degree and, as he convincingly argues, cannot be explained away as social pressure or concealed self-interest. For two reasons I hesitate to pursue this theme. It was Austin Farrer's carefully weighed opinion that 'when he (Lewis) considered man in relation to God he viewed him too narrowly as a moral will, and that relation too narrowly as a moral relation'.[35] And then, again, I am impressed by the fact that in so many anecdotes of the kind I have considered in this chapter, the *absence* of generalized ethical demand is specifically mentioned, as though with surprise. 'There was a strange but quite entire absence of any claim or compulsion', says one typical account, while another asserts with a note of relief, 'good and evil, sickness and health, fear and courage, the whole damn lot are somehow part of it and purified by it until not one of them really matters.' Before dismissing this as spiritual candyfloss, it is worth noting that if, as I am urging, many of these experiences are indeed gratuitous glimpses of everyday phenomena perceived in their true relationship to their changeless source and context and alight with the radiance of it; if, to speak in myth, these are transfigurations that give back to us 'the clear unfallen world', we should on sound theological grounds expect them to be innocent of the knowledge of good and evil. We should, at least, expect whatever divine imperative sounds through such encounters to be particular to the one person concerned but inapplicable as a general rule. In his great unfinished work on *Ethics* Dietrich Bonhoeffer wrote:

> Man at his origin knows only one thing: God. It is only in the unity of his knowledge of God that he knows of other men, of things, and of himself. He knows all things only in God, and God in all things. The knowledge of good and evil shows that he is no longer at one with this origin.
>
> In the knowledge of good and evil man does not understand himself in the reality of the destiny appointed in his origin, but rather in his own possibilities, his possibility of being either good or evil . . . Instead of knowing himself solely in the reality of being chosen and loved by God, he must now know himself in the possibility of choosing.[36]

Bonhoeffer went on to argue that Jesus Christ deliberately invalidated this life of ceaseless conflict and choice between good and evil and won back for humanity the total simplicity and freedom of knowing only God and his will. But this is a claim that must be examined further in a later chapter.

There is, however, one whole range of our experience of the ordinary which surpasses all others as a channel of the self-revelation of God, namely human beings themselves. More people encounter God and comprehend something of his nature through other women and other men than through any other experience. And this is true of our experience both of certain special characters and of humanity as such. At both levels, the particular and the general, the words of Irenaeus are accurate: The glory of God is the living man. There is no stereotype of the kind of personality of whom others can say 'That one showed God to me.' W. H. Auden wrote in his commonplace book:

> I have met in my life two persons, one a man, the other a woman, who convinced me that they were persons of sanctity. Utterly different in character, upbringing and interests as they were, their effect on me was the same. In their presence I felt myself to be ten times as nice, ten times as intelligent, ten times as good-looking as I really am.[37]

In a properly indirect way that humorous tribute tells us more about God than a library of books. So does the testimony of the French missionary priest in India who was universally known as Abhishiktananda.

> We do not of course presume to appraise the sanctity of India's great seers. That is known to God alone. Furthermore, according to an old adage, only a jnāni can recognize a jnāni. Nevertheless it is to them rather than to any book that the earnest seeker should turn when he wants to discover the call and working of the Spirit. One of these sages was with us not very long ago. His life was passed entirely in the clear light of day and could be observed by any who wished . . . and certainly most of those who met him claim to have recognized in him the unquestionable sign of the Presence and to have received from him an inspiration which has for ever illuminated and transformed their life.[38]

What greater contrast could there be than that between the *sadhu* Sri Ramana Maharishi and the British army officer, Hugh Lister, to whom Austin Farrer paid tribute in more than one of his books.

> I knew a man whose name, though uncanonized, I shall always silently mention when I recall at the altar of God those saints whose fellowship

> gives reality to our prayers; a man who sacrificed in the prime of his age a life which he had never lived for himself; a man whose eyes sparkled with all the passions, pity, indignation, sorrow, love, delight, but never for himself . . . Such a life, then, is evidence, and what other evidence could you hope to find?[39]

But humanity in general seems at first sight to offer evidence of something very different. No other species has the same propensity for destroying its own kind, the same taste for deliberate cruelty; nor does any other so threaten to destroy the life system of the world itself. It is humanity, in the main, that presents the problem of evil. Yet this is only one side of our tragically ambiguous truth. The author of Psalm 8 had evidently glimpsed the same beyondness transfiguring all humankind as others have perceived in a clump of dandelions or the Bach *Sanctus*.

> Thou hast made him but little lower than God,
> And crowned him with glory and honour.

Indeed, the very language of metaphor, our basic vocabulary for thinking about God who is beyond thought, is largely drawn from our workday experience of human beings, ourselves and others. So worn by repetition that we use them merely as words, these metaphors did not originate in a preacher's study; they were forged in some flash of illumination when the beauty and significance of a face or gesture caught someone's attention, held it and spoke, not necessarily about God, but about itself as something more than ordinary: the otherness was there. True theology is what we have learned from *really* seeing a mother teaching her toddler to walk, a school teacher explaining to a puzzled child, a potter handling the clay on a wheel, a shepherd at lambing time, the faces of women in childbirth, of a betrayed husband, of a nurse or a judge or a commander on the field of battle.

> For Mercy has a human heart,
> Pity a human face,
> And Love, the human form divine,
> And Peace, the human dress.

None of us is truly human except through relationship, neither can we speak truly of God except in terms of relationship. Therein lies the image of God in humanity. We see it everywhere defaced, but not obliterated. If ever we were to see it whole and uncompromised and self-abandoned in basic trust, as Christians believe we have, then the unknown Other, the Beyond at the heart of everything, would be made visible.

10. Today if ye will hear . . .

The purpose of this book, as already explained, is not to argue the existence of God but to elucidate what we should be talking about when we use that name. The wide range of glimpses and intimations surveyed in this chapter are pointers towards its meaning. It is notoriously easy to dismiss all such experience or perception as 'subjective', if not hallucinatory. Yet the human capacity for sensing what is 'really there', as a purely animal skill, has proved itself to be extraordinarily trustworthy. Throughout the long evolutionary processes, all living organisms have survived by having an adequate mechanism for picking up and processing, through their sense organs and their nervous systems, information about what is 'out there' in their environment. Faulty mechanisms of cognition that conveyed images of what is out there that did not match the reality could not long survive. The human creature has developed a more complex and far-reaching capacity than any other organism for apprehending, storing and processing information of a kind that extends beyond the purely material 'facts', and this should always be borne in mind in any assessment of our mystical and numinous experiences. This is not to say that, with even the most perfected sensory apparatus, we could discern God, for he is not an object 'out there' in any comparable sense at all. But we should, perhaps, be more ready to trust our occasional perceptions of the luminosity of the physical world and its apparent potentiality for becoming a Voice and a Word whereby we know ourselves to be addressed and held in relationship.

But these perceptions, however trustworthy, are only momentary visions. Though they leave an unforgettable certainty, they cannot plant anyone's feet firmly in an Eden either lost or regained. One man who corresponded with the Alister Hardy Research Centre, reflecting on 'a vaguely mystical experience he had had more than fifty years before' regretted that, while he had never been able to forget it, it had not made the difference it might have done had he made more of it. He thanked the researchers for enabling the long dormant seed, through their questions, to germinate.[40] To bear their full fruit these momentary intuitions of the truth, like all others within the process of learning, need to be reflected upon and responded to in the light of the experience and reflection of hundreds of other people. In other words, experiences of the kind we have been considering, however intense or however quietly normal, do not lead anywhere unless they are evaluated and fortified by tradition, *always provided that tradition is used to explore and build upon the individual's experience, and never merely to supplant it*. For there is no substitute for personal encounter as the mainspring of spiritual conviction and action.

How regrettable it is, how unnatural in fact, that through the centuries the confessional stalls around the walls of many churches have received the secrets of so many sins, and have not been equally available for the confidences of men and women and children who have been overtaken by the ecstasies or insights or consolations that declare the reality of God! Had this other side of personal experience been invited, no doubt there would have been the same amount of fantasy, neurosis and self-advertisement as has always been exhibited in the confessional, and wise priests would have known how to discern and guide, as they have done hitherto. No doubt they would have found the recitals of glory just as repetitive as the catalogues of sin, for the accounts of these intensely private memories are uncannily similar. But at least it might have redressed the balance and made the churches everywhere as mindful of divine initiative as of human failure. If it could become normal for people to know that a church was the place where confidences of that sort could be shared and understood; where they would be helped to reflect upon the experience and grow by responding to it; where they could learn that, just as they have known the approach of God in the strength of a tree or the swelling tide of music, others have known it in a bush lapped in flame or the action of a potter at the wheel; where they could find that the church itself was living and growing by response to such experiences; then, I believe, the Christian community would present a less mummified face towards the world and, within its own life and thought, might rediscover the more dynamic exploratory view of the knowledge of God which its own scriptures display.

3

When I Consider

Formative Reflection in the Primal, Indian and Classical Greek Traditions

1. A highly charged world

When the Gospel of Luke concludes its account of the birth of Jesus with the words, 'And Mary kept all these things, pondering them in her heart', it is not simply rounding off that particular narrative. Her secret rumination over her treasured experiences typified the process by which the new faith was shaped within the church. It is, in fact, a model of the way by which every religion has emerged. Each of them is the fruit of a long pondering, a tradition of reflection upon, and response to, certain germinal experiences. A few of these experiences in the course of human history have been of revelatory events or personalities that can justly be claimed as unparalleled, and these have given the stamp of uniqueness to this or that religion. But in the main the determining experiences have been common to humanity everywhere and at all times, like those surveyed in the previous chapter. The great differences between the religions have arisen from the diversity of cultural background against which these basic human experiences were first pondered and interpreted. This truth underlies St Paul's contention that 'what can be known about God is plain to all, because God has shown it to them: ever since the creation of the world his invisible nature, namely his eternal power and deity, has been clearly perceived in the things that have been made' (Rom. 1.19,20, RSV; cf. Acts 14.17). Any community's reflection upon the illuminating experiences must involve an attempt to relate them to its own current mythology and view of the world. This remains true even for those who only tentatively recognize the mythology: 'I thought this must be what Heaven is like.' 'If you can imagine choirs of angels, the music of the spheres, they were present.' For however novel the experience, it can be interpreted only in the terms of the existing culture.

All the incidents reviewed in the previous chapter are, in their different ways 'numinous', to use Rudolph Otto's word. The phenomenon may have been perceived either as physically stupendous, or as aesthetically arresting, or uncanny, or mystical, but in every case it conveyed the impression of a dynamic *encounter*. The effect was variously described as overwhelming, inexpressible, intense, compelling, or in similar terms all denoting an impact so powerful that the observer became aware of being the recipient and object of the confrontation. Naturally, this sense of being affected and acted upon by some independent reality leads anyone to think of it, whatever it is, as an influence or force. The poet, Gerard Manley Hopkins, sought to express this in the vivid metaphor of an electric charge:

> The world is charged with the grandeur of God.
> It will flame out . . .

This is the feature of all such experiences which members of pre-literate cultures at all times have fastened upon when they pondered over their significance. They took them as encounters with power. They reckoned that the tree, the cave or the mountain, upon which their numinous experience had centred, must have become a point of concentration for that mysterious, immanent force which permeates all things but chooses particular places, people and events from which to 'flame out'. This form of belief is known by the anthropologists as dynamism. The world is seen to be pervaded by an independent power and volition which emerges at certain points in numinous self-revelation. Wherever it has once been encountered, there it must be presumed to reside. So the landscape is strewn with sacred springs, rocks, groves, pools, caverns and hilltops. The force that lies within them is not perceived in the same way as the Catholic Hopkins understands the word 'God'. It is less personalized, and if the words 'holy' or 'sacred' are applied to it, they denote only something so strange and mysterious as to demand the utmost reverence and caution, for such power may be beneficent, but must also be dangerous, because so highly charged. In addition to its concentration points in the natural world, it is specially present within four universal experiences of the human family – eating, disease, death, and the reproduction of life – all of them commonplace, yet surprisingly fraught with emotion and symbolic significance. The strangeness inherent in them is felt to be contagious and needs to be counteracted, either by regulation, as in food taboos, or by purification and a kind of quarantine. It is not that the birth of her child has made a woman unclean in our sense of the word; it has made her too mysterious, too charged with holiness for comfort. She must be brought back to ordinariness – secularized, as we might say. The same aura of strangeness surrounds those in the community who have a certain charisma of influence over the minds of others – the chief, the healer, the musician and the sage. This is not to say that 'ordinariness' is devoid of the invisible force. The flaming out from the concentration points, the numinous encounter as such, serve to bring home the mystery pervading all life even at its most commonplace. That is the nature of all 'religious experience'.

In the south Pacific the word *mana* describes just such a hidden force displayed through innumerable local manifestations, and this term has been adopted by anthropologists to designate the same concept wherever it is found. Some of the peoples of equatorial Africa, for example, notably among those of the Nilotic stock, who knew no name for a personal God before the incursion of Muslim and Christian influences, recognized a single pervasive power, manifesting itself at many points, to which they gave a generic name similar to *mana*. In India, during the Vedic period of religion among the Aryan people from about 1500 to 900 BC, the word *brahman*, which now denotes the Absolute Godhead, carried much the same meaning as *mana*, being particularly associated with the numinous power of the highly charged rituals of sacrifice and the hallucinatory trance induced in the worshippers. In the Old Testament itself there are fascinating traces of a period, long before the Hebrews appeared on the scene, when the verbal root, *el*, which now underlies the name for God in all Semitic languages, meant something more impersonal and diffuse, like *mana* power.[1] Even the word *theos* in Greek, which we always translate as 'God' and which is so used in the New Testament, was normally used by the ancient Greeks in a much less specific sense, closer to that of the term *mana*. The underlying root of the word means 'shining', and in his book on the Greek Philosophers,

Rex Warner declares that 'as a rule *theos* means either some "force" or the personification in mythology of some force'.[2]

It is natural enough that people reflecting upon the numinous impact of beauty, of sudden comprehension, of personal deliverance or the mysteries of birth and death, should interpret these experiences as encounters with an unseen power. This has almost always led them to two further inferences about this power that seems to pervade the world. First they imagine that it is the kind of power that they themselves are most in need of, struggling as they are to survive in a harsh and often hostile environment. Then, on the assumption that they are in touch with what might be called 'the power to overcome and get things done', they look for ways of manipulating or placating it to serve their own ends. From these ideas grow the rituals of sacrifice and the techniques of magic, both beneficial and malign. There has always been, however, a logical flaw in that tradition of reflection, in that the numinous impact of beauty, the power of music, the power of inward illumination, comfort or even deliverance, is not the same thing as the power of mastery. Yet this confusion is just as prevalent in technologically developed societies as in primitive ones. In earlier times the pursuit of dominance was tempered at least by awe and wonder. It will be a savage world indeed when we find no more in beauty than pleasing sensation, and neither death's mystery nor the astonishment of birth hold any power to overwhelm us, but are as casual as we have tried to make eating and sex. True civilization is three-quarters reverence.

2. 'It' or 'Thou'?

Reflection about these existential encounters with the *mana* power in commonplace phenomena raises a further question: Was what they experienced an 'It' or a 'Thou'? It is necessary to phrase the question in that way because the use of the word 'personal' suggests a meeting of persons, and many who have had experiences of this kind would not wish to define them so explicitly or to speak of whatever had overtaken them as 'he'. The terms in which the question actually presents itself are well exemplified in another of the interviews recorded by the Alister Hardy Research Centre.[3] Two girls, college students, were asked about a sense of numinous reality, focussed upon a cluster of birch trees, which had come upon both of them together when, aged sixteen, they were walking the winter woods at night. One of them remembered, 'I felt sure it had come from outside, had sort of let me know that it was there,' and at a later point the other added, 'I don't know how we could possibly think of it as impersonal when it was something that obviously was needed so much by both of us, and made such a great difference to us.' While clinging to the word 'it', both of them wanted to insist that the experience was not self-induced, but had been initiated and intended by whatever it was that had *let them know that it was there.* The only analogy that does justice to that quality of interaction is that of the meeting of one person with another, and it is this that justifies our use of the word 'personal' to describe all such encounters.

This quality of interaction which we properly describe as personal is not limited to relationships between persons. It is present to a greater or lesser degree wherever an encounter takes place between two or more centres of consciousness, involving mutual recognition and a two-way communication. It is this that distinguishes it from our dealings with inanimate objects. In a long article entitled *Dialogue* which he wrote in 1929 Martin Buber recounted a childhood experience which brought this home to him. He used to visit the stables on his grandparents' estate to stroke the neck of a favourite horse.

> What I experienced in touch with the animal was the other, the immense otherness of the Other . . . yet it let me approach, confided itself to me, placed itself elementally in the relation of 'Thou and Thou' with me. The horse, even when I had not begun by pouring oats for him into his manger, very gently raised his massive head, ears flicking, then snorted quietly, as a conspirator gives a signal to be recognizable only to his fellow-conspirator; and I was approved.

Buber then described one such occasion when he became self-consciously aware of the 'fun' he was getting out of doing this to the horse. And at once

> something had changed, it was no longer the same thing. And the next day, after giving him a rich feed, when I stroked my friend's neck he did not raise his head.[4]

That memory contributed significantly to Buber's later distinction between the quality of relationship indicated in 'I-It' and 'I-Thou'. Through the written form of their language, the Chinese make this distinction plain. Their ideographs of the pronouns for man, woman, divinity or animal contain on the right side an element common to them all, which does not appear in the pronoun for a thing.

他	她	祂	牠	它
he	she	divinity's pronoun	animal's pronoun	it

So we might say that the personal relationship which we know in the interaction of one human being with another can be present to a limited degree in our interaction with an animal, though it is less than a person, and to a far fuller degree in our interaction with God who is infinitely more than a person. But we are indebted to Martin Buber for his emphatic reminder that even the world of things, which we rightly call inanimate, may at times give itself to us in a manner that makes us respond to it as 'Thou'. Convinced by Buber's insight, John Robinson, later to be Bishop of Woolwich, argued that it is this way of experiencing the world that compels us to speak of God as 'Thou' rather than 'It', and to treat 'God' as a personal name.

> The heart of all talk about personality is the reality of a certain quality of relatedness, of being encountered and drawn out by the grace and claim of a 'Thou'. This is the centre-point, the existential reality, which has to be given expression. And the need to speak of 'God' derives from the awareness that in and through and under every finite 'Thou' comes, if we are open to it, the grace and claim of an eternal, unconditional 'Thou' who cannot finally be evaded by being turned into an 'It'. This was the reality which the language of 'the personality of God' was trying to represent.[5]

This personal quality inherent in the whole range of numinous encounters has led different groups to different conclusions as they reflected upon it generation after generation. It is clear from ethnological evidence that in many areas people have held on to the impression that the force or *mana* which manifests itself in a wide variety of ways is one universal, pervasive power, and, from the personal quality of the encounters, have conceived the idea of a Great Spirit or supreme God, though one who is much more immanent than the term 'High God' suggests. In general, this 'He-who-is-met-everywhere' is approached for help only in the last resort, and belief in him does not preclude recognition of the more impersonal power in certain manifestations. But another way of interpreting the same experiences has been to individualize each local manifestation of the intangible power. Each tree and spring and sacred stone from within which such a numinous impact has been felt became the abode of a spirit – a nymph or *daemon* in ancient Greek mythology – often with a personal name. This is what the anthropologists mean by animism. From the association of personalized divinity with particular natural phenomena it was a short step to the recognition of greater gods in charge of the various forces of nature – a sun god, an earth mother, and gods of storm and ocean, fire, war and death.

It should not necessarily follow that those who think of divinity as personal must end by giving God, or the gods, a human likeness. But the risk is there, and it has been greatly increased by the existence of a different kind of veneration altogether, the cult of the family tree. In the harsh world of former times no human creature could survive as an individual; only the natural organism of the family and the extended clan had the physical and the psychic resources to live through its adversities. Man and woman were seen to exist only as links in the unbroken chain that stretched back through parents and grandparents to the first founders of the family, and on through the newly born to the unborn generations. A son's life is the forward thrust of his father's life, of his grandfathers', and the life of the whole past lineage. As his father is responsible for him, so also are they; and as he reveres his father, so will he also remember to placate and cajole all those forebears for the protection they can give. It is a matter of social security rather than religion, and the rituals are not usually described as worship; yet so self-sufficient is the communal human organism of the living and the dead that it almost supplants the gods. Indeed, it has often come about that the heroic ancestors of the tribe, particularly the semi-mythical founders of a royal dynasty, have become elevated to the status of gods, taking the foibles and passions of their humanity with them. The ancient Egyptians believed that the earliest dynasty of their Pharoahs had been preceded by a long line of gods and demi-gods, and only in the last century have excavations revealed that those divine rulers were, in fact, long-forgotten human kings. Greek city states likewise raised their legendary founders and heroes to the level of gods and built temples for them. Even the gods of Olympus bore the faint traces of having been an invading dynasty that usurped the thrones of a still earlier race of deities. It is well-established that, in much more recent times, the more dynamic of the tribal ancestors in many parts of Africa have become the hero-gods, with particular jurisdiction over storm, fire or war, childbirth or plague. There can be little doubt that veneration of ancestors, with its consequent deification of dead heroes, has contributed considerably to the development of polytheism in many cultures and civilizations.

It has also fostered the habit of thinking that the divine power is not only personal, but very like a human person. Anthropomorphism – visualizing God, or the gods, in the glorified likeness of humankind – is unquestionably a source of illumination. It affirms that the Absolute is at least to some extent accessible to our finite understanding, and opens a way for the discovery of some aspect of God's nature that cannot be found out by any other means. By the same token, it puts a unique value on those aspects of human nature in which our kinship to God resides. Yet anthropomorphism needs to be submitted to continuous correction – 'This Thou art, yet this Thou are not' – otherwise it leaves us with a fatally diminished idea of God. The inexpressible Other that addresses us from within and beyond the phenomena of this world and gives itself to us in such varied experiences as were described in the previous chapter, is far more than personal; we can and must respond to it as 'Thou', yet our encounters are of a vastly different quality from the exchanges between one human person and another.

3. Many or one?

In the history of religion reflecting upon those encounters has often pointed people in quite the contrary direction to the one we have so far considered. Though it can be only a matter of speculation, the reason for this may be that in certain periods people have paid more attention to a different aspect of those common experiences of encounter. The recipients of such experiences have often reported both a sense of being confronted by some separate reality or presence, and a sense of being part of an ultimate unity of all things – of being, in one example already quoted, both hailed by the buzzards and identified with them (see p. 41). It is at this point that the distinction made by Professor Ninian Smart, as mentioned in the previous chapter,[6] proves most helpful as a way of denoting, not two types of religious experience, but two elements in the same experience and, consequently, two distinct traditions of thought and spiritual practice derived from them. The sense of being face to face with something other and greater is the numinous aspect of the experience, and the last few pages have touched on the main inferences which subsequent reflection has drawn from it. On the other hand the recognition of a single oneness embracing all things, and of one's own identification with it, is the mystical aspect, and human pondering on that realization has led to the ideas and the spiritual disciplines of what has become known as the Perennial Philosophy.

This unitive perception of reality, when it breaks upon anyone unsought, brings about, at least temporarily, a drastic re-orientation that seems to stand most previous assumptions on their heads. The appearance of innumerable separate existences gives place to the one undivided, limitless entity; the contraries of good and evil, life and death, creation and destruction, are heard as distinct notes in a transcending harmony; history's interminable succession of beginnings and endings is seen to be only the rippling surface of a vast pool of completeness. With all this change of perception comes a sense of blissful fulfilment and peace. After such a revelation it is hardly surprising that the normal way of seeing the world should appear to be the merest delusion. The task of detaching one's mind from false habits of thought and trying to grasp that ultimate simplifying reality, the One which is also the All, begins to look as arduous as it is irresistible.

> From delusion lead me to Truth.
> From darkness lead me to Light.
> From death lead me to immortality.[7]

That well-known quotation from the Hindu scriptures is a reminder that the Indian sub-continent is the homeland of the Perennial Philosophy. Some features of it were present there long before the Aryan invasions that began about 1600 BC, among them the belief in the transmigration of the human soul through successive rebirths and the practice of yoga techniques of contemplation to bring the soul to self-knowledge and liberation from those endless returns. That was all submerged at first beneath the extrovert polytheism of the Aryan conquerors and their great nature gods – Varuna, Lord of the heavens who, with his companion Mitra, bestowed order; Indra the god of storm and war; Dyaus the god of the bright sky; Agni, god of fire, with his craftsman Tvashtar the blacksmith god who made Indra's thunderbolts. This all sounds oddly familiar because it was migrations of the same Aryan stock that carried their pantheism into Iran and Greece, where we can recognize Varuna in Uranus, Lord of heaven, and Dyaus in the supplanter, Zeus, Tvashtar the smith in Hephaestus and, possibly, Mitra in the Persian Mithras. But the peculiarity of the Indo-Aryan polytheism lay in the numinous quality engendered in their sacrificial rites which, as has already been mentioned, were so performed as to convey an overwhelming sense of *mana*-power, or *brahman*, which naturally became associated with the priests, or *brahmins*, themselves.

Gradually over the next seven centuries, as the complex ritual externals came to predominate over the numinous impact of the sacrifices, various movements of reaction set in. Elements of the pre-Aryan religion, never wholly forgotten, with their search for release from the treadmill of re-births, regained their appeal, and new spiritual treatises, the *Upanishads*, offered a re-interpretation of the Aryan liturgical texts, or *Vedas*, in the terms of a more individual and inward search for ultimate reality and liberation. 'I have thus laid the fire of sacrifice and, by burning in it the transient, I have reached the Eternal.'[8]

The transient was the illusory, and the first great delusion that had to be shed was the apparent multiplicity of separate beings that made up the world. 'There are not many but only ONE. Who sees variety and not the unity wanders from death to death.'[9] The capacity to grasp, or to be grasped by, the mystical aspect of religious experience, the unitive vision, has always been strong among the peoples of India.

There was a man mending the road; that man was myself; the pick-axe he held was myself; the very stone which he was breaking up was

> a part of me . . . I could feel the wind passing through the tree, and the little ant on the blade of grass I could feel.[10]

But seekers after reality could not rest content in fleeting glimpses of the essential unity which were just as transient as all other phenomena. They looked for the source of this oneness, and found it in an eternal, indivisible Self. 'Concealed in the heart of all beings is the *Atman*, the Self; smaller than the smallest atom, greater than the vast spaces . . . who rests invisible in the visible and permanent in the impermanent.'[11] How could this supreme reality, immanent in all things, be known and described, unless by looking within oneself? So began a discipline of introspection and self-knowledge whereby it was found that the journey in was as far as the journey beyond, and the final reality at the depth of the human heart seemed as inaccessible as the Supreme Reality behind all existence. For, though painful, it is not difficult to recognize the unreality of the false selves that one pretends to be; it is also possible to say of the ego that does the pretending, 'That is not the real, the permanent me.' But the unwrapping goes further and, in the last analysis, the one who finally knows the true self of a person is not that individual self, nor even some collective consciousness, but Another, a Self beyond the self, 'the unseen seer, the unheard hearer, the unthought thinker, the un-understood understander. No other seer than It is there, no other hearer than It, no other thinker than It, no other understander than It.'[12] That is the transcendent Self who alone can say 'I AM', whether in the deepest recess of the heart of any creature, where It is called the *Atman*, the Self, or in the aloneness of Its own Absolute Being, where It is known by that ancient name of power, *Brahman*.

The metaphysics of the *Upanishads* and the later scriptures was further developed into very diverse schools of thought, notably in the mediaeval period. At the beginning of the ninth century AD, Shankara stressed the doctrine of *a-dvaita*, non-duality, affirming that *Brahman* was the sole reality, unknowable because there was no real 'other' that might know It. The seeming existence of any other centre of consciousness than *Brahman-Atman* was an illusion to be overcome, there was no meaning in the exchange of 'I' and 'Thou', and blessedness came only when the sense of individual identity was dissolved into the universal ONE. Centuries earlier, while the *Upanishads* were still being composed, the

Buddhist movement had in fact shown that the path to *a-dvaita* bliss could be followed without belief either in a god or an immortal soul.

It is often suggested that strict *a-dvaita* philosophy is the one classic form of Hindu thought, but this is not so. The tradition of *bhakti*, personal I-Thou devotion, has co-existed with it. The emergence from obscurity of the two great gods, Shiva and Vishnu, as imaginable forms under which the Unknowable may be known, has allowed seekers to think and speak of It in positive as well as negative terms. So Hindu theology has recognized over the centuries that there must be two ways of looking at the Eternal. In itself It is *Brahman*, unmanifest and unaffected, but in Its relation to the universe It is the active and involved *Ishvara*. What the Western mystic, Meister Eckhart, called 'the silent desert of the divinity' calls to the human spirit as do the empty spaces of earth and sky, even to the point of self-negation. But when exploration turns to love the heart longs not for extinction but exchange, not for union, but *commu*nion. In his introduction to the *Bhagavadgita* Professor Radhakrishnan wrote:

> The *Gita* admits that the Real is the absolute Brahman, but from the cosmic point of view it is the Supreme Ishvara. The latter is the only way in which man's thought, limited as it is, can envisage the highest reality. Though the relation between the two is inconceivable to us from the logical standpoint, it is got over when we have the direct apprehension of Reality.[13]

4. The quest for the essence of things

More than half a century ago an English student, seeing Athens for the first time, and naively ignorant of what others had said before him, wrote ecstatically in his journal: 'In some extraordinary way the Parthenon is something more than the physical measurable facts, marvellous as these are. It is built of light and space, and the stone is used simply to contain, reflect and give form to the light which is the real building. You look at it and say, "This is the thing all of us are searching for: this is the heart of beauty." ' Pericles and his architects might have been pleased to know that the broken shell of their masterpiece should affect a 'barbarian' youth in those terms two and a half millennia after their day.

For no people have been more aware than the ancient Greeks were of the impact of beauty in all its numinous power. In their vocabulary one word denoted both the Lovely and the Good, and from pondering on the nature of beauty they gained their profoundest insight into the meaning of God. Yet they were haunted by beauty's transience and learned from it to distrust the passing phenomena in which our senses perceive it. They were the first to draw this distinction between loveliness and its material embodiment and to lament the poignant dichotomy in innumerable epitaphs.

> . . . your nightingale songs live on,
> and Death, the destroyer of every lovely thing,
> shall not touch them with his blind, all-cancelling fingers.[14]

The Greeks' envious veneration of the gods was evoked principally by the deathless vigour by which the calm power and perfection of those immortals was sustained at a level far above the reach of brief human lives.

So the pain inherent in beauty's enchantment led them to discriminate sharply between the loveliness that touched them so keenly and the objects in and through which they recognized it. They wanted to abstract 'the heart of beauty', which alone possessed the godlike quality of permanence, without falling captive to those beguiling sense-impressions through which beauty had laid its spell upon them in the first place. Though their sculptors and vase-painters were supremely aware of forms and outlines – what Sir Maurice Bowra called 'the plastic vision' – they seem never to have been content to reproduce what met the eye alone. It was not the bereavement of particular people that they commemorated on their funeral *steles*, but grief itself; and in reproducing the precise balance and tension of a body's movement they were trying to disclose the quintessence of young manhood, feminine grace or divine mastery. Bowra wrote:

> Artists sought to catch and express the essential nature of a subject, whether divine or human, high or humble, tragic or convivial, heroic or salacious, because they felt that the conviction of the beautiful which came to them in explicable and inspiring visitations was derived from a higher order of being and must be treated with a full awareness of its haunting and possessing presence . . . It was this sense of a

connection between the seen and the unseen, between the accidental and the essential, between the transitory and the permanent, which provided Greek art with a guiding ideal and a welcome discipline and ennobled it with an exalted detachment and a consistent, self-contained harmony.[15]

It is necessary to bear in mind always that the Greek thinkers of the classical period, in distinguishing the essence from the incidentals, were not contrasting, as we would do, the material realm with the spiritual, or physical with metaphysical reality. Greeks differed from Indian philosophers by holding to a basic conviction that the Whole, All-that-is, including the human soul and the immortal gods, was a single living organism, material in its constitution and subject to physical laws. Many scholars, especially in their commentaries on Plato, have ignored this persistent peculiarity. So, like their artists, the philosophers of Greece looked for the essence or inmost substance of the All in order to grasp what was most real and permanent amid so much that came into being, changed and passed away. What was unchanging at the heart of so much becoming? What was the unifying principle underlying the multiplicity of existence?

Their earliest guesses as to what this might be – water, air or some indefinable element devoid of qualities of its own and therefore adaptable – progressed towards less corporeal solutions: Pythagoras believed numbers to be the primary elements throughout nature, Anaxagoras was the first to propose Mind. Yet even those concepts which we would consider abstract or immaterial, they regarded as physical substances, albeit of a more rarefied constitution. The soul might be made of air or fire or, as in Plato's *Timaeus*, of a commixture of affirmation and negation; the opposed forces which Empedocles called 'Strife' and 'Love' are described by him as having length, breadth, height and weight; they tried in fact to answer metaphysical, psychological and even moral questions with deductions from the way in which solid bodies relate to one another in space. Conversely, when Melissos of Samos calls the ultimate reality 'eternal and infinite and one, imperishable and incapable of suffering pain or grief',[16] it is difficult for us to realize that what he has in mind is not God but the universe. Their world-view was what E. R. Goodenough called 'instinctively pantheistic materialism', and, by applying the logic of geometry to what we consider to be immaterial and spiritual realities, they reached conclusions that were often bizarre. They argued with such brilliant originality, however, that what they construed from those inappropriate premises was accepted for nearly two thousand years as self-evident truth about God and the human soul!

5. Is reality static or dynamic?

In about 500 BC two rival schools of thought appeared. Heraclitus of Ephesus declared that the underlying principle of existence was motion and process, which he likened to fire that is in constant change, flaring up at one point, dying down at another. Existence, he claimed, consists of a tension of opposites, or 'strife', so that the controlling soul or mind of the world (the nearest he came to an idea of God) is in a state of ceaseless becoming. In opposition to this dynamic interpretation of existence, Parmenides of Elea in southern Italy argued by strict logic that all that exists is in reality eternal, unmoving and unchanging, in spite of all appearances to the contrary. He called it 'What is', meaning the material continuum of the universe. There is no void. There cannot be such a thing as nothing, since whatever is nothing does not exist. There can be no 'coming to be' and no 'ceasing to be', since 'coming to be' implies that something was formerly nothing, and 'ceasing to be' implies that something is going to be nothing, and these are meaningless, since there is no such thing as nothing. All is an immobile, indivisible continuum, and no part of what exists can move from where it is because there is no unoccupied space, no void, into which it might go. (This was two centuries before Archimedes cried 'Eureka!' over his discovery of displacement.)

Both these rival schools of thought were elaborated by later teachers, and it was by attempting to reconcile the two views that first Leucippus of Miletus and then Democritus of Thrace hit upon the astonishingly accurate theory of the atomic structure of matter towards the end of the fifth century BC. Nevertheless the logic of Parmenides, based upon material and spatial models, proved to be the more tenaciously influential, leaving the most persistent legacy of assumptions. For, by equating existence with immutability, he confirmed the Greeks in their nostalgic tendency to regard change as loss, and predisposed the mind of Europe to place supreme value upon permanence and fixity and to disparage mutation and development. Along with this inhibiting conviction a number of other blind alleys were built into the structure of philosophical thought that was to dominate both the classical and the mediaeval world-views, namely:

that the natural state of anything is to be at rest, unless it has been attracted or impelled by some external force;

that change necessarily entails transition from a worse to a better state, or from a better to a worse;

that being and becoming are mutually exclusive, since whatever comes to be also ceases to be, but whatever is remains forever the same;

that the senses perceive the changeable, but only logical thought apprehends changeless reality;

that there is a dichotomy between the body which perceives through its senses and the soul which is the seat of rational thought.

Plato and Aristotle, though they far surpassed earlier thinkers, did not break free from these preconceptions. Plato admired Parmenides and projected what he had deduced from physical properties on to his own concept of immaterial realities. Parmenides meant by 'What is' the material continuum of the universe; Plato meant 'What *really* is', namely, the immaterial abstractions of pure thought. So he argued that only the changeless was real. He postulated a timeless realm of archetypal Ideas or Forms, those inner essences of things that the artists strove to capture, and a Mind of pure beauty, truth and goodness presiding over them. Yet those realities were inaccessible to the world of imperfect copies and sense-perceptions which was, paradoxically, the artists' stock in trade. He ended with an unbridgeable gulf between the objects of sense and the objects of pure thought, the realm of reality.

Aristotle, the realist, refused to regard the eternal Forms as independent entities. He accepted, in his analysis of any object, the presence of a paradigm, such as 'horse', 'olive-tree' or 'cloud', which gave the object definition and was *logically* distinct from the matter of which it consisted; but he resolutely confined all explanations, even of metaphysical realities, to a scrupulous observation and analysis of the phenomena of this world. He also rejected Parmenides' absolute polarity of being or not being by pointing to the reality of potentiality as a link between them. Becoming involves the actualizing of a potential in something that already is in being. Hence being must include becoming.

Artistotle's approach to truth was strictly scientific in the modern sense of the word, though with two important differences. As with all

Greek thinkers, his faith in logical deduction entailed a distrust of sense-perception, so he saw no value in submitting a hypothesis to experiment in the manner of today's scientists. Moreover, his understanding of causation was significantly different from that of the last four centuries. While recognizing antecedent or 'efficient' causes as one element in explaining why anything is as it is, he agreed with Plato that the fundamental explanation must lie in the purpose that a thing is bent on achieving or the potential it needs to fulfil. So Aristotle argued that flames rise upwards because it is their natural fulfilment to reach a higher plane, and plants produce leaves to protect the fruit they are going to bear. This is the teleological concept of causation which predominated in classical and, subsequently, mediaeval speculation. Post-Renaissance science repudiated it as an unwarranted interpretation of the facts, and has without doubt gained its greatest achievements by concentrating upon the search for antecedent causes. The new science of the twentieth century, however, by disclosing a universe of indeterminate options, has re-instated the inherent potentiality of matter as at least a quasi-teleological factor in the evolution of life and consciousness. Be that as it may, when Aristotle argued that the existence of a world of things in process of becoming and passing away requires logically some First Mover that is itself unmoved, he was not visualizing an original nudge but an ultimate magnet, a supreme Good attracting all things towards a more perfect fulfilment of themselves or, as he called it, 'blessedness'. In a good deal of his writing he seems to equate the blessedness that draws human beings with the achievement of virtue, generosity and greatness of soul. But in a few almost mystical passages, Aristotle suggests that the culmination of our rational faculty is abstract thought of such intensity as to bring about a union with its object, namely with that supreme Mind that is drawing all intelligence towards itself. Since, however, pure thought does involve an attraction towards and a participation in the object of thought, the supreme Mind cannot think anything less than the best of all possible objects, namely itself. Aristotle's God knows nothing outside itself.[17]

6. The Hellenistic developments

It is not surprising that, in the centuries that followed the break-up of the city states and their classical Greek culture, philosophical and religious speculation veered towards an agnostic fatalism, ennobled by the cultivation of a calm, dispassionate acceptance of the vicissitudes of life. Belief in an immaterial realm of changeless reality was abandoned as too remote to be significant and the theory of atoms came into its own as the prevailing account of the physical nature of all things, including the soul. This meant, in effect, that events were determined by two imponderable forces: Necessity (natural law) playing upon Chance (the random whirl of the atoms) as if in some cosmic pin-table. The rival ideologies of Stoics and Epicureans prescribed very similar techniques for eliminating fear, anxiety and illusion. Their brave but bleak ideals for human character – *apatheia* or unaffectedness and *ataraxia* or calm – were to colour the idea of God's character also for many centuries to come.

But, having argued their way to the concept of an unknowable and unknowing God and steeled themselves to eliminate all desire, even for purely spiritual consolations, the thinkers of the later Hellenism were left with the old unappeased longing for access to the essence of beauty, albeit a purely intellectual beauty detached from the illusory perceptions of the senses. So, from about the beginning of Rome's ascendancy in the eastern Mediterranean, when philosophy was becoming very eclectic and trade with India was bringing new influences to bear upon metaphysical speculation, there was a movement of return towards a mystical pursuit of fulfilment. Its leaders harked back to the more unworldly doctrines of some of the earlier philosophers and re-interpreted them in an attempt to bridge the abyss between this world of transient unreality and the realm of pure changeless being. There were those who constructed their system on what they supposed were the teachings of Pythagoras and his mystique of numbers. These Neo-Pythagoreans, as they were called, retained an unmitigated polarity of mind and matter, of the Absolute and the cosmos. Their supreme God remained totally out of reach and beyond comprehension, but, borrowing more from Plato than Pythagoras, they called him the First God and envisaged one or more less transcendent levels of divinity, by means of which matter, with its evil downward drag, could have come into being and aspiring souls might ascend towards eternal reality. The second level of divine being was, according to their scheme, the creator of the cosmos, sometimes called the Demi-urge or Fabricator, sometimes the Son or Second God, sometimes the Logos or Mind.

It is impossible to say whether intercultural exchanges were taking place or whether the same concepts came to birth independently in several different religious systems, but certainly this idea of derivative extensions or emanations from the essential being of God is reminiscent of the Indian distinction between the absolute *Brahman* and the world-related *Ishvara*. Judaism was probably under the influence of Hellenism when it began to speak of the Wisdom and the Word of Yahweh as personified agents of God. Philo, the Alexandrian Jew and contemporary of Jesus, who sought to assimilate that Jewish faith to the Hellenistic philosophies of his day, found in this development the most apt way of expressing the relationship of God's absolute transcendence to his presence in the world as its Creator and Lord.

Once the intraversible divide between rational human souls and the transcendent God had been bridged, however crudely, the way was opened for a genuine mysticism, and in the third century AD Plotinus gave it a systematic form which has survived in Western spirituality to this day. It is significant that, after nearly twenty years of philosophical enquiry in Alexandria, he wanted to pursue his studies in India, and only by a series of accidents set up his own school in Rome in the year 244. The language Plotinus uses is that of a man who has evidently experienced the unitive vision of the world and reflected deeply upon it. He taught that all existence has its origin in the One, the Alone, which is beyond being and beyond knowing. Yet out of the expansive fullness of the One flows the divine Mind, 'the image of the One which contemplates the One after its manner and in turn pours forth a lower level of Being which is called Soul'.[18] The process of outflowing involves a progressive distancing from the source and so sets in motion a vast cyclical rhythm of departure and return such as Heraclitus visualized. That part of the cosmic Soul which is nearer to its source is held in blissful contemplation of the Mind from which it came, but that part which has fallen further away is involved in the multiplicity and materiality of the world of sense which it has created. But since all things, in time, are driven to make good what they have lost, materiality is drawn back towards the spiritual and multiplicity towards the oneness from which they emerged. Within this cosmic cycle the human person is a microcosm in which the individual soul must disentangle itself from the realm of multiplicity and thereafter abandon even rational thought until it is lifted by the 'unknowing' of ecstatic love into union with the One.

This was a new note after the centuries of mathematical logic, a note that was to knit the pagan Plotinus in a strange kinship of spirit with Augustine, John Eriugena, Meister Eckhart and the whole Christian mystical tradition and, ironically, with the true beginning of the long quest of the Greeks. For Plotinus, like the artists of Attica and Ionia, was actually searching for the heart of beauty.

> What then are we to think of those who see beauty in itself, in all its purity, unencumbered by flesh and body, so perfect in its purity that it transcends by far such things of earth and heaven? All other beauties are imports, are alloys. They are not primal. They come, all of them, from it. If then one sees it, the provider of beauty to all things beautiful while remaining solely itself and receiving nothing from them, what beauty can still be lacking? This is true and primal beauty that graces its lovers and makes them worthy of love. This is the point at which is imposed upon the soul the sternest and uttermost combat, the struggle to which it gives its total strength in order not to be denied its portion in this best of visions . . . It were well to cast kingdoms aside and the domination of the entire earth and sea and sky if, by this spurning, one might attain this vision.[19]

4

God With Us

Formative Reflection in Jewish and Christian Tradition

1. The memory of a deliverance

To turn to the Hebrew idea of God that appears in the Old Testament is an entirely different experience. So, indeed, it should be, since the contrast derives precisely from the very different type of experience upon which the Jewish people focussed their formative reflection. The Greek mind, as we have seen, engaged itself with the strange impact of beauty and 'the way in which physical nature can at times grip us and hold us with an inexorable enchantment'.[1] But what launched the Hebrew tribes into their distinctive faith was an experience of the impact of rescue: the religion of the Old Testament sprang out of the Exodus from Egypt. God had kept a promise. God had saved. God was to be trusted. The stories of their earlier ancestral origins in the days of the patriarchs and of the dim, mythical period before that, as we have them in the Bible, were all told from within the settled life of the Israelites in their own land, and the telling bears the marks of the never-absent memory of that Exodus. Even their accounts of the creation of the world and the making of humankind are set down in terms that recall that definitive experience of rescue.

Without far more evidence than has so far come to light it is impossible to know as historical facts exactly what happened, or when, or to whom. There are no certain references to the event in Egyptian records, just as the crucifixion of Jesus is almost unnoticed in the annals of Rome. The intriguing, but inconclusive, correspondences that have been noticed between Egyptian writings and the Pentateuch suggest that over a long period there may have been several incidents of moonlight flitting from the Egyptian labour camps on the part of Hebrew and other Semitic clans, which then settled in Palestine by peaceful or other means. One of these escapes, probably involving at least the Rachel tribes – Ephraim, Manasseh and Benjamin – must have been accompanied by such an overwhelming sense of divine presence and deliverance as to make it an unforgettable revelation. It is inconceivable that a folk memory so powerful that it became the pivotal heritage of a whole nation should have arisen from any other source than an actual experience at a particular time and place, however few and negligible the people to whom it happened. The evocative strength with which the memory of that experience persisted through the subsequent millennium can be gauged from the number of references to it that occur throughout the Old Testament. Isolated scraps of the tradition crop up in those songs – probably the oldest material in the Bible – which have been incorporated in the narratives.

> I will sing to Yahweh, for he has risen up in triumph,
> the horse and his rider he has hurled into the sea (Ex.15.1).
>
> Yahweh came from Sinai and shone forth from Seir,
> he appeared from Mount Paran,
> and with him were myriads of holy ones
> streaming along at his right hand (Deut.33.2).
>
> Yahweh, when you set forth from Seir,
> when you marched from the land of Edom,
> earth trembled; heaven quaked;
> the clouds streamed down in torrents.
> Mountains shook in fear before Yahweh, the Lord of Sinai,
> before Yahweh, the God of Israel (Judg.5.4,5).
>
> . . . the choice fruit of the everlasting hills,
> the choice fruits of earth and its fullness
> by the favour of him who dwells in the burning bush –
> may this rest on the head of Joseph,

> on the brow of him who was prince among his brothers
> (Deut.33.15,16).

The Hebrew prophets continued to use that primitive device of remembering the past as though it had happened to those whom they were addressing.

> It was I who brought you up from the land of Egypt,
> I who led you in the wilderness forty years,
> to take possession of the land of the Amorites (Amos 2.10).

But from the middle of the eighth century BC, the prophets began to exploit the living memory in a moralistic and chastening way. So, in the passage above, Amos goes on:

> Listen, I groan under the burden of you
> as a wagon creaks under a full load (Amos 2.13).

Hosea also recalled the initial rescue and vocation of the people to bring home to the northern kingdom the enormity of its apostasy.

> When Israel was a youth, I loved him,
> out of Egypt I called my son;
> but the more I called, the farther they went from me (Hos.11.1,2b).

Some of the oracles attributable to Micah, who addressed the kingdom of Judah in the next generation, take up the same theme:

> My people, what have I done to you?
> How have I wearied you? Bring your charges!
> I brought you up from Egypt,
> I set you free from the land of slavery,
> I sent Moses, Aaron and Miriam to lead you (Micah 6.3,4).

Micah's contemporary, Isaiah, is surprisingly the exception among the great prophets in mentioning the Exodus rescue only once, and that very obliquely (10.24–26), though he often shows precise knowledge about the Egypt of his own day. But Jeremiah, who was much influenced by the reform movement which had produced the Book of Deuteronomy in the second half of the seventh century BC, frequently referred to that original liberation,[2] at least up to the time when Jewish refugees from Jerusalem began to seek asylum in the land of their ancient captivity. Of the prophets of the Babylonian Exile, Second Isaiah makes good use of the Exodus story as a paradigm of deliverance to come.[3] Ezekiel, on the other hand, writing in the earlier part of the Exile, chose to narrate the whole saga of the original rescue from Egypt and the law-giving at Sinai in the context of a single sermon designed to drive home the obdurate disobedience of the Jewish people in succumbing to polytheism, and to recall them to repentance (Ezek.20.1–44).

This new genre of homiletical recapitulations of history became a feature of Judaism after the Exile as a method of using the 'mighty acts of God' for a moralistic or didactic purpose. A good example is the Levites' public recital of the fortunes of their nation as a preamble to the communal renewal of the covenant, as recorded in Nehemiah chapter 9; and similar catalogues are found in the Apocrypha (Wisd. 10.15–11.14; 16.15–19.12; Ecclus.44.16–49.16) and in Stephen's apology in Acts 7.2–53. One might wish to include in the same category all those psalms which describe at length the events of the deliverance from Egypt and the possession of the promised land; but this would be a mistake. A closer look shows that Psalms 78 and 106 certainly share the same motive as the passage in Ezekiel 20, which is to shame the Jews for the repeated rebellion of their forefathers against the demands of God, and so may be said to belong to that later genre. But Psalms 77, 105 and 135 recall the saving events with the sole object of eliciting praise to Yahweh and confidence in his ancient promises. It is the difference between law and gospel. Reflection upon a past experience of divine rescue focussed attention in the early period upon the character of the God who had so acted, but increasingly, as time went on, upon the actions of the human beings who had been so obligated.[4]

2. *The actively present God*

The impact of divine rescue is essentially an experience of God, and each recollection of it renews the encounter with God's reality and God's nature. It is not a backward look but a fresh re-presentation. Sheila Cassidy's 'rescue' consisted in the fact that 'all the time it was happening I knew that God loved me',[5] and every memory of it must to some extent recharge that absolute and immediate knowledge. 'I am Yahweh your God who brought you out of Egypt, out of the house of bondage' is a reminder that works neither as a philosophical statement nor a moral argument, but with the multiple reverberations of a song, a war-cry or a sacrament. So ritual reiteration has been the means *par excellence* of keeping the Exodus experience alive. 'On that day you are to tell your son, "This is because of what Yahweh did for me when I came out of Egypt" ' (Ex.13.8). 'Then you must solemnly recite before the Lord your God: "My father was a homeless Aramaean who went down to Egypt and lived there with a small band of people, but there it became a great, powerful and large nation. The Egyptians treated us harshly and humiliated us; they imposed cruel slavery on us. We cried to Yahweh the God of our fathers for help and he listened to us . . . He brought us to this place and gave us this land" ' (Deut.26.1–11). Such recitations of the story are themselves a form of reflection upon it.

As time passed and situations changed the story takes on a different significance. What it 'says' about God also needs to be reiterated. Terence Fretheim, a Lutheran scholar in the USA, has drawn attention to a parallel type of recitation, more propositional in form, which appears just as frequently in the Old Testament, summarizing the essential generalization about the nature of Yahweh which reflection had derived from the story itself.

> The Lord, the Lord, a God compassionate and gracious, long-suffering, ever faithful and true, remaining faithful to thousands, forgiving iniquity, rebellion and sin but without acquitting the guilty, one who punishes children and grandchildren to the third and fourth generation for the iniquity of their fathers (Ex.34.6,7; see also Num.14.18; Neh.9.17; Pss 86.15; 103.8,9; Joel 2.13; Jonah 4.2).[6]

This might be called the creed of the Old Testament derived from the recollection of its gospel. It is a statement about the abiding presence of the God who was first known as an intervention.

The experience of an apparent intervention from beyond which implies an active presence introduces an entirely new dynamic into the previous faith, or lack of faith, in an individual or a community. Something has happened, and happened to particular people. Religions that have been born, or born anew, out of some act of God have at best a vitality, at worst a fanaticism, that even the finest system of ideas cannot generate. Judaism and Christianity are not the only examples of this. Islam owes its vigour to its conviction that the giving of the Holy Qur'ān in its perfection was the supremely saving act of God in virtue of which a welter of warring tribes was raised from a debased paganism and welded in a few decades into an empire with a new message for the world. The corporate experience of divine intervention is bound to establish so strong a sense of a special relationship with God that it feels like a new beginning, if not a new religion. This is the significance of the announcement to Moses of the name Yahweh in Exodus 3. It summed up and symbolized the new relationship and, whether in fact the Hebrews had formerly known it and used it or not, the tradition inserted later into the story by the priestly chroniclers is certainly true in a psychological sense.

> God said to Moses, I am Yahweh. I appeared to Abraham, Isaac, and Jacob as El Shaddai, the Power of the Heights, but I did not let myself be known to them by my name Yahweh. I also established my covenant with them to give them Canaan, the land where for a time they settled as foreigners. And now I have heard the groaning of the Israelites, enslaved by the Egyptians, and I am mindful of my covenant. Therefore say to the Israelites, I am Yahweh. I shall free you from your labour in Egypt and deliver you from slavery. I shall rescue you with outstretched arm and with mighty acts of judgment. I shall adopt you as my people and I shall be your God. You will know that I, Yahweh, am your God, the God who frees you (Ex.6.2–7).

There has been much discussion among Semitic scholars as to the derivation and precise meaning of the name Yahweh, and it still goes on. Now there is fairly wide agreement that it is related to the verb *hayah* or *hawah*, which resembles the Greek *ginomai* in signifying both 'to be' and 'to become or come about'. So one might say that it means to be, but not in the abstract sense of existing in oneself so much as in the concrete, relational sense of being there or being present. In the passage in Exodus 3 where the sacred name is revealed, Moses parries God's call with the protest, 'But who am I?', to which God replies 'I am with you – *ki ehyeh 'immak.*' And when Moses objects, 'If they ask me the name of the one who sent me, what am I to say?', God answers him not with '*ani asher ani* – I am what I am', but with '*ehyeh asher ehyeh*', which has variously been rendered, 'I am there; wherever it may be, I am really there',[7] or 'I will be present as I will be present'.[8] So the name Yahweh signifies, 'He who is present', or possibly, 'Ah, he is here!' It is in itself a declaration of God's free choice of his people to be the ones to whom he would be present. 'Tell them that "I am present" has sent you' (Ex.3.14). It is the same promise as was renewed to Moses later on Mount Sinai, 'my presence shall go with you' – where the word '*panim*, face', is used (Ex.33.14) – and it was to distinguish the Israelites from the other nations: 'What great nation has a god close at hand as Yahweh our God is close to us whenever we call to him?' (Deut.4.7). During the wanderings in the desert and the gradual conquest and settlement in the land of Canaan, it was that presence, and its symbols, the shining Shekinah cloud and the ark of the covenant, that rallied the easily disunited clans as if to a flag. Indeed, when for the first time they had to face a common enemy together, the commemorative altar was afterwards named 'Yahweh our banner' (Ex.17.15). Later, when the monarchy was established in Jerusalem, another potent symbol of the presence of God was the anointed king himself, God's viceregent. He was said to be seated on Yahweh's throne and acclaimed as his son (I Chron.29.23; Ps.2.6,7; 89.20–37). As the last of these references shows, however, the king's claim to represent God was conditional upon his own righteous rule.

Yet to this still primitive people, the presence of the divine was fearful as well as reassuring. God's drawing near to them did not diminish Deity in their thought. The numinous terror of God's otherness and unknowability was there from the first, both in Moses' individual encounter at the burning hush – 'Do not come near; the place where you are standing is holy ground' – and in their corporate experience at the foot of the unapproachable mountain, where all the camp trembled at the trumpeting din of thunder and lightning. Yahweh was holy, and that meant so essentially separate from earthly existence that any inadvertent contact with that presence could strike a human creature dead (II Sam. 6.3–10). So whatever pertains to God must be 'set apart', God's own rescued people most of all (Ex.19.4–6; Lev.20.26). 'The "thou shalt" is a corollary of the "I am" of Ex.3.14, for the revelation of God as a sovereign and personal presence can only have as counterpart the revelation of man as a dependent and obedient creature.'[9] The impact of their rescue, and its implication that God had thereby made them his own, was for all time to be a source of both comfort and dread. In the prophecies of Ezekiel many centuries later, the words, 'You shall know that I am Yahweh, the actively present God' could portend blessing or punishment: 'You, my people, will know that I am Yahweh when I open your graves and bring you up from them' (Ezek.3;7.13). 'On the frontier of Israel I shall bring you to judgment, then you will know that I am Yahweh' (Ezek.11.11).

3. The demands of a rescue

The continual presence of God in their midst constituted in itself a claim upon their exclusive adherence. 'I am Yahweh who brought you out of Egypt, out of the land of slavery, you must have no other god beside me' (Ex.20.2,3). That would not immediately have conveyed the idea of pure monotheism to people of those times. The fact that Yahweh was their God, committed to them and present in their midst, required of them only that they resorted to none of the other gods, not that they should deny their existence. To each nation its own divinity – that is what is technically called 'monolatry', worshipping only one. Its weakness is that, in a pluralist society such as Israel was, with many of the former ethnic groups still living in the land and kings marrying foreign wives, there is a constant temptation to try the efficacy of other gods when one's own seems to fall short. A step nearer to monotheism was taken when most Jews became convinced that their God was supreme over a pantheon of gods who formed his entourage. Two of the psalms almost certainly assume that view (Ps.82.1; 89.6,7) and there is evidence of it elsewhere in the Old Testament.[10]

The final stage of a pure monotheism is reached when the very existence of any other divine being is denied. Jeremiah was the most persistent spokesman of this refutation: 'Has a nation ever exchanged its gods, and these no gods at all?' (2.11). 'Your children have forsaken me, swearing by gods that are no gods' (5.7 16–20). Through the second Isaiah the claim is plainly stated: 'I am Yahweh and there is no other; apart from me there is no god' (Isa.45.5,6,22; cf. 44.6,8; 46.9). The pure monotheism to which the Jews eventually attained was a belief in Yahweh so absolute that they brooked no counterpart to him. Hans Küng has affirmed that this religion totally precluded not only other gods, but also any concept of a feminine partner to the deity as in most ancient Semitic religions, or of a countervailing god of evil as in Zoroastrianism. No word for goddess ever evolved in Hebrew, but male and female images and metaphors were applied with an equal seemliness to the one God who transcends gender. Here and there the Old Testament speaks of destructive demons, but it knows nothing of a personification of evil set in eternal contradiction to God, and the accusing cynic, Satan, so far from being on a par with God, is made to serve his purpose.[11]

But the exclusive loyalty to Yahweh that was to issue in this highly personalized monotheism was not the only demand laid upon the Hebrew tribes by their memory of rescue and their sense of God's commitment to their destiny. Other obligations were entailed. There were ritual requirements directly inferred from God's intervention on their behalf. 'Observe the Sabbath day to keep it holy; . . . that day you must not do any work, nor your slave, your slave girl, your ox, your donkey, or the alien residing among you, so that your slaves and slave girls may rest as you do. Bear in mind that you were slaves in Egypt, and Yahweh your God brought you out' (Deut.5.12–15). The age-old agricultural festivals of lambing, wheat-harvest and fruit-gathering were to have commemorations of the escape from Egypt, the law-giving at Sinai and the desert wanderings superimposed upon them. That commemorative aspect of these occasions must have predominated once people were required to make the pilgrimage to Jerusalem for the celebration instead of holding it at the local shrine close to their farms. But those very memories laid other social obligations upon them. 'You must not deprive aliens and the fatherless of justice or take a widow's cloak in pledge. Bear in mind that you were slaves in Egypt and Yahweh your God redeemed you from there. That is why I command you to do this' (Deut.24.17,18). 'You must use true scales and weights, true dry and liquid measures. I am Yahweh your God who brought you out of Egypt' (Lev.19.36). Their God's self-commitment *to* them demanded a reciprocal commitment *from* them. This was the meaning of the covenant and the significance of his being called a jealous God.

This vividly personal and active picture of God entailed a view of history which interpreted events as interventions. One supreme experience of rescue had clearly not ensured a perpetual exemption from trouble. So from quite an early date the Israelites began to read their own story as an alternation of chastisement and restoration in a continuous process of divine education. Any religion, however, which brings God on to the stage of history and appropriates God to that extent tends to present a very restricted concept of the divine interests. The impact of their deliverance from Egypt, fostered over the years in the national memory, led them, understandably, to regard Yahweh as their particular tribal god and, as has just been shown, they only gradually came to recognize him as the sole and universal God and the world as a single entity under him. It was probably during the second stage of this development, when they claimed his supremacy over an entourage of lesser gods, that they first hailed him as the Creator of the universe. But it may have taken their loss of homeland and holy city, and their discovery of his continuing presence with them in exile, to convince them that the Holy One of Israel was in fact the Provider and Judge and Redeemer of all.

Then how, in the light of this all-inclusive monotheism, were they to make sense of their special relationship with God as a chosen people? To this difficult question they found a variety of answers at different levels of spirituality. To the most perceptive among them the promise they believed God had made to their ancestor Abraham that, when his descendants became a great nation, all the families of the earth would pray to be blessed as he was blessed, suggested a vocation of demonstration to the rest of the world. By obeying the moral demand of their God of rescue, his people should exhibit such blessedness in the purity and joy of their worship and in the justice of their society that the other nations would turn to Yahweh and bring their offerings also to the temple at Jerusalem, the true spiritual home for them all. 'I will count Egypt and Babylon among my friends; Philistine, Tyrian and Nubian shall be here; and Zion shall be called a mother from whom men of every race have taken their true birth' (Ps.87.4,5). The Second Isaiah visualized the ultimate possibility that the chosen people, after extreme tribulation and rejection, indeed by virtue of these sufferings, would be recognized as God's servant and light to the nations (Isaiah 53).

4. From remembrance to expectation

Naturally such an exalted vocation never became the popular hope. More of the people and, indeed, more of the prophecies, looked tenaciously to the prospect of an eventual restoration of the political power that Israel had briefly enjoyed under the single monarchy of David and Solomon. In times of greatest adversity they recalled the pledge they believed God had given to David that his dynasty would never die out (Gen.49.10; II Sam.7.13; Isa.11.1; Micah 5.2; Jer.23.5–8; Ezek.37.24–5). In this vision of the future the anointed king, the Messiah, through whose agency God would reverse history, was essentially a conqueror. So the mainstream of Jewish expectation was set, not towards a voluntary conversion of the Gentiles but towards their enforced submission: 'Your gates shall be open continually, they shall never be shut day or night, that through them may be brought the wealth of nations and their kings under escort. For the nation or kingdom that refuses to serve you shall perish' (Isa.60.11,12). Jewish expectations of the future, however, were never clear and consistent. As often as not they anticipated that God would bring about the restoration of their kingdom by his own intervention with no messianic intermediary.[12] When a Messiah *is* included among their predictions he is most frequently a warrior king like David himself or like the human saviours in the days of the judges,[13] though occasionally a more peaceable leader was visualized, one vested with spiritual or even priestly authority rather than military power, to restore the Jewish kingdom in a golden age of peace and plenty.[14]

This, however, began to seem such an unlikely prospect, whether by force of arms or spiritual breakthrough, that more and more Jews postponed their expectations until the end of the present world order when, they believed, God would wind up history, sweeping away all natural structures of power, and restore Israel in a future state of *supernatural* existence – an apocalyptic scenario which, like the this-worldly restoration, did not necessarily require any Messiah at all.[15] The contrast with the earlier expectations was striking.

> Hosea, Amos or Isaiah know only a single world, in which even the great events at the End of Days run their course. Their eschatology is of a national kind: it speaks of the re-establishment of the House of David, now in ruins, and of the future glory of an Israel returned to God . . . In contrast apocalypticism produced the doctrine of the two aeons which follow one another and stand in antithetical relationship: this world and the world to come . . . There arise

> the conceptions of the Resurrection of the Dead, of reward and punishment in the Last Judgment, and of Paradise and Hell.[16]

After the time of the Graeco-Syrian tyranny and the revolt of the Maccabees, some writers, probably through interpreting the visions in the Book of Daniel literally rather than symbolically, envisaged a *heavenly* Messiah whom God was holding in readiness until the time was due for him to appear as judge and ruler of the new age. These were clearly the terms in which the earliest Christians proclaimed Jesus as Messiah after his resurrection, but it is notoriously difficult to judge how prevalent the idea of the heavenly Messiah had become before that time.[17] On balance it seems that for most Jews the title continued to mean an earthly warrior king with certain supernatural powers.

Most of the Jews, however, like the silent majority everywhere, wanted only to be left alone to enjoy a modest life and the consolations of religion without the pretensions of politics. If God's rescue was little more than a racial memory, they could still hold on to God's presence in their midst. If it seemed to be no longer such an active presence as their ancestors had known, there were calmer ways of enjoying it with as much certainty as before. The observance of the Law was a more reliable way of remembering God's presence and their identity as his people than the vicissitudes of political independence. 'Yahweh has told you mortals what is good and what it is that he requires of you: only to act justly, to love loyalty, to walk humbly with your God' (Micah 6.8). Gradually over the years Judaism of this more introverted style came to focus its grateful remembrance of God's goodness less upon the rescue from Egypt and more upon the giving of the Law at Sinai. The Torah as a way of life turned every trivial detail of daily routine into a recollection of God. Since nothing they might do was beneath his notice they must indeed be his people and he their ever-present God. Anyone who has in these days experienced a Sabbath in modern Tel Aviv and the great stillness of its car-less streets can understand the shared happiness and cohesion that such a corporate observance creates. 'God is in the midst of her, therefore shall she not be removed' (Ps.46.5).

The claim of the Law, the Torah, upon the Jewish family, then, was the point of God's contact, the pressure of God's presence, upon every happening in the day's events. His Word, his Wisdom, his Way, was like an extension of God's transcendent being into their world of mundane activity. The Glory, the Word, the Wisdom of the Lord were first simply personified as an indirect way of saying 'God himself'; but in time they came to be thought of as distinct modes of God's self-communication to his people and his presence among them. The Torah was another means whereby God was immanent, the Beyond at the heart of things. The later Isaiah had spoken of Yahweh's Word as an envoy that would not return empty-handed without accomplishing his purpose (Isa.55.11). The so-called Wisdom literature of later Judaism, and the rabbinic teaching that grew out of it, pictured the Torah as pre-existing even the creation, an embodiment of the very mind of God, working with him as agent and play-fellow. 'The Lord created me the first of his works, long ago before all else that he made . . . Then I was at his side each day, his darling and delight, playing in his presence continually, playing over his whole world' (Prov.8.22–31). Thereafter this Word and Wisdom, which was 'a clear effluence from the glory of the Almighty, the image of his goodness', was bidden to make its home in Jerusalem as 'the book of the covenant of God Most High, the law laid on us by Moses, a possession for the assemblies of Jacob' (Wisd.7.25,26; Ecclus.24.1–29). In the Torah God was keeping his promise: 'My presence shall go with you, and I will give you rest.'

5. *The impact of Jesus*

That heritage of reflection on a long-remembered experience of rescue, and the particularly confused stage in its development that prevailed in Judaea and Galilee when they became part of the Graeco-Roman civilization, was the context within which occurred the experience that gave birth to the Christian faith, namely the disciples' personal encounter with Jesus of Nazareth. It constitutes the last of those four paramount seminal experiences on which the Christian Bible hangs. It was clearly one of those experiences of the Beyond at the heart of things, mediated through a human personality, perhaps the supreme instance of all time. What was it they met with during that brief encounter some time between AD 27 and 33 which made such a far-reaching impact?

We have only their own accounts or, more probably, those of their successors, from which to derive the answer to that question. The Gospels just as much as the epistles are expressions of the faith of the first-century church. They are put together out of material that was being used in the worship and the preaching and the training of new enquirers in a variety of Christian groups, either Jewish or Gentile. There are virtually no disinterested sources against which to check their statements and so, on strictly historical grounds, no one can say beyond question that any particular episode or saying in the Gospels actually occurred just as it is reported. Yet the uncertainty concerning Jesus, his actions and teachings, has been unwarrantably exaggerated. Without plunging into the cross-currents of New Testament studies, which would require a very different style of book, it can be affirmed with integrity that the personal characteristics of this man and the broad outline of his short public career can be quite sufficiently discerned from the Gospels to make sense of the wildly improbable response of his Jewish followers to the impact he made upon them.

They knew him as a man, '*totus in nobis* – entirely one of us', as a famous letter from Pope Leo the Great was to put it four centuries later. In fact, the New Testament clearly implies that he was a blood relation to several of them, a skilled artisan from Galilee who had become a free-lance rabbi. They quickly recognized in him something exceptional, but whatever he did and whatever he was, they had no doubt but that he did it and was it as a man. With them he had inherited the undying memory and the variegated hopes and expectations of their oppressed nation, and, like many other Jewish boys through the centuries, he bore the evocative Hebrew name Yeshua or Yehoshua, which means 'Yahweh is rescue'. In their lifetime there had been several insurrections under terrorist leaders claiming divine authority and miraculous powers. Other preachers appealed for national restoration of a more spiritual kind through a strict return to the observance of God's Law. If, as Bishop John Robinson and others have argued,[18] the Gospel of John contains an early tradition of the order of events, some of the inner circle of Jesus' followers may first have become aware of him when he joined forces with John the Baptist who was proclaiming an imminent Day of Judgment and calling for national repentance. For a time it looked as if Jesus himself had accepted the role of the 'Coming One' promised by John, even to the point of acting out the part of the Elijah-figure foretold by Malachi, who, as a messenger of the covenant, was suddenly to come to his temple in purifying zeal (Mal. 3.1–4; 4.4–6; John 2.12–17).

But then, it seemed, there came a change of location and emphasis in Jesus' mission, prompted by the reaction against the Baptist's movement in certain quarters which culminated in John's arrest (Matt. 4.12; John 3.22–26; 4.1–3). Jesus came north and made Capernaum on the Lake of Galilee his headquarters for a style of ministry which John could no longer recognize (Matt. 11.2–3). His message was still the proclamation that God was drawing near to take control of events and establish his rule, his kingdom, in the land. But he made it sound more like liberation than catastrophe. It was plain that he regarded himself as God's agent, but not so much for purgation as for demonstrating God's victory over the powers of evil and disease and God's acceptance of the most unlikely and unworthy people into that kingdom. Jesus now adopted an attitude towards those who had put themselves beyond the religious pale which teachers of a stricter piety, especially those of the Pharisee party with which he had most in common, were bound to condemn as dangerously lax.

What they noticed in this new teacher was that his approach was different. He did not argue the pros and cons of behaviour by balancing one proof text against another like the jurists, but spoke like a man with direct knowledge of God's mind: 'It was said by the ancients, but I say . . .' He prefaced his more weighty pronouncements with 'Amen, Amen', similar to the prophets' 'Thus says Yahweh'. Yet, with all this inherent authority, he left his hearers free to reach the true insight by themselves, and his unique way with parables was designed to that end. Even when using a story already in circulation, he tried to involve his audience, whether friendly or hostile, by asking them to imagine how they would react in this or that situation. 'When you find that one sheep is missing from your flock or, for that matter, a book from your shelves, don't you fret over it more than all the rest until it turns up?' And he would tell an anecdote with such skill that their spontaneous response often contradicted the conventional view which they thought they held. 'You would agree wouldn't you, that anyone has the right to invoke the full rigour of the law to recover a bad debt? But suppose the creditor had just had a vastly greater debt of his own written off out of sheer generosity, what then?'

There was a difference, too, in his method of healing sickness. They did not, of course, infer from his miracles that he was anything more than a man. There were other healers and exorcists, and at that time all healing was thought to have some element of the supernatural in it. According to the Gospel of Luke, even his raising of the dead youth outside Nain elicited from the mourners only the acknowledgment that 'a great prophet has arisen among us', such, presumably, as Elisha who was known to have done as much just down the road at Shunem. But, unlike the other healers of his day, Jesus apparently recited no incantations, invoked no angels' names, and wielded no prophet's staff; he merely commanded on his own authority as the confidant of God, and the evil withdrew.

So they came to perceive the source of this man's certainty and authority. They saw him praying to God and heard him speak about God. His God was the God of the Old Testament without a doubt, and he prayed to him as a Jew; yet he appeared to enjoy an incomparably direct and intimate communion with him. To express it he himself used the simile of an ideal relationship between a human son and his father – for we should not read the familiar saying as a theological pronouncement, but as an analogy from daily life: 'Only a father really knows his son, and only a son really knows his father.' Other religions had spoken of God as the father of creation, and the Old Testament called Israel, or even Israel's king, God's son; but no teacher before Jesus had referred to God as 'my father', still less had anyone addressed him directly in prayer with the child's familiar term of affection, *Ab'ba!* And the corollary of this intimacy with God was his active imitation of God. Because he knew God to be gracious and forgiving he consorted with those who most needed compassion and forgiveness. Because he knew God to be just he denounced the hard-hearted and self-righteous. Because he knew the nearness of God in experience he announced the imminence of God's intervention to take control, lived as one already within the coming kingdom, and dared others to do so with him.

6. Who can this be?

What were they to make of a man who was unquestionably one of themselves and yet was inwardly directed by a unique consciousness of the mind of God and of his vocation as an agent of God's kingship? By this time their own thoughts about God were being coloured by continuous contact with him. His words, and especially those subtly simple parables, were habituating them to see God in a new light. It was becoming impossible for them to speak of God without thinking of this man.

> Jesus evoked or produced significant new convictions, not primarily concerning himself (however much they presented themselves in that form), but concerning God. The titles attached to him because he was the novel, tangible element; but he was in fact the agent whereby experience of God was enlarged and transformed.[19]

Some of the titles by which they may have addressed him or spoken of him among themselves were ambiguous enough to accommodate an expanding significance without their necessarily being aware of it. They would have addressed him quite naturally in Aramaic as *Maran* or as *Adon* in Hebrew, or, using the Greek lingua franca, as *Kurios*, all with the same meaning, Lord, since in common parlance it was the equivalent of Sir or Master. The word signified any superior – the employer of a steward, the owner of a vineyard or the king among his court officials, as in Jesus' parables. But, like a ladder reaching from earth to heaven, 'the Lord' was open to higher and higher gradations of meaning, as it is in English.

To those who know the title 'Son of God' only as a term of Christian doctrine it comes as a surprise to learn that it could have been given to Jesus of Nazareth without implying anything that a strict Jew could not have accepted. In Semitic usage, *ben*, son of, can be an idiomatic way of saying 'man of'. In the Bible we meet 'son of Belial' – or even 'daughter' – (I Sam. 1.16; 25.17, 25), 'son of perdition' (John 17.12; II Thess. 2.3), 'sons of thunder', in the Aramaic form *boan* (Mark 3.17), 'sons of light' (Luke 16.8; John 12.35). So, if the centurion exclaimed at the death of Jesus, 'Surely, this was a son of God', it would have meant 'a man of God'. In that sense 'son of God' is synonymous with 'servant or agent of God', and this would have been the meaning of the cries of the demented: 'What do you want with us, Jesus, son of the Most High God?' This sheds light also on the story of the baptism of Jesus as a crucial moment of inner conviction for him, expressed in the words, 'You are my son, my beloved, in whom I take delight.' The phrase actually harks back to the prophecy in Isaiah 42.1: 'Here is my servant whom I uphold, my chosen one, in whom I take delight.' In Jesus of Nazareth people met a man who knew himself called to be *God's* man, God's instrument for ushering in the kingdom and, moreover, one in whom the sense of vocation was raised to an extraordinary degree of personal intimacy and mutual love.

But that would not automatically have driven them to conclude that he was the anointed king, the Messiah of ancient expectation. For, as has already been shown, we now know, contrary to the scholarly opinion of seventy years ago, that a Messiah figure featured in very little of the literature of Jewish eschatological hope at the time of Jesus. It was quite possible to believe that God was about to judge the ungodly and inaugurate a new age without recourse to any other agent, apart from faithful preachers to warn people in advance. The image of a heavenly being coming on the clouds to judge the world on God's behalf was not widely current at the time of Jesus, even though Josephus testifies to the popularity of the Book of Daniel.[20] The Essene communities expected two Messiahs, one priestly, the other a warrior. Otherwise the only sort of Messiah referred to in the literature of the period, so far as it is known, is the conquering hero, and those who entertained messianic hopes were the ones who were reckoning on a restoration of Israel by force of arms. Was that the way in which the close companions of Jesus thought of him? The fact that so soon after his death and resurrection they adopted the title Christ (Messiah) as his most common designation suggests that it must already have been in their minds. Some of them, it seems, had been associated with the Zealot movement in Galilee; all of them betrayed a very earthy interest in their status in the coming Kingdom; if they called him Messiah, it was certainly in this unambiguous, popular sense. Yet it is equally certain that Jesus himself consistently disavowed the revolutionary role, and even though the Romans put him to death for claiming to be a king of some sort, they did not proceed to round up his followers as though they thought they were dealing with the leader of a revolt.

It is understandable, therefore, that the man who is known universally as Jesus the Christ should have avoided that title during his earthly life. Twice only is he said to have allowed it, and on both occasions his acceptance was non-committal, according to at least two accounts (Mark 8.29, 30 and Luke 9.20, 21; Matt. 26.63, 64 and Luke 22.67). He preferred the ambiguous term 'Son of Man' as a title. It is doubly ambiguous, not only as being open to more than one meaning, but also because it has the effect of extending the reference beyond himself to include others to a greater or lesser extent. When, for example, he asserted that the Son of Man was lord even of the Sabbath, his critics were justified in thinking that he was claiming some prerogative for himself. But the words could carry the more general meaning of 'The Sabbath was made for man, not man for the Sabbath.' When he says, 'If anyone is ashamed of me and my words, the Son of Man will be ashamed of him when he comes in his glory,' it sounds as though he is distinguishing between himself and that future Son of Man.

In any case, as a title, the words do carry several layers of meaning. They speak of humanity in its weakness and suffering, 'mere mortal man', as in Psalm 8.4: 'What is a frail mortal that you should be mindful of him, a human being that you should take notice of him?' But the title is also, almost certainly, derived directly from the apocalyptic vision in the seventh chapter of Daniel which was probably written during the gallant revolt of the Maccabees against the pagan over-rule of the Seleucid Greeks. In that vision successive foreign oppressions are represented by monstrous beasts; but then 'one like a son of man', in the form of mere mortal man, appears coming with the clouds of heaven to be presented to the Ancient of Days, and vested with everlasting sovereignty. In the interpretation of the vision which follows, this human image, like those of the beasts, symbolizes a *corporate* entity. It represents, not one of the super-powers, but 'the people of the holy ones of the Most High', namely the spiritually renewed Israel that was to emerge from the sacrifices of the Maccabean martyrs. This was the symbol that Jesus chose to identify his role as the agent of God's kingdom. In the weakness of his humanity and through his intimate communion with God, his *Ab'ba*, he was to be in himself the new Israel of the new age. On his lips the title always took the form 'That Son of Man'.[21] It was both a declaration of his role and an invitation to his followers to share it with him – the holy ones of the Most High, standing faithful and pure in the conflict with evil, to whom God would entrust his judgment and rule.

This self-understanding of Jesus was far beyond the level of his companions' hopes and the Gospels are remarkably frank about the divergence. What brought the issue to a head was not hostility but popularity. All four Gospels place the feeding of the multitude at the centre of the narrative as a turning point. Jesus clearly treated the occasion as a symbolic ritual. The huge crowd, interpreting it in their own way, took over and, according to the Fourth Gospel, tried to make him their messianic leader. His reaction was prompt. Unable to trust his disciples to dissociate themselves from the hysteria, he virtually pushed them into a boat and sent them off so that he could disperse the mob in his own way. Then he spent most of the night in prayer. Soon afterwards he took the disciples right away from the political hotbed of Galilee, and it was towards the end of this period of withdrawal that he asked them outright, 'What do the people think I am? And what do you think?' According to Mark's Gospel, as soon as Peter said 'The Messiah', Jesus ordered them not to spread that idea because 'that Son of Man' was destined to pass through rejection, suffering and death before being raised up. From that moment this was his recurrent theme. He had, as it were, looked into the eyes of the messiah the crowd called for, and they did not reflect the mind of the God he knew. Neither did the hopes of his companions: 'You think as men think, not as God thinks.'

This isolated him from them in a way that had not existed before. The Gospel of Mark significantly recalls Jesus walking ahead on the road to Jerusalem while the disciples followed, awestruck and afraid (Mark 10.32). But for three of them this distancing dread seems to have been the prelude to that vividly numinous experience we call the Transfiguration,[22] when they saw the mortal humanity of the man Jesus, at a moment when his thought and prayer was directed towards his death, alight with the radiance of its ultimate reality, the Beyond at the heart of all things. Unless he now chose to abandon his vocation to be God's man, making God's true nature visible in conflict with the powers of evil, the end had become inevitable. He needed neither Old Testament prediction nor profound theology to tell him that. The question was no longer whether the way ahead might end in death, but what he should make of his death.

7. *The culmination*

Considering the many facets of interpretation given to the death of Jesus in the New Testament epistles, it is surprising that so little explanation is attributed to Jesus himself in the Gospels. In order to lend weight to their claim that the one who had been publicly condemned and crucified was nonetheless God's Messiah, the first Christian groups hunted eagerly for Old Testament texts that seemed to have foretold his suffering and death. There may even have been a collection of such 'testimonies' circulating in book form at a very early date. If this activity prompted some of the words ascribed to Jesus in the records of his own predictions of his death, as may be the case, it is all the more strange that those predictions contain no theological explication. We have only incoherent hints of what may have been in Jesus' mind, and they point to a strong probability that the image of the Suffering Servant of Yahweh, the true Israel, already significant for him since the experience after his baptism, had become for him identified with that of the Son of Man, the agent of the Kingdom, who, through faithful self-sacrifice in the conflict with evil, was to be exalted as judge and ruler on God's behalf. Since neither the Suffering Servant nor the Son of Man are developed as theological concepts in the rest of the New Testament, they are more likely to be an authentic reflection of the thought of Jesus himself.

But such dwelling on Old Testament images cannot fully account for Jesus' decision that God's purpose was to be accomplished through his own humiliation and death. It is, in fact, quite out of character. It was the way of the scribes to find momentous significance and guidance in particular words in the text of scripture, a way which the followers of Jesus adopted for their later controversies with fellow Jews. But it was notably not the source of Jesus' convictions. His thought about God and God's will was drawn from direct acquaintance, and what he knew of God's nature became the model for his own practice. It was his living forth of the Father's likeness that had led him to consort with sinners and liberate the spirit-possessed, and now that likeness demanded that he let himself be turned over to helplessness and execution. The appeal to scripture seems to have been made mainly to help his disciples to accept the imperative even when they could not understand it. His own understanding of what his death was going to achieve is veiled in a reticence that we can penetrate no better than his awestruck companions on the way up to Jerusalem. As a result of his silence the figure of the Crucified is free to explain itself to humanity in new ways generation after generation. In the words of the poet Thomas Blackburn:

> Because it says nothing reasonable,
> This image explains nothing away,
> And just by gazing into darkness
> Is able to mean more than words can say.[23]

But, as has already been noted, the 'Son of Man' was a plural image and by adopting it Jesus was implying that those who were ready to become incorporated with him into that role could share in it, just as they could share in his knowledge of God as *Ab'ba*. 'Can you drink the cup that I drink, or be baptized with the baptism I am baptized with?' It is possible that his action with the bread and the cup at the Last Supper was intended not only as an anticipatory self-oblation ('Take; this is my body') and an inauguration of a new relationship with God ('My blood of the covenant, poured out for many'), but also as a means of including them with himself in the sacrificial self-giving of the Son of Man. And, if that was meant to be a symbol of their drinking his cup, the Gospel of John may have substituted the feet-washing for the institution of the eucharist partly as a symbol of their undergoing the baptism with which he was baptized: 'What I am doing you do not know now, but afterwards you will understand. If I do not wash you, you have no share with me.'

They were not ready then to follow where he was going. They were too confused and trapped. He must have known long before that he would have to endure the ordeal uniquely and alone. And they for their part had to face this most glaring proof, not only that he had never been the Messiah they had envisaged, but also that they had never been the pioneers of the Kingdom he had tried to make them. Yet after that disastrous, God-forsaken debacle, very soon after, they knew he was more alive than ever, closer to God and yet present to them as never before. He who had shown God to them now showed himself to them, and from that time they would never think of God without thinking of him. To proclaim the Kingdom of God was to proclaim Jesus. Their certainty of his exaltation by God, which was also a certainty of his presence in their midst, convinced them that his knowledge of God as Father had been true, his representation of the Father in his words and behaviour had been true, his message that the new age of God's rule was about to break in had been fulfilled, his defiance in setting himself above certain customs and his disturbing acceptance of outsiders and outcasts was confirmed, and even his decision to let himself be handed over to helplessness, apparent failure and death was truly vindicated. By raising him from death into glory God had acknowledged it all. The one who had called people to believe had become the object of faith, and to decide for or against God's rule was identical with a decision for or against Jesus. Thinking about Jesus and thinking of God had become inseparable. Their sense of his nearness, though invisible, was like their sense of God's nearness. And this original conviction of those who experienced the resurrection appearances seemed strangely transmissible, so that others who never knew him 'in the flesh' were as profoundly affected by the story told to them as the immediate companions of Jesus had been by his resurrection.

They were Jews, and those who succeeded them as the writers of the New Testament were Jews or Jewish proselytes. Nothing in the New Testament remotely suggested that a divinity like Dionysus had been walking the roads of Palestine in disguise. They were at pains to safeguard the distinction between the risen Lord and the God who had raised him, between Jesus Messiah – for now they gloried in that title with the new meaning he had given it – and him who was his God and Father, between the one who was sent and the one who sent him. Yet within thirty years or less after the death of the man Jesus, their reflections upon their experience of him had crystallized into all the essentials of later christology: 'May our God and Father himself and our Lord Jesus open the way for us' (I Thess. 3.11); 'God sent his Son . . . God sent into our hearts the Spirit of his Son' (Gal. 4.4–6). 'There are many such gods and many such lords, yet for us there is one God, the Father from whom are all things and we exist for him, and there is one Lord, Jesus Christ, through whom are all things and we exist through him' (I Cor. 8.5, 6); 'In Christ God . . . ' (II Cor. 5, 19); 'He was in the form of God, yet he laid no claim to equality with God' (Phil. 2.6).

Later generations of Christians, arguing their creed in the setting of Greek thought, were going to run into great difficulties over explaining the relation of Jesus to God in a way that kept human and divine distinct; so that it seems extraordinary that those earliest Jewish Christians found it comparatively unproblematic to say the things they did say about Jesus. This was largely because they had known him as a man, so that whatever his resurrection and their experience of the Holy Spirit might add to their perception of him, they started with the knowledge that, whatever he was in relation to God, he was it *in* his humanity, so their Jewish faith was not compromised. This is reflected in the primitive preaching of the Jerusalem church, inasmuch as we discern this from the early chapters of Acts: 'Men of Israel, listen to me: I speak of Jesus of Nazareth, a male person singled out by God and made known to you through miraculous portents and signs which God worked among you through him, as you well know' (Acts 2.22). The Epistle to the Hebrews, which clearly reflects a Jewish-Christian background, even while presenting Jesus as the son whom God had sent 'at the end of these days', and as the high priest who ever lives to intercede for us, speaks of him as someone 'taken from among human beings, of one and the same stock, sharing our flesh and blood, beset by weakness, who in the course of his earthly life offered up prayers and petitions with loud cries and tears to the one who had the power to save him from death, but who learnt obedience through his sufferings, son though he was' (Heb. 5.1–2, 11, 14; 5.2, 7, 8). Whatever else the exaltation of Jesus of Nazareth meant to those first Christians, it did not give the lie to their experience of him as a human being. They applied to him phrases from the Old Testament which had originally been written about God (Phil. 2.10; cf. Isa. 45.23; Heb. 1.10–12; cf. Ps. 102.25–27), yet they instinctively avoided naming him God as such.[24] St Paul constantly paired 'God our Father and the Lord Jesus Christ' as together the recipient of his praise, thanksgiving and prayer, yet he always spoke of the Son as the agent through whom God had acted and in whom God is approached.

It is not difficult to understand how their recognition of Jesus as God's human agent grew into their belief that he is God's eternal agent. His resurrection had brought home to them the conviction that God had raised him to the realm of his own transcendence. This in itself might not have led them to believe that he had come from that realm in the first place had they not already known his matchless intimacy with God and the authority he derived from it. Having experienced God in him, it was not an unthinkable next step for them to feel that the exaltation of Jesus was in some sense a return, a home-coming. The idea of a heavenly Messiah held in readiness until the appointed time was probably, as we have seen, current in some circles and St Paul was applying that imagery to Jesus in the earliest of his epistles only twenty or so years after the crucifixion. It does not follow that they gave a crudely literal interpretation to that imagery any more than they did to other mythological symbols available to them in Jewish thought – the figure of God's Wisdom or Word, the eternal Torah, assisting at the creation of the universe; or the older notion of Shekinah-glory, making God's essence visible. They used them all to express their understanding of the relationship of Jesus to God (I Thess. 4.16; II Cor. 8.9; John 1.1–3, 14; Heb. 1.2–4; Col. 1.15–18). He was the image, the energy, the self-expression of the transcendent God, reaching out in immanent presence towards the world. They claimed that through him God's long-awaited intervention had come about to bring a new order into being; through him the age-long estrangement and conflict of wills between God and the self-determining world had been reconciled; in him humanity had been restored to its original pattern and Adam re-created; through his continuing presence within the life of the church, manifested in that superhuman assurance and love they called the Spirit, God's own covenanted presence in the midst of his people was established for ever. They had no coherent doctrine of the Trinity as yet, but they proclaimed out of an inmost experience that salvation is *from* the Father *through* the Son who is the perfect image of his self-giving, *in* the Spirit; and that true prayer is *in* the Spirit who is the spirit of sonship, *through* the Son *to* his Father. The Three were clearly seen to be distinct, but the Logos, the meaning of them all, had been revealed in Jesus of Nazareth. In the familiar words of Archbishop Michael Ramsey: 'God is Christlike, and in him is no un-Christlikeness at all.'[25]

5

How Shall This Be?

The Christian Experience Confronts European Philosophy

1. Storming the ramparts

St Paul's brief encounter with the city of Athens is narrated in the Acts of the Apostles as a strongly symbolic event, a prototype of Christianity's prolonged struggle to win acceptance by the cultural and intellectual world of the Roman empire. He was a Jew with an irreducible conviction about Jesus based upon an experience of him that he could not deny and profound subsequent reflection upon it. Temporarily deflected, as he thought, from his mission to Macedonia, he was waiting for fresh news from there (I Thess.3.1,2), but he could not refrain from sharing his faith and, with the striking versatility that was later to be his boast, he argued like a rabbi with the congregation in the synagogue and like a latter-day Socrates with bystanders in the public square. Though outraged by the polytheism of Greek religion, he did not scruple to adapt the rhetoric of Greek philosophy to his presentation of the gospel. This seeming inconsistency was perpetuated by later generations of Christian apologists who railed against pagan idolatry while accepting pagan metaphysics as self-evident truth. Only their over-riding allegiance to the Jewish and Christian scriptures gave them a foothold from which to challenge, occasionally and reluctantly, the classical dogmas.

The apostle's failure to impress the sneering philosophers – 'This snapper-up of grains of learning' – drove him to disavow with characteristic vehemence the subtleties of the intellectual and focus his teaching more narrowly on the significance of Jesus and his cross. But his was only the first skirmish in a war of words that has gone on to this day, and the issue could not be so simply abandoned. Yet Paul's Athenian affray did at least identify the real bone of contention in this stubbornly ambiguous dispute. On the one side stood those definitions of God's nature and God's relation to the world which Middle Platonism established upon the foundations of the earlier philosophies: God is inaccessible to thought or description and can never be the object of anyone's experience; God is one, indivisible and alone; God is immutably and eternally what he is and can never become other; God can neither be affected nor limited. These axioms have stood as impervious bulwarks in defence of the absolute uniqueness and inviolable perfection of God, forbidding those confident, unqualified declarations in which the New Testament writers passed on the implications, as they saw them, of the apostolic experience of Jesus Christ: 'God was in Christ reconciling the world to himself.' 'God's only Son, he who is nearest to the Father's heart, he has made him known.' 'The Word became flesh.' 'In him the Godhead in all its fullness dwells embodied.' In those and similar statements Christian faith is insisting that in and through the humanity of Jesus, God, and nothing less than God, has revealed himself and acted for the redemption of the world.

If we compare these two sets of assertions, the philosophical axioms and the Christian claims, it can soon be seen that, although they are in effect mutually exclusive, they are not contesting precisely the same ground. The former are pronouncements about the supposed nature of God, the latter are affirmations about the being of Jesus Christ. They contradict each other only by implication. So the parties to the quarrel have always been meeting at a tangent rather than head-on and have, therefore, always been inclined to suppose that a reconciliation of their two positions could be found. Indeed, those who were from time to time condemned as heretical have invariably thought that they were proposing an acceptable compromise.

For this reason the conflict from the beginning was never a simple confrontation of Christian believers against pagan philosophers. The great teachers of the early church, like all serious thinkers in that Roman empire, whether at Lyons, Alexandria, Carthage or Caesarea, took for granted the classical presuppositions about God. The magisterial decrees of the great ecumenical councils were a victory for Plato and Aristotle no less than for the Judaeo-Christian revelation and left the philosophical ramparts apparently intact. And this is not really surprising since Christianity throughout its history has advanced by a succession of dialogues whereby it has both penetrated a new cultural milieu and, at the same time, received its impress. The struggle to embed the Christian faith into the very foundations of European thought has enriched the church with concepts it could not have hit upon in any other way, and also lumbered it with fixed ideas it has still to unlearn. That unlearning will eventually he brought about by the continuing process of dialogue between the gospel and culture, for, during the past four centuries and especially in the last sixty years, further logical analysis of what is actually meant by 'to be' and 'to know' has exploded many of the basic assumptions of classical and mediaeval philosophy. Meanwhile, as though this has not happened, the battle drags on around each of the four bastions of the older theistic philosophy like a military pageant staged amid castle ruins.

2. The first bulwark: the inaccessible God

The foremost of those dogmas stood in defence of the infinite difference of God's mode of being from that of the world. For the past three centuries the 'problem' of God's relation to the universe has lain in the universe itself, in its unbroken continuity of causation that seems to offer no room for divine action. Previously, however, and for far longer, the problem was found in God, in the impossibility of his being involved in interaction with the world, or, indeed, in any action whatever, without impairing his absolute distinctness and self-sufficiency. Plato, building upon the quasi-physical metaphysics of earlier philosophers, had fabricated a total dichotomy between this world of transitory impressions perceived through the senses and a transcendent realm of changeless immaterial realities apprehended only through the logical thought of rational souls. He wished to set his pupils upon the quest for mental perception of the ultimate beauty and goodness, but his logic fixed such a chasm between the two realms as to make each virtually inaccessible to the other. It was unthinkable that the eternal changelessness should itself be the creator of mortality, so in his myth of the making of the world Plato supposed that the Father of the universe delegated that task to the lesser divinities he had brought into being.[1] By the same token none of the qualities or categories of this mundane existence could be predicated of that 'heaven above the heavens' where 'abides the very Being with which true knowledge is concerned, the colourless, formless, intangible essence, visible only to mind, the pilot of the soul'.[2] That Being was 'beyond words or the human power of thought'.[3] With that exasperating flexibility of opinion that was his peculiar glory, Plato allowed himself on occasion to doubt this categorical conclusion.

> Are we really to be so easily convinced that change, life, soul, understanding, have no place in that which is perfectly real – that it has neither life nor thought, but stands immutable in solemn aloofness?[4]

Aristotle, with no such hesitation, sealed the dogma of divine inaccessibility for centuries to come. He reinstated the reality and value of the material universe, but his Prime Mover, setting all things in motion by attraction towards itself, was locked into the still centre of that centripetal movement in an absolute self-absorption.

The Christian apologists and theologians saw no reason to doubt that God is wholly beyond the reach of human thought. Scripture and experience appeared to say as much. 'The Almighty we cannot find; his person is beyond our ken' (Job 37.25). 'He who alone possesses immortality, dwelling in unapproachable light, him no one has ever seen or can ever see' (I Tim. 6.16). Then as now those who had experience of the impact of the Beyond in any form protested that it could not be put into words. Some time after 138 AD Justin Martyr wrote in Rome, 'No one can declare the name of the inexpressible God, and if anyone presumes to say that he has any, he commits an act of incurable madness.'[5] And he argued that the Lord who appeared to the patriarchs must have been the Logos, the Word, since the Father could have no intercourse with this world. Towards the end of that second century Clement of Alexandria asked

> How can that be expressed to which we can apply neither type nor differentiality nor species nor individuality nor any of the logical categories? He is neither a quality nor one to whom a quality may be attributed; neither all, nor part. If we say he is infinite it is because he has no dimension.[6]

As time went on great divines of the church asserted more emphatically that God is unknowable. In the fourth century Gregory of Nyssa declared in one of his expository sermons,

> The divine nature, whatever it may be in itself, surpasses every mental concept. For it is altogether inaccessible to reasoning and conjecture, nor has there been found any human faculty capable of perceiving the incomparable, for we cannot devise a means of understanding inconceivable things.[7]

In our own day it must strike us as strangely arrogant to assume that only God is so uniquely beyond the grasp of human thought. There is much more, including our own selfhood, which we can never know as it really is, but only as we are constituted to see it. The philosopher Immanuel Kant (1729–1804) showed that the human mind perceives reality only by making our experience of what is there conform to certain preconceived categories of thought and measurement such as subject and object, cause and effect, number, position, direction and duration. We assume that these must be categories of things as they are, and the assumption seems to be justified by the remarkably effective relationship with our environment which it has enabled our human species to develop, even to the point of our present exploration of the constitution of matter and the nature of the universe. Kant believed that these *a priori* categories of thought were intuitively known realities simply because rational argument is impossible without them. Gottlob Frege and more recent philosophers of this century have demonstrated that the categories of thought are just that and nothing more, propensities of the human mind that determine the way we are bound to see things; and all our marvellous instruments of scientific observation are only extensions of that way of seeing. The mathematical formulae which today's physicists and cosmologists use as the only medium of discourse that remains valid for their field are, like much theology, a purely symbolic idiom that can specify how things behave but not what they are. Werner Heisenberg, the originator of matrix quantum mechanics, wrote of his fellow physicist from Denmark, Niels Bohr:

> He did not look upon the electrons in the atomic shell as 'things', in

> any case not as things in the sense of classical physics, which worked with such concepts as position, velocity, energy or extension.[8]

This is not merely the relative incomprehension of things that elude our present state of knowledge, which may, in principle, be overcome in the future. However much we know, it will forever be limited to our human ways of knowing. Scientific man, probing the mystery of the physical universe, confirms the ancient contention of philosophers, theologians and mystics that there is a chasm between what is humanely thinkable and reality itself, and no means of measuring how wide it is. We are thrown back upon the insight of *The Cloud of Unknowing* (applicable to other things besides God himself): 'By love he may be gotten and holden; but by thought, never.'

The Fathers of the Church, then, had inherited, and were confronted by, a concept of the incomprehensible One who was intrinsically unknowable, and from the beginning there have been many theologians who readily took to a language of all-round negation as the only form of statement that did justice to God's total difference and separation from all created existence. John of Damascus wrote in his digest of Orthodox theology early in the eighth century:

> Neither men nor the celestial powers nor the cherubim and seraphim can know God, other than in his revelations. By nature he is above being and therefore above knowledge. We can designate his nature only by negations. Whatever we say about God affirmatively indicates not his nature but his attributes, the periphery of his nature.[9]

A century later the Irish philosopher, John Eriugena, who taught under the patronage of Charlemagne's grandson and greatly influenced mediaeval spirituality, explained how it was appropriate to describe God as 'Nothing'.

> By that name is signified the ineffable and incomprehensible and inaccessible brilliance of the divine Goodness which is unknown to all intellects, whether human or angelic, for it is beyond being and beyond nature; which, contemplated in itself, neither is nor was nor ever shall be, for it is understood to be in none of the things that exist because it surpasses all things.[10]

One representative of this tradition in Britain today is Professor Nicholas Lash who, extrapolating the terms of an argument of Martin Buber, has said:

> The nature of God is unknown to us. It can neither be pictured, depicted, narrated, nor described. We could go a step further and say that it is far from clear what the right answer would be to the question: 'Does God have a nature? . . . For surely not to be able to be taken under the basic word I-It is not, as it were, to have a nature of a rather peculiar kind but, as a matter of definition, not to 'have a nature' *at all*?[11]

This, then, was the first of the philosophical bulwarks that Christian thinkers had either to breach or find their way round. Affirming, as they have never ceased to do, the impenetrable mystery of God, they had nonetheless to qualify and counterbalance all categorical definitions of it, and this for three reasons.

1. The biblical doctrine that God is himself the creator precluded all notions of his non-involvement.
2. The Jewish faith in that same God's immanent action in historical events meant that divine incomprehensibility is only half the truth, and self-disclosure is of the essence of God's being no less than his hiddenness.
3. Loyalty to the apostolic experience of God in Jesus, perpetuated in the life of the church, demanded a God of whom it was not inconceivable that he should take our nature upon him.

Some of the Jewish thinkers of this century seem to have got the balance between God's mystery and God's accessibility more truly adjusted than some of the Christian exponents of the divine Otherness. Abraham Heschel, for example, has expressed it in truly biblical terms:

> The God of the prophets is not the Wholly Other, a strange, weird, uncanny Being shrouded in unfathomable darkness. . . . Silence encloses Him; darkness is all around Him. Yet there is meaning beyond the darkness. God *is* meaning beyond the mystery.[12]

3. A two-tier model

The earliest Christian attempts to reconcile God's absolute difference and beyondness with his accessibility and relatedness with the world, especially in the form in which this had been experienced in human encounter with Jesus Christ, relied heavily on the Greek idea of a ladder of intermediate gradations of divinity. Plato had spoken of Mind, and Logos-Reason and the eternal Forms or divine concepts, as derivatives of God, and in more mythical terms had described how the Father of all, having made lesser divinities, committed to them the creation of all that is mortal. Philo, the Jewish Middle Platonist who was teaching at Alexandria during the life-time of Jesus, fitted the biblical images of God's Wisdom and Word into this hierarchical pattern of divine powers. He thought of Yahweh as the inaccessible Absolute of the philosophers who delegated to the subordinate Logos both the making of the universe and every subsequent action of self-communication. Every visitation of God to human beings recorded in the Old Testament he attributed to the Logos. Indeed, in Philo's view it was the Logos who took upon himself the whole burden of divine immanence, just as in Hinduism it is Ishvara who has disembarrassed Brahman of it.

Christian apologists of the second and third centuries, with the prologue of the Fourth Gospel to support them, seized on this two-tier model of God's relationship with the creation to make sense of their proclamation that, in the humanity of Jesus, deity had not only made itself visible but had acted for the salvation of the world. Whether by deliberate borrowing or not, Justin used Philo's term, 'powers', to denote the knowable intermediate levels of God's being.

> As a beginning before all created things God begot of himself a certain Power of rationality which is also called by the Holy Spirit (i.e. in the scriptures) the Glory of the Lord, at another time Son, at another Wisdom, at another an angel, at another God and at another Lord or Word . . . For he has all these appellations both from his ministering to the Father's will and from his being begotten by the Father's intent.[13]

> For the first Power after God the Father and Lord of all things, even his Son, is the Word who took flesh and was made man.[14]

It seemed that a smooth reconciliation of the Greek Logos and the incarnate Lord had been effected, and Clement of Alexandria based his more sophisticated theology on the theme of the Logos as divine principle of rationality creating and directing the universe, illuminator of human minds, dispenser alike of Jewish Law and Greek philosophy, finally incarnate in Jesus as universal Saviour – something resembling the cosmic Christ of modern thought. Origen, the first of the great Christian mystics, put it in a brief definitive form: 'The Father as the Absolute is incomprehensible; he becomes comprehensible through the Logos, the expression and image of the essence and basic nature of God.'[15]

The use of the Logos doctrine by the early Christian theologians, and especially their exploration of the metaphor of self-communication and the communicated self inherent in the biblical term, Word, undoubtedly opened the way into a rich and lasting understanding of God as Trinity. But by resorting to the Platonic hierarchy of divinity as a means of bridging the supposed chasm between God and the world they committed the church of their day to what Professor Henry Chadwick has called 'a *faux pas* for which (their) successors had to pay a high price in blood and tears'.[16] By regarding the hierarchy as a necessary ladder they endorsed the idea of the gulf between the Absolute and the creation and left intact the bastion of an essentially uninvolved and inaccessible God. Latent in the first quotation from Justin above is the thought that the Logos is not intrinsic to the being of God but was begotten out of God's 'intent' to create a world. In effect this means that the Second and Third Persons of the Trinity are functional rather than essential to the Godhead.[17] Tertullian, writing at Carthage in about 213, argued from scripture that God the Son had been generated in two stages, first as a thought in the mind of God, and then as active agent at the moment of creation.

> It was then that the Word itself received its manifestation and completion, namely sound and voice, when God said: *Let there be light.* This is the perfect birth of the Word when it proceeds from God. It had first been produced by him as thought under the name of Wisdom. *The Lord created me the first of his works* (Prov.8.32).[18]

That is tantamount to saying that the Logos is more intrinsic to the existence of the world than to the being of God, and within a decade or so Origen was challenging such a train of thought: 'How can it be said there was a time when the Son was not?'[19] Yet even Origen could write

> We say that the Saviour and the Holy Spirit are incomparably superior to all things that are made, but also that the Father is even more above them than they are themselves above created things.[20]

The concept of different levels of divinity is bound to imply that what is immanently present within the whole of creation is something less than God, and that something less than God was revealed, and acted, in Jesus Christ. Within the church it played into the hands of Arius and his later exponents, with their subordinate Logos and adopted Christ; and on the fringes of the church it seemed to give the nod to Gnosticism with its 'trickle down' emanations between God and an evil world, and its corresponding ladder of esoteric illuminations for the spiritual elite.

Consequently the theologians of the fourth and fifth centuries, while they jealously clung to the enriching perception of distinctions within the being of God, staunchly refused to have them defined as differences either of degree or of function and activity. Athanasius, Bishop of Alexandria, dismissed the idea of a merely functional Trinity in which the Logos and the Holy Spirit took their being from the divine intent to make a world. 'If they shall assign the toil of making all things as the reason why God made only the Son, the whole creation will cry out against them as saying things unworthy of God.' And, with an eye on the Platonist tradition, he thundered on, 'And if God made the Son alone, as not deigning to make the rest, but committed them to the Son as to an assistant, this on the other hand is unworthy of God, for in him there is no pride.'[21] Didymus, the blind principal of Alexandria's famous theological school, insisted that Father, Son and Holy Spirit 'do not differ from one another either in divinity or in what they do',[22] while Gregory, the Bishop of Nyssa in Cappadocia, argued that, in any work of God, Father, Son and Spirit act indivisibly:

> We do not learn that the Father does anything by himself in which the Son does not work conjointly, or again that the Son has any special operation apart from the Holy Spirit; but every work . . . has its origin from the Father and proceeds through the Son and is perfected in the Holy Spirit.[23]

So, by a progressive unfolding of the truth, the trinitarian concept, which originated from existential human experiences of God as universal Deity, incarnate Lord and indwelling Presence, was pushed back behind those functional 'operations' or 'energies' of God *vis-à-vis* the world, and located in the depth of God's eternal being. We must not equate God-in-his-essence with the Father alone. The only real distinction we may draw between the three identities within God lies in their reciprocal relation one to another: the Father is wholly the eternal source, the Son is eternally *from* that source, and the Spirit also *from* the source *through* the Son. Gregory of Nazianzus insisted, 'There is complete identity among the three divine Persons except for the relations expressive of origin.'[24] Accordingly, no one can rightly say that the Father is incomprehensible and the Son accessible, but only that, in so far as the Father is mystery beyond all knowing, so is the Son, so is the Spirit; and in so far as the Son is self-revealed and knowable, so equally is the Father.

Unhappily, even after achieving this fully unified and equal concept of the trinitarian God, many of the Fathers of the Church allowed the two-tier model of God's relation with the world to survive surreptitiously, as it were. Augustine of Hippo, for example, transferred to the angels those operations and energies within created things which earlier theologians had attributed to the subordinate Logos. God's immanence was still inferior to his transcendence.

4. A common ground model

The impregnable axiom of God's absolute inaccessibility was, and is, open to assault from another quarter – the evidence of what the Bible calls the image of God in human nature. Infinite as the difference must be between God and all that is, yet the very creatures that recognize this have in themselves something that belongs to the same order of being as God. At different periods of thought philosophers have variously identified this 'likeness to God' which is in humanity; however defined, it is an area of common ground on which the infinite and the finite meet, a common language in which God communicates himself to us.

In the preface to his treatise on prayer Origen wrote, 'Who would not admit that it is impossible for a human being to trace out what is in the heavens? Nevertheless, this impossibility has become a possibility by the boundless excellence of the grace of God.'[25] Athanasius identified this grace with the divine image and likeness implanted from the start, which, true to the Greek tradition, he equates with the gift of rationality, 'making them in his own image and giving them a share in the power of his own Logos, so that, having as it were shadows of the Word and being made rational, they might be able to remain in felicity'.[26] But he also recognized that this special human endowment entailed the gift of a self-transcendence comparable to God's: 'Through its likeness to himself he made humanity in such a way that it could behold and know that which really is, giving it also an idea and knowledge of its own eternity.'[27] A passage from Gregory of Nyssa was quoted earlier in this chapter to demonstrate the absolute terms in which God's inaccessibility was upheld by Christian theologians; yet in the same sermon he disclosed the other side of this truth:

> When you hear that the divine majesty is exalted above the heavens, that its glory is inexpressible, its beauty ineffable and its nature inaccessible, do not despair of ever beholding what you desire. It is indeed within your reach; you have within yourselves the standard by which to apprehend the divine. For he who made you did at the same time endow your nature with this wonderful quality. For God imprinted on it the likeness of the glories of his own nature, as if moulding the form of a carving into wax.[28]

And Thomas Aquinas, the definitive teacher of the later Middle Ages, found in this divinely given capacity of human beings to know God the warrant that God is inherently accessible.

> God is wholly actual; he contains no unrealized potential. So nothing in him poses an obstacle to knowledge. Nevertheless what is in itself knowable may be beyond the understanding of some particular mind . . . and for this reason some people think created minds can never see God as he really is. This is a mistake. Man's ultimate happiness consists in his highest activity, exercising his mind; and if created minds cannot see God then either men will never be happy or their happiness must be elsewhere than in God. That is not only opposed to our faith but makes no natural sense.[29]

Aquinas saw the difference between saying that God is knowable, but not wholly, and saying that he is wholly unknowable; and he rejected the latter.

What then, is this image of God, this factor common to the Creator and his human creature? Gregory of Nyssa thought it was the gift of freedom and self-determination. 'How could a nature that was subjugated and enslaved to any kind of necessity be called an image of the nature of the King?'[30] But Augustine of Hippo saw this emphasis, especially as Pelagius developed it, as an incitement to the primary sin of pride, and reverted to the classical belief that what humanity shares with God is rationality which, 'although so dimmed as almost to cease to be, never utterly disappears'.[31] Aquinas too followed the same tradition but explored more analytically what we mean by 'knowing'. In his view, to know an object is to receive it into oneself in an immaterial form and co-exist with it as present in one's mind. The same must also happen, he thought, if we are to know God, but because God can never be merely the object of our observation, the initiative must be his: 'Unless God himself, by his grace, enters a created mind and makes himself intelligible to it, no such mind can ever see God.' And, he adds, no created mind whatever can understand God fully, without the limitation that is inherent to it.[32] It would seem on the face of it that Christian thought had not advanced beyond the Greek idea that we approach God through the same kind of rationality as that by which we perceive mathematical truth. If human rationality is the image of God in humanity it seems a poor one, not only because it is so often flawed by irrational intrusions, but also because it is absurd to attribute to God mental processes as we know them.

It is clear, however, that what theologians through the centuries were identifying as the image of God, whether under the name of self-determination, reason or spirit, was self-transcendence, the capacity to surpass or step forth beyond one's own being. Augustine marvelled at the power of memory to transcend time and individuality.[33] Aquinas found human self-transcendence in our capacity to abstract the general from particular instances (as recounted on pages 6ff. of this book), to stand back and see the world as a whole and to perceive the activity of our minds.[34] In our own day, Karl Rahner has built his philosophy of human nature upon this insight. He, like Aquinas, assumes without warrant that our grasp of generalities or categories is an innate intuition that actually precedes and facilitates our perception of particular instances. Nonetheless he has shown compellingly that our capacity to learn to abstract makes us into creatures 'with an infinite horizon' reaching willy-nilly for 'more' as the context for our mundane existence.

> Man is spirit, ie. he lives his life while reaching unceasingly for the absolute in openness towards God. And this openness towards God is not something which may happen or not happen to him once in a while, as he pleases. It is the condition of the possibility of that which man is and has to be and also always is in his most humdrum daily life. Only that makes him into a man: that he is always already on the way to God, whether or not he knows it expressly, whether or not he wills it. He is forever the infinite openness of the finite for God.[35]

This is the nature of our self-transcendence. Humanity is inescapably oriented towards that which lies beyond the horizon, towards its own fulfilment in the limitlessness of God. Henri le Saux, the Benedictine missionary who took the Indian name of Abhishiktananda, wrote out of a mystic's lifelong reflection:

> Only when man realizes that he himself is an inscrutable mystery – that is, that his true being lies beyond any thought or consciousness that he may have of himself – only then can he discover in the depths of his experience the inscrutable mystery of God. Man's unknowable being is of the same order as God's, for man comes from God and has been created in his image.[36]

Rahner is saying exactly the same thing when he describes our self-transcendence as the capacity 'to be given away and to be handed over, to be that being who realizes himself and finds himself by losing himself once and for all in the incomprehensible'.[37]

But if this is the nature of our self-transcendence, and if this is the image and likeness of God, what is the nature of *God's* self-transcendence? How can the Absolute surpass *itself*? Whither does the Limitless step forth beyond its own being? Not, like the rich fool, by pulling down the barns of his infinitude to build greater, but, like that other landowner, by running to meet his 'other' while he was yet afar off. He who has all and is all surpasses himself only by overflowing in self-dispossession. That is *his* transcendence. Rahner concludes:

> The Absolute, or, more correctly, the absolute One, in the pure freedom of his infinite unrelatedness, which he always preserves, possesses the possibility of himself becoming the other, the finite. He possesses the possibility of establishing the other as his own reality by dispossessing *himself*, by giving *himself* away.[38]

Human transcendence images and reciprocates God's in that both consist in being given away, handed over, by way of dispossession.

5. A dialectical model

As human beings we are aware of this capacity within ourselves to receive and respond to the approaches of God, aware of this common ground where his self-giving elicits our own. Our power of self-transcendence gives us a unique relationship with God. 'The glory of God is the living Man and the glory of Man is the vision of God.'[39] But God's self-giving, his overflow of being, is not limited to humanity, and the history of his relation to the universe has been, it seems, continuous and all of a piece. The inwardness of all other modes of being than our own is a closed book to us, yet our introspective recognition of God's action upon ourselves may offer a clue to the nature of his immanent presence in everything else.

> There is only one point at which we can possibly touch the nerve of God's creative action, or experience creation taking place, and that is in our own life . . . Because we have God under the root of our being we cannot help but acknowledge him at the root of all the world's being.[40]

Self-transcendence may seem a pretentious word to describe the processes we can observe at work in nature, yet the science of this century has taken to describing things not simply by enumerating the laws that govern their behaviour, but also in terms of their unpredictable openness to the future through a capacity for spontaneous reorganization into more complex systems which behave quite differently.

> Every determined level and order of being is from the very start open towards a higher level and order and can be incorporated into it, without its own laws thereby having to be suspended.[41]

When we acknowledge that there is more to a living organism than the atoms and molecules it consists of, more to consciousness, self-awareness, creativity and spirit than all the neurophysiological interconnections of the brain, more to music than the carefully structured arrangement of sound waves that are its physical totality, we are identifying examples of self-transcendence as a principle of development inherent in the fabric of the universe.

Yet, if we ask what this 'more' consists of, the answer must be 'Nothing whatever that is identifiable or measurable'. The scientist knows that 'no extra "substance" or ontological entity is added to atoms and molecules when they adopt the complex organization which is characterized as "living".'[42] Potentiality is not a physical force, not an additional element in a compound, nor is it written into a genetic code. Potentiality is, by definition, a 'not yet'. For no sooner is the latent possibility realized than a further potential lurks within, unfulfilled. It is forever a non-existent. Yet it appears to play a crucial role in determining the course of events. It is the beyond in the midst – the equivalent within the rest of nature of what in ourselves we call the image of God. It is the common ground of creation's affinity with its Creator, for the hidden potentiality of things precisely images the immanent presence of God.

Life itself and our reflection upon it, experience of the world around in its normality and strangeness, or 'transfigurations' like those recorded in chapter 2, all convince us, as they have convinced the generations before us, that God is in all things and all things in God. Gregory of Nyssa asks

> Who, surveying the whole scheme of things, is so childish as not to believe that there is divinity in everything, clothed in it, embracing it, residing in it? For everything that is depends on Him-who-is.[43]

Aquinas also seized upon that idea of God as immanent Being itself:

> Since existence itself is what God is by nature, he it must be who causes existence in creatures. During the whole period of a creature's

> existence, then, God must be present to it in the way its own existence is . . . more intimately and profoundly interior to things than anything else.[44]

And he added as a necessary caution against pantheism: 'Wherever God exists he exists wholly.' But this concept of God's immanent presence in all things, the gift of Being itself within all beings, can be too static unless it is linked to the truth of the potentiality and openness of all things, which in turn implies indeterminacy and possible frustration.[45] The biologist, Charles Birch, wrote in the 1960s:

> In his primordial nature God is 'the absolute wealth of potentiality' of the universe. God confronts the world in his primordial nature which is the lure of unrealized possibility. The world experiences God as the world is created.[46]

This must mean that the immanent God preserves his incognito. Like the potentiality of things, God's presence within them is strictly undetectable. If you ask what is actually there beside the physical facts you must answer 'Not a thing'. And if something in the way things are alerts you to the 'more', then receive that 'more' by faith, for it leaves no trace by which you can convince others.

For God in his involvement in the world *is* the transcendent One, the Beyond. There is no going back to the subordinate Logos of the early apologists nor to the intermediary angels of Augustine. The triune Being is not divisible. 'Wherever God exists he exists wholly.' In his infinitude he cradles the universe, yet knows every atom of its structure from within. The truth of God transcendent and of God immanent, his mystery and his availability, must be held together as a single reality, dialectical to human thought but indivisible in itself. The God who is within things is not secondary nor less than the God who is beyond. His unfathomable otherness addresses each of us with an intimacy surpassing all other relationships. This is not poetical paradox but the dialectical truth forced upon us by the fact that the transcendence of God consists in an inexhaustible self-giving.

> I know that the Immovable comes down;
> I know that the Invisible appears to me;

> I know that he who is far outside the whole creation
> Takes me into himself and hides me in his arms.[47]

Christians have never found it easy to hold this dialectic in balance. According to the climate of thought, or in reaction to it, they have at certain times opted for a naturalistic view of God and chattered about him with either academic or merely sentimental familiarity, and at other periods have scurried to reconstruct the ancient stronghold of divine inaccessibility with an equally one-sided emphasis. Perhaps because both the science and the philosophy of the early years of this century made all God-talk sound ridiculous, the recent trend has been a return to the *via negativa* which dares to know only what God is not, and may end in knowing only that he *is* not. In its most convincing form it concentrates on the absolute 'non-objectivity' of God, by which two related truths are intended – that God is not to be regarded as an additional being, not even the Supreme being, among all other beings, for he is Being itself, the source of all being; and that God can never be the object of another's observation, but is necessarily the initiator and subject. Both things need to be asserted; they are rooted in Christianity's traditional stand against domesticating God, which is idolatry. But the assertion must be counterbalanced in order to be true. So, for example, Bonhoeffer wrote in his doctoral thesis, 'A God who is there is not God' – meaning that the true God cannot be 'there', as a mountain or a mathematical truth is there, to be discerned. But he immediately added: 'God "is" in relation to persons, and his "being" is being personal' – so denying no less firmly the concept of an unrelated, inaccessible mode of being.[48] With the same intention Rahner has written, '*That* God really does not exist who operates and functions as an individual existent alongside other existents and who would thus be a member of the larger household of all reality.'[49] Without qualification, that statement can be taken to imply that God is non-existent and unreal. In order to be true it needs the counterpoising explanation that all 'existents' in the true meaning of the word, have a derived being, whereas God alone *is* absolutely, and so is the source of all being and the very abode of all reality.

For, unless it is thus counterbalanced, the *via negativa* leads to such an emptied definition of God as to be indistinguishable from nothing. Paradoxically it also results in a very objectified God, a mental construct like those of the Renaissance philosopher, Nicholas of Cusa, who played games with the idea of infinity. The hidden mystery of God is not to be argued but to be experienced. Martin Buber, that great exponent of the approaches of the Other and of those unbidden moments when we become aware of being addressed, does confuse the matter by disallowing the word 'experience' in respect of them. To experience is not necessarily to turn something into an 'It' and objectify; and the kinds of experience that were considered in chapter 2 are always distinguished by their essential givenness and the passivity of the recipient. Reflecting upon them afterwards inevitably entails objectifying but need not imply manipulating, using or imposing oneself upon the memory. The memory becomes an 'It' of which we can speak with others; but the experience itself was of an inexpressible 'You', a Presence towards which one is still present, though the awareness may have faded.

6. The second bulwark: the one God

The second of the ancient philosophical axioms standing in contradiction to the Christian gospel has been the basic assertion of all monotheism, God is one. The words carry several layers of meaning. In their simplest, numerical sense they make the exclusive claim, God is the only God. Oriental mysticism goes further, making the words mean that God is *the* One, the sole Reality pervading all. The philosophical meaning of the words is that God is indivisibly himself and cannot by any thought be analysed into distinct elements or attributes. This is a concept that stems naturally from the Platonic polarity between being, as an eternal and unmoving state, and becoming, as a state of flux and impermanence. Since material objects are very evidently composite and manifold it was deduced without further evidence that whatever really *is* must be indivisibly simple. Christian orthodoxy has taken this as axiomatic up to the present day.

Over against this tradition came the Christian experience of God in the humanity of Jesus Christ and in the indwelling Spirit within the church, realities which could not be denied though they seemed to imply a plurality in God, if not an outright plurality of Gods. It is essential to recognize that it was, and is, an experience, not merely a dogmatic formula, which calls for some modification of the bald assertion that God is one. By insisting on the inclusion of Jesus Christ and the Holy

Spirit as distinct entities within their definition of God, Christians have been witnessing not merely to past events but to the pattern of their own relationship to God in prayer. This is an insight which has recently commanded wider attention but which, if true, must have been a fact of Christian prayer throughout the centuries.

> Usually it dawns bit by bit on the person praying that this activity, which at first seems all one's own doing, is actually the activity of another. It is the experience of being 'prayed in' . . . graciously caught up in a divine conversation . . . the Spirit himself bearing witness with our spirit (Rom.8.16) . . . But second, and more specifically, in allowing the divine activity of prayer to happen, the one who prays begins to glimpse what it might be to be 'in Christ' or to 'have the mind of Christ' (I Cor.2.16)[50]

These empirical grounds for thinking of God as triune, as distinct from conceptual argument, are reflected in some of the early Christian writings. Irenaeus clearly has more than salvation-history in mind when he says, 'The Spirit prepares man for the Son of God; the Son leads man to the Father, the Father gives man immortality.'[51] In his treatise on prayer Origen promises that the person who prepares for prayer by purging the heart of distraction and resentment 'becomes more ready to be mingled with the Spirit of the Lord' and 'will partake of the Logos of God . . . who prays to the Father with the person whose mediator he is'.[52] And Athanasius reflects the same spiritual progression in his oft-repeated phrase, 'to the Father, with and through the Son, in the Spirit', which is, in his thought, a reciprocation of God's constant action upon the world 'from the Father, through the Son, in the Holy Spirit'.[53]

Had Christianity been free to witness to its experience of the saving potency of Jesus and the inner process of prayer without resorting to metaphysical definitions, it need never have turned God into an object of logical definition, nor taken up a position so incompatible with simple monotheism. Judaism, as already noticed (pp.87f.), is not unacquainted with the idea of God's emanations or separate modes of self-communication; and even in Islam the Spirit is named, as in the Old Testament, as a distinct power of the one God. Unfortunately experiences have implications, and implications cannot be discerned without subsequent reflection. Unless the implications of experience are pondered corporately and integrated into a growing tradition they remain subjective and idiosyncratic. There is no escape, therefore, from some measure of objectifying God by talking about him as an 'It' and thereby setting up opposing theologies. The antidote is to alternate metaphysics with adoration, 'It' with 'Thou', and to observe so far as possible the advice of Wittgenstein: 'Whereof one cannot speak, thereof one must be silent.'[54]

We can, without religious chauvinism, be profoundly grateful to the early theologians of the church, apart from their anathemas, for pursuing so relentlessly the metaphysical implications of the Christian experience because, properly understood, their trinitarian conception of the being of the one God does wonderfully enlarge and illumine the meaning of divine transcendence. An earlier section of this chapter recounted briefly how their trinitarian doctrine first grew out of the adoption of the hierarchical model of God's relation with the world, and how, to avoid suggesting that the Logos and the Spirit were less than God, being associated more with the world and its creation than with the timeless Godhead itself, thinkers from the fourth century onwards argued that the terms 'Father, Son and Holy Spirit' define equal and eternal modes of being within the one God, distinguished only by their unalterable relation one to another. In simple, and therefore inexact, terms the great benefit of the doctrine, apart from other things it enables us to say, amounts to something like this. We human creatures attain our highest fulfilment only as persons, and we can exist as persons only in the richness of mutual exchange with other persons, giving and receiving, knowing and being known, including and being included. God, who transcends our idea of personhood by being more than person, cannot in the unimaginable fullness of his perfect being lack this joy of mutual exchange. Hence he must possess it within the pure oneness of himself, being both knower and known, giver and recipient, encompassing all the facets of love. This is not a denial of God's indivisibility, but a further glimpse into the depths of his transcendence.

Tragically this insight has been formulated in such ambiguous terminology as to mislead many Christians and heighten the affront to other monotheists. To start with, the words Father, Son and Spirit, are all metaphors. God is Father inasmuch as he is eternally the origin, source, initiator. God is Son, or Word, inasmuch as God is known to himself and self-expressed; he is Son inasmuch as he is eternally derived from that self-knowing. God is Holy Spirit inasmuch as he recognizes and goes out in affirmation towards the perfection he sees through that self-knowing. If this depiction looks unpleasantly narcissistic it needs further explanation, but it does serve to demonstrate the metaphorical nature of the names Father, Son and Spirit. Confusion, however, was worse confounded by the philosophical terms chosen to denote these relationships within the being of God. Greek-speaking theologians used two of them almost interchangably. The first, *hypostasis*, originally meant the underlying reality or essential being of anything, as it does in the New Testament (Heb. 1.3 and, possibly, 11.1). Its Latin equivalent was then *substantia*, substance. But by the middle of the fourth century *ousia*, or essence, was preferred as the more exact word for underlying reality, and *hypostasis* took on a different nuance, denoting particular individuality. As Basil the Great put it: '*Ousia* and *hypostasis* have the same distinction as the general has in respect of the particular, as, for example, "a living creature" has in respect of "a particular man".'[55] The obvious danger in applying that analogy to the distinct relationships within the being of God is that it may imply three gods – three instances of the genus, 'God'. So they also took the word *prosōpon*, face or presence, as another term to denote the same thing. Like its Latin equivalent, *persona*, it could also mean a mask or a character in a play. Taking all these nuances into account, it might be better to avoid the English phrase 'Three Persons', which suggests three autonomous personal beings or centres of consciousness, and translate *prosōpon/persona* as 'identity', and *hypostasis* as 'particularity'.[56] So, speaking of the relationships that God contains within his own being, Basil said 'It is necessary to confess that each Identity (*Prosōpon*) exists in a true Particularity (*Hypostasis*).'[57]

Teachers of the Christian faith have always looked for analogies that make it easier to conceptualize the interrelation of Father, Son and Holy Spirit within the one being of God without either making them interchangeable or turning them into three divine beings. The earliest comparisons, drawn from the physical world – three torches lit one from another, the three primary colours in a rainbow, or the sun, its radiance and its warmth – pointed to the experience of God as Trinity in his self-communication to the world (known technically as the functional or 'economic' Trinity). Augustine of Hippo realized that if we were to attempt to understand God as Trinity in his innermost being (called, as if deliberately to confuse, the 'immanent' Trinity!) it was necessary to look for analogies from the only innermost being of which we had any knowledge – the human mind. The brief explanation of Father, Son and Holy Spirit, at the beginning of the previous paragraph, summarizes the imagery that he, and Aquinas long after him, drew from that source. It remains extraordinarily coherent and convincing because it speaks of God as personal, dynamic being, and the hint of divine self-complacency in it vanishes when one starts with the crucial revelation of the gospel that the transcendence of God lies in his self-giving.

Human beings, on their infinitely smaller scale of measurement, know what it is to mirror that self-giving. In our own self-giving, as we have seen, is our own self-transcendence. The mother living for her children, the scientist committed to a particular search, the liberator dedicated to an oppressed people, the artist giving form to an inner vision, the devotee pursuing the vision of God – each of them is simultaneously in three distinct states of self-awareness, though only fully conscious of one of them at a time. There is the self-giver absorbed in willing the welfare of the children, the discovery of the truth, and so on, fulfilled in pure *generosity*. There is the given self, conscious of the imperative 'I must', fulfilled in *obedience* to it. And there is the 'in-othering' self that is so identified with the child, the work of art, the victims, the presence of God, as to know them from the inside and be fulfilled only in *their fulfilment*. These are three modes of consciousness in one person but each is distinct and characteristic so that only one prevails in the mind at any instant. Ask the in-othered self why, and it will speak of the sheer worth of the other, be it child, undiscovered fact, disregarded people, artistic concept or vision of God. Ask the given self why: it may tell of an inner drive, a love of the work, a charge to carry out, or a sense of vocation. Ask the self-giver why, and the reply is likely to be, 'I am what I am.' It is not difficult to apply this analogy to God's relation to humanity and to the world, in the Father whose self-outpouring purpose and will establishes the relationship; in the Son, the given self of God, obedient to love's imperative, delighting in response to it; and in the Holy Spirit who is God's empathy with creation, affirming and indwelling, and fulfilled in its fulfilment. Can the same analogy apply to God's being in himself? Does it answer the question, 'What was God doing, what was God loving, to what was God giving himself in the absence of a universe?' There is enough arrogance in such a query from those to whom even the universe is strictly unknowable to warrant Augustine's famous retort, 'Preparing hell for people who ask such questions.' Perhaps the 'immanent' Trinity is inherently unknowable. Yet, we must affirm, even of this mystery of God's being, that it encompasses all the facets and all the exchanges of love, knowing and being known, giving and receiving. The simplest of Augustine's analogies is also the best: 'Here we have three: a lover, a beloved and love . . . We have not yet found what we are seeking, but we have found where to look for it,'[58] and where we must look is to the pitifully fragmentary understanding of mutuality in love which is our highest human faculty. If the One that is before and beyond and within all is self-giving, self-abandoning love, there must be within that love a ceaseless reciprocity between that which is ever anew pouring forth love from its inexhaustible fullness, that which ever receives and recognizes and responds with love, and that which, in love with love, as it were, delights in the very goodness of that mutual exchange.

7. The third bulwark: the unchangeable God

The Bible bears consistent witness to God's changelessness. In contrast to human moodiness God is constant. In contrast to human fickleness God keeps faith. In contrast to the transitoriness of human endeavours God abides for ever. Without this stability God would be as arbitrary as any pagan deity and there would be no warrant for trusting him. That is what every assertion of divine immutability in the Old and the New Testaments is saying. Changelessness is not propounded in the Bible as a necessary attribute of divinity itself, but invariably refers to God's actual relationship to the creation, to humanity, and to his people Israel in particular. Throughout the Bible, therefore, the changeless God does not exhibit the fixity of an idol or of a philosophical definition but is liable to display those variations of response whereby the stable party in a relationship preserves his constancy in the face of every vacillation of the other. Consequently, like a parent to a child or a teacher with a pupil, this God remains dependable by adapting to the other's change of behaviour, and his face or seeming may be one of mercy or severity, presence or absence, justice or caprice, since he is the God not of logical deduction but of experience. Yet even at his most inscrutable he evokes confidence: 'Though he slay me, yet will I wait for him' (Job 13.15). Such is the paradox of God's reliability.

But that is not what classical philosophers or Christian theologians have meant by divine immutability. What they have had in mind was rooted in Parmenides' contention that, since whatever does not exist is a nothing, it makes no sense to say of anything that *is*, either that it was not or will cease to be; so all becoming must be an illusion. Plato could not deny that things do actually come into being and pass away, but like Parmenides he insisted on an absolute polarity between this world of things that become but can never truly be, and the immaterial realm of what really *is* and never becomes. Aristotle refuted the polarity by introducing the middle term of potentiality. In order to become anything the subject must in some sense already be: actuality is prior to potentiality. Hence being includes becoming. This is an insight of immense significance, as we have already glimpsed;[59] yet it does not contradict Aristotle's more powerful argument for God's unchangeability, namely that change implies the addition of some property formerly lacking or the loss of some property formerly possessed; since God's perfection can neither lack nor lose, God cannot change. Augustine was wholly convinced by Plato[60] and Aquinas by Aristotle.[61] Both arguments, however, assume that 'to be' is to be essentially inert, and that each distinct being is what it is, an immutable self-contained 'substance' with variable 'accidents', or properties. A state of rest is regarded as normal.

That is the metaphysics of a universe in which there is no evolution, only a multiplicity of disconnected elements and 'types', each for ever the same. It is an image we can no longer sustain. For we know the universe to be a single, vast interflow of energy by which each entity derives its being from that of others in ceaseless give and take, and our human personhood emerges only from its relation with other persons. A persistent traditionalist might argue that this perception of a whole creation in flux only confirms the absolute difference between it and the God who abides in immutable stillness. But such a blatant antithesis would make God's immanence within the world impossibly problematical.

Gregory of Nyssa saw that the actual experience of prayer and spiritual progress turns our idea of change and stability upside down. The seeming change and movement of human life, he said, is actually a futile standing still, like a convict on a treadmill or a traveller climbing a dune of loose sand; whereas those who move on and up by continual change towards God are the ones who are participating in the divine stability.

And this, he believed, shows us the true nature of God's changelessness.[62] We do see, in fact, a natural concord between the universe and its trinitarian Creator who, in the words of the ninth-century philosopher, John Eriugena, 'moves from himself in himself to himself'.[63]

> The motion of the supreme and threefold and only true Goodness, which in itself is immutable, and the multiplication of its simplicity, and its inexhaustible diffusion from Itself, is the cause of all things, indeed *is* all things.[64]

The classical definition of change, however, and the denial of any becoming on God's part remained axiomatic throughout the centuries of Christian thought until the present day. Logically it demands a radical qualification of the straightforward statement that the Word *became* flesh. Irenaeus had found no such difficulty in affirming 'the Son of God become Son of Man',[65] and later Athanasius, who reiterated that formula, was at pains to make the point that 'He became man and did not just come into man'.[66] The contrast Athanasius is drawing in that statement is between 'becoming' and 'entering', and not, as many of his interpreters have tried to make out, between being human and being a particular man, since the word *anthropos*, without the article, is the same in both parts of the phrase. But the view which he was refuting by those words prevailed none the less as the more typical christology for centuries to come. Tertullian sets out the accepted argument in these terms:

> Everything that is transformed into something else ceases to be what it was and begins to be what it was not. God however does not cease to be nor can he become something different . . . If he is not capable of conformation to something else it follows that he must be understood to have become flesh in the sense that he comes to be within flesh and is manifested and seen and touched through flesh.[67]

So began the centuries-long struggle to get over the impossibility of God becoming man by hitting upon some way whereby divinity and humanity, each retaining its utterly incompatible and exclusive particularity, might be said to co-exist in Jesus Christ without splitting his singleness of identity. No exercise could have been better calculated to turn both 'God' and 'humanity' into objects to be manipulated in a delicate balancing act. The philosopher Schleiermacher in the nineteenth century objected to the incongruity of applying the term 'nature' to God and to humanity as though they were on the same plane, and then trying to co-ordinate them as two of a kind.[68] What those involved in the argument were all trying to say, of course, was that the single personal reality of Jesus Christ was both truly man and truly God, but they were saying it in 'It' terms instead of in terms of relationship.

Both Tertullian and Athanasius were careful to explain that in all talk about the person of Christ the Logos could mean nothing less than God, and 'flesh' or 'body' meant nothing less than the whole human being.[69] But the thinking of the church was still heavily influenced by the Platonic conviction that mind and soul had a superior reality compared to the physical part of human personhood, and this inclined all of them, including Athanasius, to equate the humanity of Jesus with his bodily frailties and sufferings, and his divinity with miraculous power and knowledge.

> Let it be said in each case, as is fitting, Christ hungered and thirsted for our sakes *in the flesh*, Christ said he did not know, and was beaten, and toiled, for our sakes *in the flesh*, and Christ was lifted up, and was born, and grew up *in the flesh*.[70]

> It is not the human nature that raises up Lazarus nor is it the impassible Power that weeps when he lies in the grave: the tear proceeds from the man, the life from the true Life.[71]

> He willed to offer prayer to his Father, not now as lacking power in himself, but for our instruction and as an example of prayer for us.[72]

Every attempt to describe the unity of God and man in Jesus in terms of a strictly parallel juxtaposition of two elements results in an unconvincing figure, lacking integrity. For a truly human person is an indivisible nexus of body-mind-spirit. He or she does not *have* a body but *is* a body. Spirit or soul is involved in our most animal experiences no less than body, and probably more involved than body in our sins; body shares no less than spirit in our purest aesthetic or religious encounters. It is this inseparable totality we must keep in mind when we think of the humanity of Jesus. Had the earlier theologians been able to do so, they might never have slipped into the habit of regarding his manhood as merely the body or garment or instrument of the Word, taken up or 'assumed' as the means for carrying out his task. Nor could they have spoken always of the Logos/Son as the essential subject or consciousness of the God-Man, and the humanity as an attribute.[73] Cyril of Alexandria, in spite of falling into the same habits from time to time, strove to emphasize the interpenetration and union of the humanity and divinity of Jesus, and protested against the common method of distinguishing them.

> If anyone distributes to two identities or particularities the expressions used both in the Gospels and the Epistles . . . attributing some to a man conceived of separately, apart from the Word which is of God, and attributing others, as befitting God, exclusively to the Word which is of God the Father, let him be anathema.[74]

Another element in the old Platonism, namely the idea of Forms or eternal archetypes, may have lent an ostensible credence to the strange notion that a generality can exist objectively apart from particular instances, so that God the Son could be said to have assumed human nature without becoming *a* man. Cyril has been quite unjustifiably credited with this dogma which, Professor Henry Chadwick assures me, was introduced in the sixth century as an attempt to reassure those who could not reconcile themselves to the formula of the Council of Chalcedon. The idea is, in fact, untenable, as Aristotle knew. Generalities exist nowhere but in their instances, unless one refers the word, incorrectly, to something like R. J. Mitchell's design of the Spitfire before the first plane was built, or to our knowledge of dodos subsequent to their extinction, and these belong to the category of potentials, something between being and coming (or ceasing) to be. The need to perpetuate such an illogical concept arose from the church's determination to use the language of 'assuming' rather than that of 'becoming', for 'assuming' presupposes that something is already there to be picked up. So Aquinas argues:

> The human nature taken on is not already the nature of some person, but comes to be such as the result of being taken on. Any pre-existent person would have to be destroyed by the union . . . for otherwise

there would be two persons, one taking on and one taken on, which is heresy.[75]

John Henry Newman endorsed the dogma on the same grounds.[76] But though it was officially decreed by the Second Council of Constantinople in the year 553, it remains a contradiction in terms, since it is only by becoming a particular instance of human nature that either God or man can be said to have assumed human nature. It is, moreover, philosophically questionable whether any generalities exist in the mind of God. According to the Jewish theologian Abraham Heschel, that kind of categorizing has no place in God's manner of knowing.

> Pure reason comprehends a concrete fact as if it were an abstraction, a particular being in terms of a generalization. But it is the greatness of God according to the Bible that man is not an abstraction to him, nor is his judgment a generalization. Yet in order to realize a human being not as a generality but as a concrete fact, one must feel him, one must become aware of him emotionally.[77]

God's relation to the world is personal and particular. He knows each thing only as a 'thou', and his knowing is not by cognition but by communion. Only by becoming this one man has God brought humanity in general into such communion with himself.

In this long-drawn-out endeavour to make sense of the Christian conviction that the historical reality of Jesus must be thought of both as truly a man and as truly God, neither the subtlety of theologians nor the jurisdiction of ecumenical councils has been able to bring the matter to a satisfactory conclusion. Talk of two contrasting 'natures' running in tandem presents a single person so divided up as to be unreal. To speak of divinity taking up humanity robs the manhood of a human centre and runs counter to the Old and New Testaments. Wolfhart Pannenberg has perceptively pointed out that the Gospels clearly portray, not a humanity possessed and inwardly directed by the Logos, but a man consciously dependent on, and answerable to, the Father.[78] Perhaps it is time for the language of juxtaposition and of assumption to give place to that of translation.

8. God translates himself

Is it after all so impossible for God to alter – that is, to become something 'other', even something less – without ceasing to be what he always is? Even Plato asked, 'Are we really to be so easily convinced that change has no place in that which is perfectly real?',[79] and Tertullian was not the only one of the great teachers of the early centuries of Christianity whose perplexity over divine unchangeability led him to contradict his own theology.

> If things from which God is far removed lose what they were in process of being changed, where will the difference be between deity and other natures unless it is that the contrary obtains, that is, that God *is* able to change into everything and yet to continue such as he is.[80]

There lies the nub of their difficulty. Though they did not always see it clearly, what the theologians felt bound to deny was not that God might choose to change but that he might thereby cease to be what he is. So Hilary of Poitiers, whose orthodoxy none impugned, argued that the Creator of a universe in which stability is preserved through development might be thought to share the same propensity.

> Man always advances through increase: he does not contract by diminution; but his increase does not mean that he ceases to be himself. Even if he fails through advancing years or is cut off by death . . . it is beyond his power to cease to be what he is . . . So it was appropriate for God to be other than what he continued to be, while not ceasing to be what he had always been; for God to be born in human nature and yet not to cease to be God.[81]

It is significant that St Hilary assumes some affinity between the Creator and what he creates, because it is in the realm of human creativity that examples, or at least analogies, of 'alteration without essential change' are to be found. The transcription or arrangement of a musical composition with a good understanding of the intention of the original, demonstrates how a thing can become something else without ceasing to be what it was. Bach's arrangement for the organ of Vivaldi's set of concertos for violin and orchestra is a case in point; and anyone fortunate enough to have heard Dame Myra Hess's performance of her own setting for piano of the chorale, *Jesu, joy of man's desiring*, will remember the clarity with which she conveyed the musical values of the three distinct sounds of four-part choir, oboe obligato and small orchestra for which Bach composed it, without in the least detracting from the integrity of the solo piano. Even the joyful impression clearly intended by the trumpet doubling the soprano part was suggested through the attack with which she brought in the chorale. The aesthetic communication was identical, though now in purely pianistic terms.

Again, many would say that it is impossible to translate the sense and the beauty of a poem into any other language, and Dante certainly detested the very idea. Yet Anne Ridler, herself both poet and translator, has kindly drawn my attention to T. S. Eliot's opinion that in the Elizabethan Thomas Heywood's translation of Seneca's play, *Hercules Furens*, the chorus at the end of Act IV was 'very fine' and in the last six lines 'perfect'.[82] She has also told me of Germans who declared that they understood their own poet Rilke's *Duinese Elegies* more profoundly after reading the English version by Leishmann and Spender.

Symbolic actions also are a kind of incarnation: a kiss or the touch of fingers are able to convey the entire gift of someone's love as no words can do. Sacraments are derived from this principle. Our capacity to embody and convey a relationship in a symbol is one of the faculties that make us human, and it arises from our intuitive recognition that there is more to things than meets the eye.

We have seen already that, in acknowledging this 'more', this potentiality of things to go out from and beyond themselves (a potentiality that is inherent to their reality yet never an identifiable 'extra'), we are being made aware of the God who is 'more intimately and profoundly interior to things than anything else'.[83] Many of the Fathers of the Church found in God's immanence in the created world a clue to the possibility of his becoming man.

> If the Word of God is in the universe, which is a body, and has entered into it in its every part, what is there surprising or unfitting in our saying that he has entered also into human nature?[84]

> If all things are in the divinity, and the divinity is in all things, why are

> people embarrassed at the divine economy displayed in the revelation which tells us of the birth of God in humanity, since we believe that God is not outside mankind even now?[85]

Modern thinkers also are drawn to dwell upon the immanence of the transcendent God as the key to many problems.

> Our only way of being present to another's suffering is by being affected by it, because we are outside the other person . . . Now, the creator cannot in this way ever be outside his creature . . . If the Creator is the reason for everything that is, there can be no actual being which does not have the Creator at its centre holding it in being. In our compassion we, in our feeble way, are seeking to be what God is all the time: united with and within the life of our friend . . . The Lord has no need of compassion; he has something more wonderful; he has his creative act in which he is closer to the sufferer than she is to herself.[86]

The birth of every child is a new emergence from the very stuff and continuity and history of the human race and of the material universe itself. The same must be said of the birth of Jesus also. To think of the eternal God, already committed to space, time and history, being inwardly present to each instant of every thing's existence, yet not as something additional to it, and then to think of that immanent God emerging, in total identification with the emergence of a particular human child, to be one with him in each instant of his life, though still not as something additional to his humanity, does not differ essentially from saying that 'he came down to earth from heaven'; it is, in fact, less misleading. We have no warrant to disallow God's freedom to bring this about. His changelessness means that he cannot cease to be what he is, but it does not preclude his doing some new thing to express what he is. God's sameness is not monotony.

> Immutability says too little, since God not only establishes and maintains present reality in its lawful course, but has within himself an infinite plenitude of ever new possibilities in the realization of which he manifests the freedom of his invisible essence.[87]

So, within the boundless possibilities of his infinitude God does not cease to be what he is; and what he is is total self-giving. He is the eternal Source.

We are back, then, with the common ground of self-transcendence by self-dispossession which human nature, in its incomparably lesser, finite way, shares with God. Karl Rahner, who has identified this common ground with special clarity, sees it as the clue to the incarnation. Human beings are creatures with an infinite horizon and, though they have become so flawed as to settle for the self-centred here and now, they still possess the instinct to reach out towards the limitlessness of God. They find fulfilment only by going out of themselves in self-abandonment to God. Human nature is so created as to match and reciprocate on its finite scale the infinite self-giving of the God who transcends, goes out of himself, in eternally giving himself away.

> God expresses precisely *himself* if he empties himself. He discloses himself as love if he conceals the majesty of his love and manifests himself in the ordinariness of man.[88]

In the earlier section of this chapter on the oneness of God there was a re-statement of Augustine's exposition of the Trinity as a three-fold relationship in love: the inexhaustible source out-pouring love, the answering love responding to the gift, and the loving delight in the goodness of that exchange. Or, putting it another way, there is the Self-giver, eternally fulfilled in pure generosity; there is the Given Self, fulfilled in dependence upon and obedience to the will and purpose of the Giver; and there is the 'In-othered' Self, fulfilled in the effect of that self-giving. It is the second of these identities, God's *Given* Self, responding to the Father's love, obedient to its imperative, who became flesh. What we can see as the human reality of Jesus is the Word, God's eternal self-expression, so translated into the language of that man's truth, God the Son's eternal relationship to the Father so transcribed and performed on the creaturely instrument of that human response to God, God's limitlessly Given Self so embodied in the symbolic action or physical gesture of that human life and death, as to have lost thereby nothing of what he essentially is for ever. The very Word of God was being spoken, God the Son was present in their midst, yet what was heard and seen was nothing but human. The 'becoming' was complete.

As with the divine immanence in all creation so now with the incarnation, his being 'here' does not exhaust his being both everywhere and beyond all place. And again, as with the immanent presence so with the incarnate, there was no extra 'substance', no additional element of divinity alongside the human fact. The human and divine aspects of Jesus are distinct only as two equally true ways of understanding this human being whom God has become.

How else would that in the Godhead which is eternally begotten, God *from* God, Light *from* Light, be transposed for the instrument of a human consciousness but as a man who knowingly derived his existence and took his direction moment by moment from God in total dependence? 'Father, if it is possible . . . yet not my will but yours.' 'The son can do nothing of his own accord but only what he sees the father doing' (Matt.26.39; John 5.19).

How else might God the Son's eternal response to the love of God the Father be translated into truly human speech and human prayer but in that intensely intimate communication with God which Jesus seemed to take for granted and which he expressed, not as a demi-god conscious of his divinity, but as a man in terms of filial devotion? 'Father, your name be hallowed, your kingdom come.' 'Everything is entrusted to me by my Father and no one knows the Son but the Father, and no one knows the Father but the Son, and those to whom the Son chooses to make him known' (Luke 11.2; Matt.11.27).

How else might the Given Self of God, conscious of the imperative purpose and fulfilled in obedience to it, become embodied in purely human action but in such a sense of mission and such ultimate self-sacrifice as we see in the life and death of Jesus? 'Whoever receives me receives not me but the One who sent me.' 'I have a baptism to undergo and what constraint I am under until it is over!' 'The Son of Man is to be handed over into the power of men' (Mark 9.37; Luke 12.50; Matt. 17.22).

And where could the ultimate mystery and otherness of God rub shoulders with the human throng without ceasing to be what it eternally is except at the place in which we always find it imaged, in the final unknowability of the human person, which, as the Gospels testify, was peculiarly baffling and beyond reach in the manhood of Jesus. He eludes the grasp of biography, and the silence of his solitude when he withdraws for prayer, walks ahead on the road or hangs from the cross, is wrapped in a cloud of unknowing. Kierkegaard called it 'the most profound incognito', but in fact it was not a concealment but a revelation. Precisely by becoming nothing but man God disclosed the whole truth of himself, all we shall ever see; and, as a man, God did and does for humankind that which he alone can do.

9. The fourth bulwark: the unaffected God

The last of the philosophical bastions that have challenged the proclamation of a Christlike God is structurally linked with the third. The axiom that God cannot be changed and the claim that he can neither be affected nor limited by anything other than himself stand together as one sprawling and formidable edifice. The proper name of this fourth dogma is divine *impassibility* and its various connotations are all derived from the Greek and Latin verbs that mean 'to undergo'. To call God impassible is to say that he cannot be the *passive* object of any external cause. There are three distinct aspects of this claim.

1. *God cannot be affected by any eventuality.* The long shadow of Aristotle's God who thinks only himself still falls across Christian theology at this point. 'No real relatedness to created things exist in God,' says Aquinas, 'though a real relatedness to God exists in created things,'[89] and he explains that basic lack of mutuality with an analogy that reduces God to an inert object more thoroughly than any other in the literature of theology! 'Seeing and understanding really relates us to things, but being seen and understood by us is not something real in the things; and similarly a pillar to the right of us does not itself have a left and a right.'[90] If such misrelation were really the truth concerning God and the world, if, in short, God could remain untouched by the world's annihilation, then nothing is of any consequence. Abraham Heschel has argued powerfully that a state of real moral indifference must logically follow from the doctrine of divine unaffectedness that both Aquinas and Marmonides derived from Aristotle.

> God does not reveal himself in an abstract absoluteness, but in a personal and intimate relation to the world. He does not simply command and expect obedience; he is also moved and affected by what happens in the world, and reacts accordingly. Events and human actions arouse in him joy or sorrow, pleasure or wrath. He is not conceived as judging the world in detachment. He reacts in an intimate and objective manner *and thus determines the value of events*.[91]

Furthermore, if God is unaffected either by our love for him or by our sin, he may still condemn or acquit as a matter of disinterested judgment, but he could not be said to forgive. Aquinas tried to make room for mercy in an unaffected God by arguing that in God's case, unlike ours, mercy resides solely in the effect that it produces, not in any effect that sympathy might have upon himself – *secundum effectum, non secundum passionis effectum.*[92] To which the modern French theologian, Jacques Maritain, has objected:

> Love is attributed to God not only because it is the cause of good in others. Love, not according to what it *does* but according to what it *is*, is a perfection of God, and is God himself. Is it not the same with mercy? It is found in God according to what it *is* and not only according to what it *does*, but in that state of perfection *for which there is no name.*[93]

2. *God cannot be subject to passions, emotions or sufferings of any kind.* The divine nature,' wrote Origen, echoing Irenaeus, 'is remote from all affection of passion and change, remaining ever unmoved and untroubled in its own summit of bliss.'[94] The most obvious reason for this almost unanimous judgment is that feelings appear to belong to the corporal side of our being and cannot appropriately be ascribed to God. Hence the Fathers of the Church went to absurd lengths to limit the sufferings of Christ to his body alone, and even there to reduce them to unreality.

> Though blows fell on his human body and wounds were inflicted on it, though it was lashed with scourges and lifted up on the cross, all these brought the onslaught of suffering, but they did not convey its pain.[95]

> Christ's soul did not repel from his body the hurt inflicted on it but was willing for his bodily nature to suffer.[96]

It has already become clear, however, that no such absolute distinction can be drawn between soul and body, and spiritual suffering can be the most intense of all. We may not preclude it from the being of God on that score. But the resistance rests on tougher foundations than that. Stoics and Epicureans alike had held up the ideal of *apatheia*, being free from emotion, and Christian ascetics pursued the same discipline as the way to draw closer to the passionless God. At the heart of such rigorism and the theology that supports it lies the suspicion that emotions are essentially *dis*ordering and so tending towards sin. The various meanings we attach to the word *passion* betray this understandable ambivalence. Augustine suggested that the unruly quality of human feelings, together with the limited capacity of human knowledge, are the legacy of Adam's fall,[97] while in this century Baron von Hügel has written: 'Suffering and Sin are, indeed, not identical, yet they are sufficiently like to make the permanent treatment of Sin as intrinsically evil exceedingly difficult when suffering is treated as not really evil at all.'[98] So it is all the more remarkable that Melito of Sardis in the second century could boldly preach about the divine Logos as the perennial Victim.

> He is the one who in many folk bore many things. He is the one who was murdered in the person of Abel, bound in the person of Isaac, exiled in the person of Jacob, sold in the person of Joseph, exposed in the person of Moses. This is the one who was made flesh in a virgin, hanged upon the wood, entombed in the earth, raised from the dead, lifted up to the heights of heaven. He is the speechless lamb.[99]

No less startling are Origen's comments on passages from Deuteronomy and Ezekiel.

> The Father himself, God of the Universe, he who is full of longsuffering, compassion and mercy, does he not suffer in some way? Or do you not know that in his concern for human affairs he suffers human passion? For the Lord your God has taken upon himself your fortunes as he who carries his child (Deut. 1.31). God, then, takes upon himself our fortunes as the Son of God takes our sufferings. The Father himself is not impassible.[100]

The very fact that neither writer holds consistently to the theology of these passages is evidence of the undercurrent of unease that has always accompanied the traditional assertion of God's impassibility and has in our day gathered to a concerted rejection of it. For the real flaw lies in the projection on to God of a defective analysis of the human person. Since we understand now that we achieve personhood not by solitary thought but through relationships involving every aspect of our human nature; since also we know that our thoughts are no more immune than our feelings from refraction by physical influences; there is no valid reason why we should not attribute to God some pre-eminent equivalent of our emotional life just as we have attributed to him some pre-eminent equivalent of the power of thought. God's pain may be no more metaphorical and no less actual than his wisdom.

3. *God cannot suffer any limitation*. He is totally free from restraint and never driven by any necessity. All this is commonly subsumed under the term *omnipotence*. That is a word that is often bandied about with very little examination. 'Since God is the Creator he must be all-powerful' is a truism that begs the question. Do we understand the act of creation so clearly as to be sure that it requires 'power' in any sense in which we use the word? It is less misleading to talk about God's *freedom*. God's omnipotence means his freedom to do what he wills. 'Power', says Aquinas, 'is the ability to execute what will commands and mind plans; but in God the three are identical.'[101] What God wills is determined by his nature, for he cannot be untrue to himself. For this reason we lead ourselves astray if we talk about God 'choosing' to do either this or that, or ask why he did this rather than that. God has no choice but to do what is according to his nature. Anything that God has not willed can never be and never could have been, so it was never an option for him. God's freedom does not consist in being able to bring about an infinite choice of possibilities, but in being able to turn everything to the service of the one purpose that he wills to bring about. And if his nature, his essence, is the inexhaustible self-giving of love, then his one purpose, whatever that is, must have been formed by that love alone. In that case, as Professor John Macquarrie has said,

> This would mean that humility and the form of a servant are not disguises of God and not unnatural to him, but of his very essence. And this would mean that he cannot draw near as a prince or even a professor,but only in some lowly and obscure form.[102]

God has absolute freedom *to be what he is* in his self-giving, even in his self-abandonment, and what he does is identical with what he is. God *is*: all created things are *derived* from his self-giving. Their being is something they have received, something they *have*. They exist by having, not by pure being, and consequently what they have is also something they can lose. We humans are distinct from all other creatures in knowing this: we know that we shall die, we know the reality of non-being. And that knowledge either throws us upon God in absolute trust, accepting our being as a gift for so long as it is given, or it incites us to a more desperate will to have and to hold. Since we exist by having, not by being, what we grasp at is a substitute for being, namely power in one form or another. Power to control our own destinies and have our own way staves off the dread of non-being. Our weakness in infancy sows in us all the seeds of fantasy whereby we imagine ourselves becoming all-powerful. We grow up admiring the strongest, the fastest, the one who can outsmart the others. Traditions, fairy tales and modern comics alike delight us with ever-conquering heroes. 'Some talk of Alexander and some of Hercules', and the weakest peoples of the world dream of liberators. So naturally the human race throughout its history has projected those frustrated, disappointed images of mastery out into the skies and called it God, 'than which no greater can be thought.' God must be the supreme potentate among the world rulers, the master-mind above all the clever controllers. God, unlike us, can do exactly as he pleases in the world at any time. God, like our private wishes, fixes everything. Only get him on your side and you can't lose.

Yet such a God, though we imagine he is what we most need, has never been one we could trust. Austin Farrer has expressed this truth in a striking passage:

> We have so mishandled the sceptre of God which we have usurped, we have played providence so tyranically to one another, that we are made incapable of loving the government of God himself or feeling the caress of an almighty kindness. Are not his making hands always upon us, do we draw a single breath but by his mercy, has he not given us one another and the world to delight us, and kindled our eyes with a divine intelligence? Yet all his dear and infinite kindness is lost behind the mask of power. Overwhelmed by omnipotence we miss the heart of love.[103]

10. A revelation of the unguessed

Farrer completes that particular passage with the words, 'Love is the strongest instrument of omnipotence for accomplishing those tasks he cares most dearly to perform; and this is how he brings his love to bear on human pride, by weakness not by strength, by need and not by bounty.' The church has prevaricated for two thousand years rather than accept the implications of the gospel concerning the nature of God. The words, 'He who has seen me has seen the Father', attributed to Jesus in the Fourth Gospel, are not a claim made about him but a declaration made about God. 'Have I been with you so long? How can you still say, Show us the Father?' When he is treated with contempt for consorting with undesirables, when they put him out of the city for including non-Jews in the divine concern, when he is powerless to heal in the face of disbelief, we are seeing God's true relation with the world. When Jesus casually asks friends to lend him their property, when he shares his powers with them and invites them to share his burden, when he knowingly perseveres in his misplaced trust in Judas, we see God's true relation with humanity. When he mourns, 'How often would I have gathered you, but you would not have it,' when he sets his face steadfastly towards conflict and suffering, when he rejects 'this shall not happen to you' as a devilish, not a divine veto, then he is most truly God.

Yet it seems that Christian piety cannot accept that simple equation, but down the centuries has echoed St Peter's protective protest: 'Frustration, suffering, powerlessness? heaven forbid! These shall never happen to our God.' With endless ingenuity theologians have identified a saving disconnection at some point along the line from the Crucified to the Almighty to relieve them of having to draw the terrifying logical conclusion. There were some early on who denied any real similarity between even the body of Jesus and the physical functions of ordinary human beings. Others imagined a break between the spirit or soul of Jesus, which the divine Logos had possessed, and his flesh, which was merely the vesture or tool of divinity. Others drove the wedge between the divine and the human natures of Christ, the one impassible and all-powerful, the other vulnerable, so that nothing about God could be construed from the humanity. Then there were those who forced a strange hiatus between the abstract humanity attributed to Jesus and the individual personality that is the unique possession and burden of every other human being; and those who, with similar intent, misused the belief in the virginal conception of Jesus to interpose a *cordon sanitaire*, as John Robinson called it, between Jesus and the hereditary past from which the rest of us receive our humanity. And, as if that were not break enough, some doubled the quarantine by propounding the sinless conception of the Virgin Mary herself. And, finally, there are those who, against all past orthodoxy, drive the wedge between the first and second Persons of the Trinity, allowing that in Jesus of Nazareth God the Son did indeed suffer and die even as we do, but insisting that this tells us nothing whatever about the nature of the eternal Father in himself.

There is another way of bracketting off the incarnate Christ so as to make him inadmissable as evidence of the essential nature of God. It is possible for anyone who is thus inclined to argue that the Uncreated is so fundamentally other than anything we can deduce from events inside the created world, and that eternity so transcends the categories of time, that what happened in the historical lifetime of Jesus, even though he is Son of God, can throw no light into the ultimate mystery of God's inmost being, nor contradict the assumption that he is, after all, primarily power. So the thirty odd years of incarnation can be regarded as a period of exile for God the Son, or an under-cover assignment he had to undertake, roughing it like a millionaire's son on a secret mission. In that case the vulnerability and conflict conceal the truth more than they reveal it, and the victim on the cross was simply enduring the worst patch of the adventure before winning through, when he threw off his disguise, mission accomplished, and resumed the throne of omnipotent incomprehensibility.

That is, of course, a caricature; but what it parodies is the way in which the church has sometimes told the story. It ignores one essential element of orthodoxy, which is that God the Son has never put off the humanity that was his in Jesus Christ. That much of the 'adventure' still goes on within the being of God; not the flawed and incomplete thing we are familiar with, but humanity fulfilled as God intended it, the common ground of transcending self-abandonment which we all potentially share with God. We cannot protest that there is no common discourse between our minds and the mind of God, no self-communication from God to humanity. For it was his Word, his self-revelation, that became flesh in Jesus Christ – only a translation, no doubt, of the eternal mystery into the inadequate language of human intercourse, a translation of the invisible Light into the lesser lights of creaturely perception, but a translation none the less that we must believe gives us true equivalents of the Original.

> If it is now that God is creating, it is now that he risks himself, that he accepts the prospect – the reality – of tears and blood. Not our tears and our blood only! Not only the tears and blood of Christ! Would the Creator wish to be outside the struggle? Can there be, can there not be, at the heart of pure Spirit something unnameable that is analogously equivalent to our tears and our blood?[104]

But if the incarnate Word was indeed a revelation of God we must give full weight to the newness and the discontinuity of the understanding of God which the gospel conveys. The *new* covenant means at the very least a renewal or restoration of something not known or overtly acknowledged before. If it were not startling but the same as before we should have no right to call it a revelation. It is the concept of revelation that compels us to see the Bible as a saga of progressive unfolding through successive revelatory experiences of which, as was outlined in the first chapter, the last was the experience of Jesus Christ. His God was the God of the Old Testament, but his relationship to that God and the events that issued from it amounted to a radical redefinition of the divine sovereignty.

I believe this view is justified by the studied reversal of the normal categories of status and authority which occurs throughout the New Testament. 'God chose the foolish things of the world that he might put to shame them that are wise; God chose the weak things of the world to put to shame them that are strong' (I Cor. 1.27). 'Did not God choose them that are poor in the eyes of the world to be rich in faith and inherit the kingdom?' (James 2.5). Again Paul writes disparagingly of the figures of absolute sovereignty, human and divine, the many gods and many lords, in contrast to whom we know one God and one Lord – a contrast not merely between the many and the one, but between the styles of godhead and lordship: we have the God we know as Father, the Lord whom we find in Jesus (I Cor. 8.5,6).

These contrasts, drawn so sharply in the epistles, reflect the reversals that Jesus himself emphasized, according to all the Gospels: the first last, and the last first; the high humbled and the humble exalted. 'In the world kings lord it over their subjects and those in authority are called their country's "benefactors". Not so with you. On the contrary . . . Who is greater, the one who sits at table or the one who waits on him? Yet here I am among you like a servant' (Luke 22.25–27). It is however the Fourth Gospel that links these reversals with a new insight into the eternal nature of God himself, and it does so through its characteristic use of the word *doxa*, glory. Glory means always the outward shining of an inmost nature, the grace and truth of any being. Jesus, the Word, was identical with the outward shining of the Father. It was the passionate desire of the Son, according to this Gospel, to reveal to the world the outward shining of his Father's inmost truth, and that the Father, for his part, should make the world see the inmost truth of the Son, since these were the same truth. 'Father, the hour has come. Glorify thy Son, let the inward being shine out, that thy Son may glorify thee' (John 17.1). But what was this hour in which the inward being, shared eternally by the Father and the Son, was to shine out? It was the cross and, through the cross, the resurrection. 'The hour has come for the Son of Man to be glorified: unless a grain of wheat falls into the ground and dies it remains that and nothing else, but if it dies it bears a rich harvest' (John 12.23–4). That is the secret at the heart of the Christian revelation, if revelation it is. Therein lies both its continuity with the past and its staggering novelty. 'The God who said "Out of darkness light shall shine" has caused the light to shine in our hearts, the light which is knowledge of the glory of God in the face of Jesus Christ' (II Cor.4.6).

6

And All the Prophets

The Christlike God in the Old Testament

1. A new teaching!

There will certainly be those who object to the proposition that to speak of Jesus Christ as a revelation of God implies that his life and his teaching made known an aspect of the truth about God that had not been grasped before. He was a child of his time, and what he would have learned from his home, the village rabbi and the routine homilies in the synagogue was the orthodox belief in the God of the Old Testament. 'You, non-Jews, worship you know not what; we worship what we know. It is from the Jews salvation comes' (John 4.22). When he himself took to preaching, he brought a distinctive emphasis to his portrayal of God and spoke with a startling degree of authority, but he did not talk like someone consciously introducing a radically new image of deity. 'Do not suppose that I have come to abolish Torah and the prophets: I did not come to abolish, but to complete. I tell you this: so long as heaven and earth endure, not a letter, not a stroke, will disappear from the Torah until all that it stands for is achieved' (Matt. 5.17 REB mg).

Yet even such a protestation of continuity prompts, rather than answers, the question: How different will the *completion* of Torah and prophets be from their present incompleteness? Later Judaism certainly understood that it was to be the particular glory of the messianic Kingdom

> to perfect what cannot find expression in the *Halakhah* (regulations) as the law of an unredeemed world. Thus, for example, only in

> messianic times will all those parts of the law which are not realizable under the conditions of the exile become capable of fulfilment[1]

When all that the Law and the prophets stand for is achieved, will their present devotees recognize it as the same thing? 'No one drinking old wine wants new, for he says, "The old is better".' All four evangelists agree that early in the Galilean ministry Jesus was harping upon the theme of radical innovation. The Fourth Gospel records the first 'sign' as an acted parable with that intent. In response to his mother's insistence upon the crisis of deficiency at the wedding feast Jesus first attends to the water jars, those symbols of the old observances, 'the purification of the Jews', which he fulfilled 'up to the brim'. Then he gives a fresh order: Draw (*antlēsate*) now. The word, as used again two chapters later, means, Draw from the well. There is nothing to suggest that the servants had to decant from the water jars. Those had been 'full filled'; they belonged to the past. For this marriage feast the servant must go back to the original source of the old tradition and draw from it afresh for the needs of a new day.

> No one tears a piece from a new cloak to patch an old one; if he does, he will have made a hole in the new cloak and the patch will not match the old. Nor does anyone put new wine into old wineskins; if he does, the new wine will burst the skins, the wine will be wasted, and the skins ruined. Fresh skins for new wine! (Luke 5.36–38).

That is not the imagery of reformism and restoration; and, indeed, had Jesus' preaching been about revival and return, the Pharisee party would have welcomed it without reserve. Their hostility is inexplicable unless the words and, even more, the behaviour of Jesus towards those who were conspicuously contravening the ritual and moral law, had already begun to exhibit the anarchic novelty and freedom of one who did actually cherish a radically different idea of God's expectations from their own.

The Fourth Gospel, from its maturer and more theological reflection upon the real nature of the controversy between Judaism and the Christian movement, recognizes that what was at stake was not so much the importance each attached to religious regulations as the image of God which their opposing attitudes represented. Every sensitive

Christian must grieve over the anti-Semitism of the Fourth Gospel's indiscriminate term, 'the Jews', to denote the opponents of Jesus. Yet we should note that the evangelist does not impute legalism or hypocrisy to them, as the synoptic evangelists do, but ascribes their hostility, rightly or wrongly, to the more radical difference in their understanding of the God whom they and he both worship. That is what the central controversies of chapters 5, 7, 8 and 12.37–50 are about: Is God in truth such a God that this man, with his actions, can be recognized as his beloved emissary and representative?

> You are bent on killing me, a man who told you the truth as I heard it from God (8.40). I do not speak on my own authority, but the Father who sent me has himself commanded me what to say and how to speak (12.49). A son can do nothing by himself; he does only what he sees the father doing: whatever the father does the son does, for the father befriends (*philei*) the son and shows him all that he himself is doing (5.19, 20). No doubt you know me; no doubt you know where I come from. Yet I have not come of my own accord. I was sent by the one who truly is, and him you do not know. I know him because I come from him and he it is who sent me (7.28) . . . he of whom you say, 'He is our God', though you do not know him. But I know him; if I said that I did not know him I should be a liar like you (8.54–55).

The same deep difference in understanding pertained also between Jesus and even his most intimate followers, and it is this that the Synoptic Gospels mainly emphasize. 'You think as men think, not as God thinks' (Mark 8.33). 'You do not know what kind of spirit you represent' (Luke 9.55 mg.).

Once we have conceded the fundamental novelty and challenge of that conception of God which Jesus had in mind as the true completion of the Law and the prophets, we are in a position to recognize that that is actually what it was – the full flowering of a truth about God the seeds of which had already been planted among the insights of the older dispensation. The confident understanding of God's nature which, out of his intimate personal communion, Jesus both possessed and proclaimed, sounded forth like the first full orchestral announcement of a theme that had been already hinted at and explored by some of the prophets long before. At the time of Jesus it may have been the discontinuity and innovation of his understanding of God's nature that most impressed his contemporaries, but we should not ignore its continuity with the earlier prophetic movement in Israel.

2. A sentient God

It has often been remarked that the God of the Old Testament, whose transcendent otherness is declared in terms of surpassing majesty, is none the less far removed from the Absolute of whom it is permissible to say only what he is not. Yahweh is supremely positive – the Living God, *'Elohim chayyim.*

> The Israelite felt God as an active power before positing him as an eternal principle. God is never a problem, nor is he the ultimate conclusion of a series of speculations; on the contrary it is he who questions and from whom the initiative always comes. Strongly typical in this respect is the sudden and unexpected appearance on the scene of history of the prophet Elijah, who justifies his intervention simply by the words, 'Yahweh is living'.[2]

The activating and responsive presence of this God who is alive is constantly contrasted with the non-response and deadness of all other gods. The same Elijah taunts the prophets of Baal with their great Lord's evident insensibility:

> Call louder, for he is a god. It may be he is deep in thought or otherwise engaged or away on a journey; or maybe he has fallen asleep and must be woken up! (I Kings 18.27).

Jeremiah and the Second Isaiah make play with the immobility of inanimate idols as symptomatic of the unaffectedness of pagan deities (Jer. 10.8–10; Isa. 46.6, 7), and the psalmist does not shrink from ridiculing the concept of non-responsive divinity in vividly physical terms – mouths that cannot speak, eyes that cannot see, hands and feet without feeling or movement. The worshippers of such a god come to share the same deadness, while the servants of Yahweh participate in his supreme quality of aliveness: 'It is not the dead who praise Yahweh, not those who go down to silence, but we, the living, bless him, now and for evermore' (Ps.115).

On first consideration it is actually something of a puzzle that the Hebrew prophets should draw the comparison between Yahweh and the other gods in terms of vitality. For throughout the Semitic world the power of the holy gods, their separateness from all mundane beings, lay in their possession of an unearthly energy that was essentially life-bestowing. As was pointed out in chapter 3, every local *el* or *baal* was originally a focus of the dangerous *mana* force, and this was the primary meaning of the word *qedesh*, holy, which was applied to sacred places, persons or objects infused with numinous energy. By association the same force was also identified with the fertility of all living creatures. So it seems contradictory that the prophets of Israel should choose impotence as the slur with which to defame the other gods. The reason, however, is not hard to find. The Hebrews' faith in Yahweh had not evolved out of any numinous awareness of the energies of nature nor did it depend upon a world order of supernatural powers. Instead, it had arisen from the impact of a historical experience of divine rescue, and it depended on the continuing history of their special relationship with the God who had chosen them. Their main religious objective, therefore, was not to secure their corporate well-being by integrating themselves with the mysterious forces of nature and avoiding the ritual taboos, but, rather, to adjust their way of life as a people to reflect the moral character of their God. The Holy One of Israel is committed to this world and to historical events within it, and is to be known only in the terms of that relationship.

> Judaism, in all of its forms and manifestations, has always maintained a concept of redemption as an event which takes place publicly, on the stage of history and within the community. It is an occurrence which takes place in the visible world and which cannot be conceived apart from such visible appearance.[3]

There is, therefore, something far more significant than primitive naiveté or poetic licence in the anthropomorphism that runs through the whole of the Old Testament. If the inability of the man-made idols to see or hear or feel is symptomatic of an essential lack of historical purpose or action in the gods they represent, then the consistent will and redemptive activity of Israel's God is clearly attested by the Hebrew writers' attribution to him of eyes that do see, ears that hear and an arm that is stretched out. Yahweh's readiness to act in order to bring about what he had purposed and promised was for them the sign and substance of his absolute difference from any god that had not, like him, staked his divinity on the outcome of historical events.

> Gather together, come, draw near, you survivors of the nations, who in ignorance carry wooden idols in procession, praying to a god that cannot save. Come forward and urge your case, consult together: who foretold this in days of old, who stated it long ago? Was it not I, Yahweh? There is no god but me, none other than I, victorious and able to save (Isa. 45.20,21).

And the same characteristic of dependable action within the uncertainties of this world distinguishes Yahweh from all his creatures, including human kind:

> God is not a mortal that he should lie, not a man that he should change his mind. Would he speak and not make it good? What he proclaims, will he not fulfil? (Num.23.19).

The anthropomorphic metaphors do not contradict the transcendence or the incorporeality of this God. The absolute veto against making any image of him was meant to ensure that verbal imagery would not be interpreted literally. But to diminish the thrust of the metaphors as though they were a merely figurative device with no precise theological significance is to stop one's ears to what the writers were saying. The point of the Old Testament analogies, especially the metaphors drawn from human experience, is that they are the most appropriate form of speech for talking of a God who, as they fundamentally believed, is committed to a reciprocal relatedness with the world and has an affinity with it. Every such metaphor is intended to affirm that in God's relationship with the world there really is a divine equivalent to the essential feature of the chosen image. So far from excluding anything corresponding to human feelings from their concept of God, their belief in his transcendent will, which to them was inseparable from his action, led them to think of him rejoicing, regretting, yearning, repenting, delighting, and feeling disgust, anguish, jealousy, frustration, anger and pity. For without such language they would have missed the most essential quality of his godhead, which was, they believed, a changeless commitment to a chosen purpose that must be fulfilled in the contingencies of a particular relationship.

3. Why a chosen people?

This understanding of God stemmed – and it cannot be too often repeated – from the Hebrews' folk memory of divine rescue from slavery and from their continuing relationship with the God who had chosen them. 'I am Yahweh unchanging, and you too have not ceased to be sons of Jacob' (Mal.3.6). The recollection of an extraordinary deliverance, culminating in a compact initiated and bestowed by God, gave to this people an indestructible sense of election and of standing in a special relation to their God. This they expressed in a rich variety of similies: mother and baby, father and first-born son, housewife and servant, husband and wife, landowner and inheritance, farmer and vineyard, king and people, shepherd and flock. Some of these might be applied to God's relation to all humanity but Israel was the jewel in the crown, the *segullah* (Ex.19.5).

To understand the Old Testament it is essential to acknowledge that special relationship as real. If it irks our more inclusive idea of divine concern, we should look at Israel as we look at Hecuba or Hamlet, born to live out a story that is peculiarly theirs alone as an archetype of our own and all humanity's condition *vis-à-vis* the God of all flesh. Israel is the paradigm of God's relationship with all peoples. The prophets were not unaware of this. Amos recognized that other nations besides Israel had experienced some divine rescue and vocation. 'Did I not bring Israel up from Egypt and the Philistines from Caphtor and the Aramaeans from Kir?' (4.7). Just as God, in punishing Israel, suffers with his people's sufferings, so also does he grieve over other nations that bring nemesis upon themselves. 'I know his arrogance, says Yahweh; his boasting is false, false are his deeds. Therefore I shall wail over Moab, cry in anguish for the whole of Moab. I shall moan over men of Kir-heres' (Jer. 48.30,31; see also vv.35–6). It is, therefore, concerning ourselves that we ask the question which Israel's history thrusts upon us: Why did God commit himself so irrevocably to an insignificant and constantly unresponsive people?

The question was answered in different ways as time went on. There was never any doubt that it was not for special qualities of their own that the Israelites became the object of Yahweh's favour and choice. 'Know that it is not because of any merit of yours that Yahweh your God is giving you this good land to occupy; indeed, you are a stubborn people' (Deut.9.6). It was even proposed that the boot was on the other foot and the land was given to Israel as a punishment for the previous inhabitants! (Deut.9.5). More often it was said that God chose to raise up his people that they might possess the Eretz Isra-el, the land of God's righteousness, 'the glory of all lands', and hold it in trust for himself (Ex.3.8; Deut.8.7–9; Josh.22.19; Ezek.20.6.15; 36.5).

Another answer was to push back the origins of the special relationship to the times of the patriarchs, and to see the Exodus from Egypt and the covenant at Sinai as the fulfilment of a solemn promise given to the patriarchs by God five hundred years earlier (Ex.6.8; Deut.1.8; II Chron.20.7; Neh.9.7; Ps.105.8–11; Isa.41.8). Whether those august ancestors were historical or legendary, the story of Abraham, 'the beloved' to whom Yahweh confided his intentions and to whose advocacy he gave heed, became another model of the relationship God was seeking to establish with human beings. The memory of Abraham was to have the same function as the example of the chosen people in demonstrating the nature of that relationship. In that sense 'all the peoples of the earth would wish to be blessed as Abraham was blessed' (Gen.12.3). Up to the time of the Babylonian exile, however, the prophets make virtually no reference to the traditions about the patriarchs, so it seems more likely that the Sinai covenant was the original historical experience which later generations read back into the stories of Abraham. In any case the question still stands: What prompted God to choose this one?

Though it is never possible to say with certainty when any particular thought first entered the theology of the Old Testament, there are firm grounds for claiming that the prophet Hosea was the first to propose that it was a spontaneous outflow of unqualified love that bound God for ever to Israel and her destiny: 'When Israel was a youth I loved him, out of Egypt I called my son' (Hos.1.11). The verb *ahab*, to love, and the noun derived from it, are ardent words in Hebrew signifying the unpremeditated self-giving which carries one person towards another with delight and desire for communion; the word frequently refers to human loves and friendships, and twenty-five times in the Old Testament it is used of our love for God – 'Thou shalt love the Lord thy God.' 'I love the Lord.' The use of this root with God as the lover, however, occurs mainly in the prophesies of Hosea and in the book Deuteronomy, which owes so much to Hosea verbally. All other instances belong to the period after the exile in Babylon. So it is at least possible to infer from this that it was suffering – personal in Hosea's case and communal during and after the Exile – which disclosed the most profound answer to the question why God should have committed himself to this people.

> It was not because you were more numerous than any other nation that Yahweh desired you and chose you; for you were the smallest of all nations; it was because Yahweh loved you and stood by his oath to your forefathers (Deut.7.7,8).

The love which the Hebrews attributed to God is just as passionate an emotion as the jealousy, joy, anger or compassion which they also considered appropriate words to apply, and we cannot expurgate the ardour from the term *ahab* without destroying its meaning. This is corroborated by the synonyms which the Old Testament uses to speak of the divine love: *ḥaphetz*, delight, *ratsah*, pleasure, *ḥashaq*, desire (as in the verse quoted above) and, most profoundly, *yada*, to know, which, as we shall see, is equivalent to what in chapter 5 I called 'in-othering', or finding one's being within the experience of another person. It is in that sense that Amos hears God saying to Israel: 'You alone have I known among all the clans of the world' (3.2). Yet, while the Old Testament writers clung to this warmly sentient conception of the divine love, they instinctively avoided insinuating in any way that God was surprised or taken over by his love. They recognized that God's passions have no life of their own, as ours have. God's fervent love is God's very self, all one with God's burning will and purpose. He sets his love upon Abraham, upon Israel, as an example of how he has set it upon humanity, upon all creation, voluntarily, as a gift, because self-giving is God's way of being.

The God of the Old Testament establishes the sovereign freedom of his passionate loving (or to put it more crudely, shows that he is in control and not *driven* by love) in two ways. First, God's love, because it is God's very being, is changeless. Once given, it can never be revoked, for God cannot be untrue to himself. As God's ardent affection and God's unswerving will are indistinguishable, divine love entails divine faithfulness, and the rescue from Egypt must be followed by the covenant at Sinai. 'I have loved you with a love that is age-long; my enduring constancy still keeps faith with you' (Jer.31.3). The second fact that precludes all arbitrary impulse from God's loving is that it is deliberately directed towards a community. Only three times does the Old Testament name individuals as the objects of God's love – Solomon twice and Cyrus once! – and they stand as representative heads for their nations. Every other mention refers to God's people or their capital city. Like a mother who cares for each child yet finds her completest fulfilment in watching the whole family living, playing, arguing together, so this God delights not so much in the piety of the few as in the justice and harmony of the whole. The response Yahweh awaits in return for his gift of love is not the mystical ascent of the saint, but the ethical intercourse of the commonwealth. 'If only you will now listen to me and keep my covenant, then out of all people you will be my prized possession. For the whole earth is mine, but you will be to me a kingdom of priests, my holy nation' (Ex.19.5,6).

4. *The God of the covenant*

There are many instances in the Old Testament of a *berith*, or covenant-bond, made between human beings. Almost always the partners were on an unequal footing, and it was the stronger who took the initiative, so that the compact was, at least overtly, an act of grace. So we are told how Ahab, the king of Israel, after a surprise victory over the more powerful Aramaeans, unwisely granted treaty to the captive king, Benhadad (I Kings 20.20–32). After David's triumph over Goliath, Jonathan, the king's son, made a covenant of friendship with him which contributed to the king's growing jealousy (I Sam.18.1–4). Whatever the consequences, once a *berith* was sealed it remained binding, even when it had been obtained by fraud. During Joshua's conquest of the land the citizens of Gibeon and its neighbouring towns, seeing they would be the next to be attacked, are said to have deceived the Israelite leader into supposing that they lived far away and wished to make a covenant treaty. Afterwards, when their ruse was discovered, the Israelites had to honour the bond and spare the lives of the Gibeonites for all time, though they took some revenge by imposing on them a regular levy of firewood and water for the local shrine (Josh.9.3–27). A distant sequel to that story further illustrates the binding force of the *berith*. Because of his former covenant with Jonathan, David spared his lame son Mephi-bosheth and took summary vengeance on the two rash men who murdered Jonathan's step-brother, Ish-bosheth. But King Saul, in his lifetime, had broken the ancient *berith* between Israel and the gentile citizens of Gibeon and tried to exterminate them; so when the surviving Gibeonites demanded expiation, David was bound by that older covenant to hand over to them for execution the last seven of Saul's descendants, though he still protected Mephi-bosheth, Jonathan's son (II Sam.4.5–13; 21.1–9).[4]

It was, then, Israel's belief that Yahweh had bound himself to his chosen people with just such a covenant at Sinai. The most detailed account of that long ago event has been re-touched many times and reveals traces of several traditions; but the original salient elements seem to have been (a) a revelation granted to Moses who was the interpreter of the whole episode, (b) a ritual blood-sharing, (c) a reading of the laws or terms of agreement, and (d) a sacramental meal. During my experience of teaching theology in Uganda, I came to recognize that the rituals of the *berith* in the Pentateuch were very similar to those of blood-brotherhood in its various forms in east and central Africa. The Bantu languages speak of 'cutting' a blood-brotherhood, which is the exact meaning of the Hebrew term for making a covenant, *karath berith*. The intention of every such ritual in Africa is to bring two parties to share one blood and so become kin. In its crudest form both will wound themselves and let the two trickles of blood mingle; or each may chew a coffee berry smeared with the other's blood. In its more sophisticated forms the bond is sealed with the blood of animal sacrifice, but always with the intention of uniting the two parties in a single blood-stream, a single life. The similarity to the rituals recorded in the Pentateuch is impressive though the actual imbibing of blood was *tabu* among the Hebrews. In the making of the Sinai covenant the law had been proclaimed, then the blood of the sacrificial bulls was collected; half was flung against the altar at the foot of the mountain, representing God, and, when the assembled people had sworn their obedience, the other half was flung over them (Ex.24).

Even more striking is the ritual of God's covenant with Abraham who was ordered to divide the sacrificial victims into halves and stand between the two lines of severed carcasses. There, within that enclosure as it grew dusk, the Lord appeared to him in likeness of smoke and flame and made *berith* with him and his descendants (Gen.15). It is clear that the same basic ritual was followed when Zedekiah, the last free king of Judah, led his people into a renewed covenant with God to proclaim the emancipation of all Hebrew slaves. When the dignitaries of both palace and temple went back on their undertaking and forced their former slaves into bondage again, Jeremiah castigated them all with the words:

> You have violated my covenant and have not fulfilled the terms to which you yourselves had agreed before me; so I shall treat you like the calf which was cut in two for all to pass between the pieces, the officers of Judah and Jerusalem, the eunuchs and priests, and all the people of the land. I shall give them up to their enemies who seek their lives (Jer.34.18–20).

That passage introduces a negative, perhaps more primitive, aspect of the intention of covenant-making. Those undertaking the agreement place themselves under an oath which works like a self-imposed curse: 'If I speak false or break this bond, let me suffer the fate of these sacrificed victims.' Perhaps some such bloody ritual was the context, at least in the mind of the speaker, of that frequent Old Testament oath, 'God do so to me and more also if I fail in such and such respect.' Vestiges of that ancient style of oath linger even in the speech of these days when anyone protests, 'Cross my heart', or murmurs 'God's truth' while drawing a finger across the throat.

However that may be, it is not the theme of retributive justice that is paramount on God's side of his covenant with Israel, but the contrary. God had bound himself to this people in a contractual kinship with all the obligations of blood-relationship: 'I shall adopt you as my people and I shall be your God (Ex.6.7; Lev.26.12; Hos.2.23; Jer.24.7; 30.22; 31.33; Ezek.11.20; 14.11; 16.28; 37.27; Zech.8.8;13.9). Familiarity breeds contempt, and it is fatally easy for modern readers of the Old Testament, as it was for the ancient Hebrews, to hear the constant reiteration of that divine commitment as though it were a child's chorus. But the great prophets that repeated the words in succeeding generations had a lofty concept of God's transcendence. It was the invisible and everlasting Creator, whom the heaven of heavens could not contain, who had pledged himself to an unbreakable reciprocal relatedness to this people. In neither of its parts does the Book of Isaiah use the phrase, 'They my people and I their God', but it conveys precisely the same thought in the oft-repeated title, The Holy One of Israel. That paradoxical name for Yahweh witnesses to the fact that this God does not cherish as his own his immeasurable distance from all created things, but reveals and shares it by drawing near; he whose thoughts are higher than ours makes his absolute difference the means whereby we may become different. He is holy in his self-commitment, by being in the midst, by sharing, as it were, his life-stream with that of human beings.

The commitment to share together a common life meant that God had taken upon himself his people's destiny and his people's sufferings. In the encounter at the burning bush Yahweh had said to Moses, 'I have witnessed the misery of my people in Egypt . . . I *know* what they are suffering'. The word here used is *yada* which, according to Abraham Heschel, signifies always a profound inner engagement and attachment.[5] It means knowing from within, so that in Exodus 23.9 the people are enjoined to show mercy to aliens with the words: 'Do not oppress the stranger, for you *know* the heart of a stranger, seeing you yourselves were strangers in the land of Egypt.' To know in that intimate sense is to undergo the same experience; it is the 'knowing' of sexual union. Such is God's knowledge of human suffering. Even when the sufferings are those his people have brought upon themselves as retribution for folly and sin, the very God who condemns them suffers at their side. Their defeat is his humiliation; their exile deprives God of home and heritage, and in all their afflictions God is afflicted (Jer.12.7–11; Isa.63.9). So real is God's kinship with his adopted people that he is called their *go'el*, the near relative who exercises the right and duty of redemption, as Boaz did even for the half-alien Ruth. That image of the rescuing kinsman is present in every occurrence of the word 'redeemer' as a description of Yahweh.

> Thus says the Holy One, Yahweh, the *go'el* of Israel, to one who thinks little of himself, whom every nation abhors, the slave of tyrants: when they shall see you (that is after you have been bought back into the family) kings shall rule, princes shall stand up and bow, because of

Yahweh who has kept faith, because of the Holy One of Israel who has chosen you (Isa.49.7; cf. 41.14; 43.14; 48.17; 54.5).

Keeping faith – that is what was expected of a responsible kinsman, that is what a covenant bond laid upon the participants, especially the stronger, initiating party. The Hebrews had a word for it, *ḥesed*, constancy (the *ḥ* sounding like the *ch* in the Scots word 'loch'), and it is the crucial term in the theology of the Old Testament. God's immovable faithfulness to the relationship with Israel, his commitment to the covenant, is the core of the Jewish understanding of deity.

5. *Faithfulness and infidelity*

In the older English versions of the Bible, for reasons that will appear, the word *ḥesed* was most often translated as 'kindness' or, especially in Miles Coverdale's glorious rendering of the psalms, with the hyphenated term, 'loving-kindness'. Both 'mercy' and 'goodness' were also used frequently. But, comforting though these familiar terms are, they somewhat conceal the real nuance of the Hebrew expression and give a decidedly un-Hebrew slant to our reading of the Old Testament. For the root sense of *ḥesed* is durability, and exactly the same meaning is conveyed when God is called 'the Rock' – not quite the equivalent of loving-kindness! This rock-like quality is brought out in the psalm couplet:

> One thing God has spoken, two things I have learnt:
> 'Power belongs to God, *ḥesed*, Yahweh, to thee' (Ps.62.11,12).

It is essentially a moral durability that is attributed to God, and in comparison to it human strength is unreliable:

> All flesh is as grass, and its *ḥesed* as the flower of the field (Isa.40.6).

Innate unreliability, the moral equivalent of physical transcience, is the flaw in human nature from which the drama of the Old Testament arises.

> How shall I deal with you, Ephraim? How shall I deal with you, Judah?
> Your *ḥesed* to me is like the morning mist, like dew that vanishes early (Hos.6.4).

But the particular durability to which the word invariably refers is that of loyalty to a relationship; so *ḥesed* is best translated as faithfulness or constancy. Sometimes the word is coupled with *berith* quite directly: 'The God who keeps covenant and constancy, *ḥesed*' (I Kings 8.23; cf. Deut.7.9; Neh.1.5; 9.32; Dan.9.4). More often we find it linked with *emeth* or *emunah*, which share the same root as 'Amen', and mean 'reliability' – usually rendered as 'truth' in the older versions: 'The greatness of your faithfulness reaches to the heavens and your reliability to the clouds' (Ps.57.10; cf. Gen.24.27; Ex.34.6; II Sam.15.20; Pss 85.10,98.3).

Loyal constancy is the virtue of keeping one's promises and was highly valued by the peoples of the ancient world, so it was a supreme reassurance to know that one's God was not arbitrary and fickle, but ever faithful and utterly reliable. Abraham's steward, sent to find a suitable bride for Isaac the favoured heir, prays: 'O Lord God of my master Abraham, give me good fortune this day; keep faith, *ḥesed*, with my master Abraham' (Gen.24.12). Again, David sends word to the city which risked giving honourable burial to the exposed bodies of King Saul and three of his sons: 'Yahweh bless you because you kept faith, *ḥesed*, with Saul your overlord and buried him; for this may Yahweh keep *ḥesed* and *emeth* towards you' (II Sam.2.6). As a philosophical principle the Greeks fastened upon the changeless immovability of the Absolute within itself almost as a law of physics, certainly as a logical necessity. To the Hebrews on the other hand God's changelessness was entirely a moral disposition and a matter of relationship. And this they knew by experience. God had bound himself to their nation by promise and commitment and must remain true to himself. 'I, Yahweh, your God, am a jealous God, punishing children for the sins of the fathers . . . but keeping faith, *ḥesed*, with thousands, those who love me and keep my commandments'(Ex.20.6). 'O give thanks unto Yahweh, for he is gracious and his *ḥesed*-constancy endures for ever' (Ps.136.1).

Covenant, and the faithfulness that sustains it, are meant to be reciprocal, as in a bond of kinship or of marriage. A mutuality of loyalty, an exchange of trust and confidences, and a sharing of plans and responsibilities are more esteemed than feelings of affection. The God of the Hebrews actually calls humanity into a partnership of mutual trust and co-operation. Terence Fretheim has drawn attention to the theological significance of the various stories of what he calls 'divine consultation' which have previously been regarded as delightfully naive. He instances the quaint 'bargaining' conversation with Abraham before the doom of Sodom and Gomorrah: 'Shall I hide from Abraham what I am about to do?' (Gen.18.7–22), the similar negotiation with Moses after the worship of the golden calf (Ex.32) and again after the return of the spies from the land of Canaan (Num.14.11–25), and God's several consultations with Samuel over the making and unmaking of King Saul (I Sam.8.4–22; 15.10,11,34,35). The claim that Amos makes, 'Indeed, the Lord God does nothing without revealing his plan to his servants the prophets' (Amos 3,7) anticipates the Johannine declaration of the same truth: 'No longer do I call you servants, for a servant does not know what his master is about. I have called you friends' (John 15.15). God's commitment to his people is a commitment to a mutual relationship. He surrenders his unilateral sovereignty in order to involve *them* in responsibility for the future.

> What God will do at least in part depends upon what Israel does. God's actions are not predetermined. Thus, Israel's response will contribute in a genuine way to the shaping not only of its own future, but to the future of God.[6]

But Israel, no less than humanity as a whole, proved to be tragically incapable of responding to God's trust with comparable faithfulness. It was precisely that exchange and reciprocation which Israel as a people failed to realize in her relationship with God in Old Testament times. The word *ḥesed* is used 102 times to speak of God's loyalty towards his people, 47 times of the loyalty of human beings to one another, but twice only of human loyalty to God, and in both cases as of something that did not last. So much for the divine hopes for mutuality! The enormity – one is inclined to say the hopelessness – of the human condition as revealed in the Old Testament lies in the all-too-evident truth that love is not loved, loyalty does not win loyalty and generosity begets ingratitude.

> What baffles the prophet is the disparity between the power and impact of God and the immense indifference, unyieldingness, sluggishness and inertia of the heart. God's thunderous voice is shaking heaven and earth and man does not hear the faintest sound.[7]

With supreme moral insight the Hebrew prophets perceived that the sin of this nation was something far more serious than its inevitable slowness to adopt a pure monotheism. Lapses into the practices of the surrounding paganism, and transgression of the ethical code prescribed in the Torah, were things that shocked the temple priests and religious reformers; but the prophets saw beyond such disobedience to the heart of the matter: all sin is a sin against love, and it defeats the long-laid plan and purpose of creation itself.

> The universe is done. The greater masterpiece, still undone, still in the process of being created, is history. For accomplishing His grand design God needs the help of man. Man is, and has, the instrument of God, which he may or may not use in consonance with the grand design. Life is clay, and righteousness the mold in which God wants history to be shaped. But human beings, instead of fashioning the clay, deform the shape. The world is full of iniquity, of injustice and idolatry.[8]

The God, who has staked his total commitment on an enterprise that requires the loving co-operation of humanity, endures a functional dislocation of his purposes which is at the same time a personal rebuff to his generosity. And, say the prophets, he is not, he cannot be, unaffected by the continual frustration of his desire for the life of this world.

> Man's sense of injustice is a poor analogy to God's sense of injustice. The exploitation of the poor is to us a misdemeanor; to God it is a disaster. Our reaction is disapproval; God's reaction is something no language can convey.[9]

God's 'reaction' – if that is the right word – is, of course, strictly beyond human comprehension because, reiterating once again what must never be forgotten, God is not a supernatural person, not the supreme entity among other beings, but the Source, the Context, the Beyond, of all that is. We can only grope blindly to imagine the disappointment and frustration of that cosmic will and benevolence. Love unrequited, trust betrayed and good will frustrated become, in biblical terms, wrath.

—

6. *The wrath of God*

Those who are fastidious over ascribing anger to the deity, because they have made God out to be either too cosy or too remote, may allay their distaste by recalling that every anthropomorphic analogy is, at best, only an indicator pointing to that in the Godhead which is equivalent to whatever feature of human experience has provided the imagery of the metaphor. Up to a point we may also say that the language of wrath is describing what we as human beings *feel* that our disobedience has done to our relationship to God: 'The Lord has become like an enemy' (Lam.2.5). 'The Lord's arm is not too short to save, nor his ear too dull to hear; rather, it is your iniquities that raise a barrier between you and your God' (Isa.59.1,2). But, having said that, we cannot deny that the Old Testament authors clearly believed that the divine equivalent to anger, whatever that is, was a real aspect of God's being, inasmuch as it was an aspect of his love. Unless we give full weight to the frustration, pain and outrage suffered by God in the face of human indifference, we shall find no substance in God's forgiveness, since either both mean something real or both are empty terms.

> To experience divine anger 'as if' God were provoked is a subterfuge alien to the biblical mind . . . The word about the divine anger points to a stark reality, to the power behind the facts, not to a figure of speech.[10]

Yahweh's relation to his beloved people is represented as a battle of wills precisely because it is love – his hope and purpose and promise pitted against their stubborn inertia, their preference for the second rate, the less exacting way, the status quo. So their true God is ceaselessly working upon them, within the terms set by their freedom, to shape them towards a total commitment to himself. In this battle Yahweh never responds to their refusals by retreating into himself or breaking off the relationship. His wrath is the divine determination to keep the channel of communication open.

God is represented in the Old Testament as the good teacher who has recognized the latent gift in a promising pupil but has to fight with every weapon in his armoury – promises and threats, praise and rebuke, rewards and punishments. So the child is often hostile and sees the teacher as a tyrant or a judge. The divine teacher's wrath is genuine, not feigned, but it is far more complex and painful than it appears to the angry child, and the Old Testament gives full weight to both Yahweh's and Israel's perception of it.

Anyone determined to hold on to the truth that God is love needs constant reminding that love's opposite is not animosity but indifference. The alternative to a keen sense of the reality of divine wrath is the sad mutual disinterest conveyed in Heinrich Heine's reputed last words: 'Dieu me pardonnera, c'est son métier.' Such an attitude entirely misses the point that God's anger is the negative assertion of an unchanging care and concern whereby the divine love insists, 'This matters. You matter.' The casual assumption in Heine's witticism that God, if he bothers at all, will be easy-going identifies God's wrath with the threat of punishment and fails to understand that it has to do with the pain and the hope arising from a broken relationship. The divine will is set upon this relationship with humanity and, when it is broken, God's sole intent is to bring about its restoration.

So God is essentially 'slow to anger'. This phrase is included in all those 'credal' recitations concerning the unchanging nature of Yahweh to which reference was made in chapter 4.[11] Like the New Testament word *makrothumia*, long-suffering, it describes a God who, while enduring the outrage of rejection, contains it in the hope that the human partner may yet turn back. Yahweh is always reluctant to give expression to his indignation. When he does so it is because nothing else has brought home to his people his concern for them or made them aware of the broken relationship. God's wrath issues in punishment only for the sake of what punishment says about the enormity of human indifference and what it does to God. The penalty reflects in its violence and devastation the strength of God's solicitude (Jer.23.19,20) but, though it is God who calls it up, what befalls is always a natural or human occurrence: sword, famine or pestilence (I Kings 8.37–39; Jer.14.10; 24.10 etc; Ezek.6.11,12). Divine retribution in the Old Testament is never a mere unleashing of vengeance but always a restoration of order by ordered means. That is the significance of the imagery of legal process in which God is presented as the plaintiff in a great assize (Isa.3.13–15; Hos.4.1–6; Joel 3.1–17; Micah 6.1–16) and penalties match the crime with strict poetical justice (Isa.33.1; Jer.30.16; Joel 3.6–8). The punishment itself is calculated to bring home to the offenders the true nature of their sin. Hence, because sin is essentially a withdrawal from relationship with God, its inevitable penalty is the desolation of what appears to be the withdrawal of God (Ps.78.59–62; I Sam.4.11–22; Jer.7.12–14).

Yet, whether by longsuffering or by judgment, God's unfailing purpose is to reverse the mutual withdrawal and transform it into return. 'Return unto me, saith the Lord of hosts, and I will return unto you' (Zech.1.3; Mal.3.7). The word *shub*, return, recurs again and again with many resonances of restoration. As the destroying flood subsides, the water returns to its proper place; things return to normal; the penitent nation returns to its rightful relationship of covenant with God. When their punishment has consisted of exile, return naturally means a physical restoration to their own land and so the theology of return in Judaism has taken on a strongly political tone. Yet its essential meaning is that of reconciliation with God (Pss 6.4, 90.3; 116.7; Isa.44.22; 55.7; Jer.18.11; 24.7; Hos.2.7; 3.4,5). Moreover, besides Yahweh's unflagging hope for a lasting return on the part of his wayward people, there was his own irreversible promise to them which worked against the full discharge of his wrath. God's hands were tied by a countervailing commitment expressed in his covenant bond. The Old Testament saw this seeming contradiction as a conflict within God, one which was afterwards summed up in an early Christian verse quoted in the Second Epistle to Timothy:

> If we disown him, he will disown us;
> yet if we are faithless, he remains faithful,
> for he cannot disown himself (II Tim.2.11,12).

The antithesis between divine loyalty and divine judgment accounts for the *ḥesed*-faithfulness of Yahweh being so frequently rendered as mercy, kindness or love in the English translations, although, as has been shown, the true meaning is constancy. That is its overriding sense even where the word is translated differently – 'slow to anger and of great *kindness*' (Neh.9.17 RV); 'for his *mercy* endureth for ever' (Ps.136 BCP); 'now have I pitied you with everlasting *love*' (Isa.54.8 REB). In the context of human infidelity divine steadfastness takes on the quality of infinite forgiveness and patience.

So in the light of his undying hope God's judgment is always contingent. There is a place in Yahweh's thought for a 'perhaps': 'Perhaps they may listen and everyone may return from evil ways' (Jer.26.3). 'It may be they will realize that they are rebellious (Ezek.12.3). It was this open-endedness in God's judgment that put the tight-lipped Jonah out of countenance when the great city repented (Jonah 4.1–3). The wrath of the Old Testament God is therefore strictly conditional and so, in principle, temporary. 'He will not always accuse, or nurse his anger for ever' (Ps.103.9). 'For a passing moment I forsook you, but with tender affection I shall bring you home again. In an upsurge of anger I hid my face from you for a moment, but now I have pitied you with never-failing faithfulness, says Yahweh, your kinsman-redeemer' (Isa.54.7,8). The forgiveness of this God is never in question; all that is uncertain is the human repentance, the return, which will open the door to that forgiveness and let reconciliation take effect.

But while the forgiving God waits for that return he pays the price of love in what we can only call pain. Forgiveness does not make light of evil. It knows the swelling sense of outrage, the shock and shame of injury. But instead of venting it in retaliation or nursing the grievance, forgiveness 'owns' the wrong that is being done, lives with the injury and shame and, by continuing to love, turns an evil event into a demonstration of ultimate good. There are, perhaps, depths of meaning in any act of complete forgiveness which the Old Testament does not plumb. But no other literature in all the religious scriptures of the world is more daring or more convincing than the insight of these Hebrew prophets into the love that endures all things, believes all things, hopes all things, outlasts all things and is never exhausted.

7. The ordeal of faithfulness

Yet the Old Testament, taken as a whole, reads very much like a tragedy, Israel's (which means humanity's) and God's. Only the unwavering chorus of faith in God's ultimate victory saves it from that, and the conclusive dénouement is still unwritten. For the history of Israel shows that intermittent punishment is not the answer.

> The people did not return to him who struck them, nor seek guidance from the Lord of hosts (Isa.9.13).

> Yahweh, will your eyes not face the truth? You punished them, but they paid no attention; you pierced them to the heart, but they refused to learn. They made their faces harder than flint; they refused to repent (Jer.5.3).

Again and again reforming leaders in Israel enthused the citizens to enact some recommitment of themselves in covenant with Yahweh (Ex.29.1; Josh.24.25; II Kings 11.17; Jer.34.8,16; Ezra 10.3; Neh.9.38). But none of these humanly initiated conversions, except that of Josiah, held for long. Jeremiah knew the difference between a sincere return to God and one that was only a pretence (3.10), and eventually there was such despair of the human capacity to make a lasting change of heart that people began to fix their hopes upon the *shub shebut*, the climactic return at the end of all things, the universal restoration that should usher in the coming new age (Ezek.16.53–55; cf. Matt.17.11; Acts 3.21). This shift of expectancy into the eschatological dimension was a way of saying that God alone could make a permanent change in human hearts; but it also signalled an abandonment from the human side of the divine purpose to create a reciprocal co-operative partnership between God and God's people within the historical process. The strength and the weakness of every other-worldly faith lie in the fact that it establishes the true horizon of human transcendence only by cutting the nerve of human response to the challenge and invitation of God's sovereign immanence within world history.

But, on his side, the God of the Old Testament could not surrender the original commitment to history, and the prophets, as spokesmen for the divine faithfulness, gave voice to what they perceived as a turmoil of conflict within God because God, whose will was inseparable from act, could neither override the unending frustration of his love nor abandon his commitment to it.

> How can I hand you over, Ephraim? How can I surrender you, Israel? . . . A change of heart moves me, a longing to comfort kindles within me. I am not going to let loose my fury, I shall not turn to destroying Ephraim, for I am God, not a mere mortal; I am the Holy One in your midst (Hos.11.8,9).

The unchangeable commitment of Yahweh cannot be debased to the level of human fickleness, whatever the provocation and however long that fickleness persists. The same determination appears in the familiar words in Isaiah:

> Let the wicked be the one to forsake his thoughts and the evil man his ways, and let them return to Yahweh who will be moved with compassion for them, return to our God who will freely forgive. For my thoughts are not your thoughts, nor are your ways my ways – such is the word of Yahweh (Isa.55.7,8).

Yet the fact remains that humanity does not forsake its ways, or, if it does return, its new commitment is not steadfast like God's. So the question stands: How long is the impasse to persist, how long can Yahweh keep faith with the unfaithful?

> How much longer will this people set me at nought? How much longer will they refuse to trust me in spite of all the signs I have shown among them? (Num.14.11).

The Hebrew prophets had no doubt that this continuous disregard of the divine self-giving must cause God the unimaginable equivalent of human suffering and sorrow. If this living God could take pleasure in human response to his love, he must be equally affected by human rejection, and so subject to *pathos*, pain. 'The prophet', says Abraham Heschel, 'is stirred by intimate concern for the divine concern. The *pathos* of God is upon him. It moves him.'[12] In passages that are unique in the world's religious literature the transcendent God of purest monotheism cries out at human betrayal in the very tones of anguish and incomprehension in which the tragic heroes of Greek myth cried out against the fickle gods.

> My people, what have I done to you? How have I wearied you? Bring your charges (Micah 6.3).

> What more could have been done for my vineyard than I did for it? Why, when I expected it to yield choice grapes, did it yield wild grapes? (Isa.5.4).

> I remember your youthful loyalty, your love as a bride, how you followed me in the wilderness, in a land unsown . . . Have I been a wilderness to Israel, or a land of thick darkness? Why, then, do my people say, 'We have broken away, we shall come to you no more'? Will a girl forget her finery, or a bride her wedding ribbons? Yet times without number my people have forgotten me (Jer.2.2,31,32).

All the most painful analogies of broken relationships are called into play to convey the prophets' sense of what humanity is doing to God. But human unresponsiveness seems to be obdurate.

> I was ready to reply, but no one asked, ready to be found, but no one sought me. I said 'Here am I! Here am I!' to a nation that did not invoke me by name. All day long I held out my hands, appealing to a rebellious people who went their evil way in pursuit of their own devices (Isa.65.1,2).

If God's wrath effects no lasting return and God's pleading love does not break through human resistance, it may mean that spiritual death has occurred. Fretheim, though he does appear to put more of the prophets' words into the mouth of Yahweh himself than the text warrants, has nevertheless drawn attention to several passages in which God is certainly presented as a mourner lamenting the recent, or at least imminent, death of the beloved nation and its land.[13]

> Over the mountains I shall raise weeping and wailing, and over the open pastures I shall chant a dirge . . . These are the words of the Lord of hosts: Summon the wailing women to come, send for the women skilled in keening to come quickly and raise a lament for us, that our eyes may stream with tears, and our eyelids be wet with weeping (Jer.9.10,17,18).

Professor Phyllis Trible of Union Theological Seminary, New York, has made a detailed analysis of one very striking poem by Jeremiah,[14] the first stanza of which is more familiar to most people than the rest, since it is quoted in the Gospel of Matthew. In it Jeremiah compares Yahweh's agonizing inability to relinquish his age-long commitment to

Israel with a bereaved mother's inability to accept the reality of the death of her children.

> Lamentation is heard in Ramah, and bitter weeping; Rachel weeping for her children and refusing to be comforted, because they are no more (Jer.31.15).

In the second stanza Yahweh answers the distraught mother with the promise that sons will return (*shub*), and in the next Yahweh hears the voice of Rachel's child, like a prodigal son who could not manage a genuine return in his own strength, imploring God to *make* him do so. Then follows the extraordinary fourth stanza in which Yahweh looks at the prodigal through his mother's eyes and, from within her maternal yearning, resolves the conflict between abandoning the son who is too fickle to make his way back decisively, or holding fast to his commitment to love. (Here I borrow largely from Phyllis Trible's version that brings out the starkly literal meaning which is played down in most translations.)

> Is Ephraim my dear son, my darling child? For the more I speak against him, the more I remember him. Therefore my inner parts are convulsed for him, my womb kindles in compassion for him (v.20).

The significance of this resolution of the inner conflict is thrust home in the gnomic saying with which the last stanza ends:

> Yahweh has created a new thing in the earth:
> Female encompasses male (vv.21,22).

In other words, the irresistibly compassionate attachment that is associated with feminine response has, in Yahweh, overwhelmed the more judicious detachment commonly attributed to masculinity – a point that this final stanza quaintly underlines by changing the prodigal son into a wayward daughter! (vv. 21, 22). The imagery of the prophets remains always a kaleidoscope of analogies and never becomes a myth. They never suggest that Yahweh, like the gods of the surrounding nations, can either engender or give birth to his people. God is no more male than female, so the prophets are free to employ any metaphor of human pain or ecstasy, struggle or stress that may convey the intensity of feeling they attribute to their living God.

The colourful Hebrew language itself is infused with powerfully visceral symbolism. The word *rachamin*, which is usually translated as 'mercies' or 'tender mercies' is actually the plural of *rachem*, which means womb. The well-known Rabbi Hugo Gryn has told me that the phrase 'The Father of mercy' is, literally, 'The Father with a womb'. Hebrew speakers often use this more emotive image when we English prefer to say 'heart'. We may go so far as to talk of guts or gut-reaction, where our seventeenth-century forebears said 'bowels', as a synonym for strong feelings; either will serve as a fair translation of another Hebrew word, *meim*. Both *meim* and *rachamim* are used by Jeremiah in the stanza that describes God's yearning compassion for Ephraim (v.20), and the same combination in parallel occurs in Isaiah 63.15,16, a prayer that addresses God in his absolute transcendence:

> Look down from heaven and behold from the heights, where thou dwellest holy and glorious. Where is thy zeal, thy valour, the convulsion of thine inward parts and the yearning of thy womb? Do not stand aloof, for thou art our Father.

The juxtaposition of male and female terms which startles us sounds more natural to Hebrew readers for whom the words speak about intensity of feeling rather than distinction of gender. Kindling or warming of the womb, for example, is attributed indiscriminately both to the true mother of the living infant in the tale of King Solomon and the two harlots (I Kings 3.26) and to Joseph in Egypt when he saw his own mother's son among the step-brothers and retired to an inner room to weep (Gen.43.30). So, as the prophets try to convey the turmoil of the divine struggle between retribution and restraint, their tumbling images can swing from battlefield to childbed and back, contrasting the sounds and the final outcome of each.

> Yahweh will go forth as a warrior, a soldier roused to the fury of the battle; he will shout, he will raise the battle cry and triumph over his foes. Long have I restrained myself, silent and held in check; now I groan like a woman in labour, panting and gasping. I shall lay waste

mountain and hill and shrivel up all their herbage; I shall change rivers into desert and dry up every pool (Isa.42.13–15).

8. The divine tragedy

But why were men of such insight as these prophets intent upon presenting in these tormented terms God's incomprehension of human indifference, God's anger at the betrayal of his longsuffering love, God's desolation over the loss of his people and the tearing choice between letting them go or holding on? There can be no doubt about the style of speech into which they cast what they believed to be the word of God, God's self-communication to his people; it belongs to the universal genre of tragic pathos and protest, as old and as new as human sorrow itself. This style grew out of the instinctive keening of people afflicted by inconsolable loss and it echoes the repetitive cries and poignant images of primitive lamentation. It has persisted as a literary form throughout the history of the written word. From the social breakdown and misery of the transition from the Old to the Middle Kingdom of Egypt in about 2400 BC comes this lament:

> To whom can I speak today?
> Faces are averted,
> And every man looks askance at his brethren.
> To whom can I speak today?
> Hearts are rapacious,
> And there is no man's heart in which one can trust.
> To whom can I speak today?
> The wrong which roams the earth,
> there is no end to it.[15]

There are passages of tragic protest in Homer's *Iliad*, but the form reached its summit in the Greek tragedies of the fifth century BC. In his *Philoctetes* Sophocles showed a man racked between unthinkable alternatives.

> Can I not die? Ye gods, can I not die?
> What can I do? I cannot turn deaf ears
> To my kind counsellor. But can I go

From this long wretchedness back to the light of day,
Back to the sight of men? Can eyes of mine,
Seeing such things as they have seen, see this,
My meeting again those two, my murderers?[16]

In different vein, Euripides, the master of human emotions, voices the ultimate despair of a woman for whom there are no choices.

O Troy, my Troy, that breathed forth such splendour
Among barbarian cities, your splendour now is gone.
They are burning you and driving us from our homes to slavery –
Oh Gods! Why call on gods?
When I called on the gods before, they never heard.[17]

One is unavoidably reminded of the two laments recorded in the Gospel of Luke of which the second enlarges on the city's approaching destruction. The first is more personal.

O Jerusalem, Jerusalem, which killeth the prophets
and stoneth them that are sent unto her!
How often would I have gathered thy children together,
As a hen her own brood beneath her wings,
and ye would not!
Behold, your temple is left unto you, desolate.[18]

The Chinese tradition has always preferred delicate understatement, though it can be charged with just as much poignancy. This is from the third century of our era.

I climb to the ridge of the Pei-mang Hills
And look down on the city of Lo-yang.
In Lo-yang how still it is!
Palaces and houses all burnt to ashes,
Walls and fences all broken and gaping.
How sad and ugly the empty moors!
A thousand miles without the smoke of a chimney.[19]

It is invidious to choose only a single example from the enormous range of Shakespeare's tragic music. Within the closing scenes of *King Lear* he calls into play every tone of voice in the register of pathos from the unbearably quiet 'I am a very foolish fond old man' to the last raging anguish of

> Howl, howl, howl, howl! O! you are men of stones:
> Had I your tongues and eyes, I'd use them so
> That heaven's vaults should crack. She's gone for ever.
> I know when one is dead, and when one lives;
> She's dead as earth.[20]

In our own century the genre of genuine lament lives on, not so much in the theatre where tragic protest clothes itself in low-key ironical dialogue, as in the novel. There the form is often recognizably the same.

> Cry for the broken tribe, for the law and the custom that is gone. Aye, and cry aloud for the man who is dead, for the woman and children bereaved. Cry, the beloved country, these things are not yet at an end. The sun pours down on the earth, on the lovely land that man cannot enjoy. He knows only the fear of his heart.[21]

In all the literatures of the world this natural rhetoric of grief is used to express the pathos of human sufferers and elicit compassion. Those who hear these lamentations are drawn by sympathy to see the situation from the sufferer's point of view. By daring to put this style of speech into the mouth of the holy transcendent Lord God the Hebrew prophets were appealing to the same power of pathos to win sympathy and open the hearts of a stubborn people to see what their defection was doing to God. Fretheim sees it as another example of the divine will to share responsibility with the human partner and elicit participation. 'It is such a portrait of God, a suffering of God, that, it is hoped, will prompt repentance.'[22] In a well-known *bon mot* E.L. Mascall condescendingly derided the very thought of sympathy for God,[23] but he has the concerted genius of the Hebrew prophets against him. For they either believed that these tragic lamentations represented some equivalent reality in God or they were exploiting the mere rhetoric of grief like professional beggars or electronic evangelists – and in all this literature there is no note of any such lack of integrity. Abraham Heschel convincingly presents the more rounded Jewish understanding of God's nature:

> When the divine is sensed as mysterious perfection, the response is one of fear and trembling; when sensed as absolute will, the response is one of unconditional obedience; when sensed as pathos, the response is one of sympathy.[24]

The voicing of God's sorrow brings home to human hearts the truth about sin and forgiveness when neither demonstrations of divine favour nor visitations of divine punishment have succeeded in doing so. A God who, as God, is unaffected by anything we may do can be concerned with human sin only as a judge and his pardon means a remission of the penalty and no more. But to recognize that what we are sinning against is the love which is God's very being amounts to a massive turn about. It is the true *shub shebut*. For then we know we are dealing with a relationship we have abused and broken, and forgiveness must mean reconciliation and the restoration of mutuality. Heschel returns to the real meaning of *daath elohim*, the knowledge of God, which the Old Testament sets forth as the true human response to God's knowledge of us. He insists that our knowledge of God is meant to reciprocate God's knowledge of us by having at least some such quality of intimate sympathy, of entry into God's inner experience, as God has for our sufferings.[25] There is no superficial sentiment in such sympathy for God; it arises, rather, from that profound transference of identity which great works of tragedy are able to bring about. This is why the resemblance of the divine lamentations in the Old Testament to the universal language of tragedy is significant.

For tragedy does more than arouse our pity or our horror. The protagonist's cry of anguish, outrage or despair moves us to identify ourselves with him or her at an emotional level below consciousness and thereby to find in that individual predicament the universal truth of our human condition. 'We take upon's the mystery of things.' Nearly seventy years ago Macneile Dixon wrote, 'There is no use in tragedy beside this – to make a disclosure of the loyalties in our blood.'[26] By its appeal to our sympathy tragedy forces us to recognize with surprise whose side we are on. But by a still more wonderful alchemy we are persuaded to recognize in these shattered representatives of our race a greatness that soars above the catastrophe, and even the evil flaw that brought it about. Achieving such surpassing stature at the very moment of their fall, they revive in us, through our identification with them, our own mysterious transcendence. In Anouilh's play *Antigone*, the heroine says of her dead father, Oedipus:

> When he could no longer doubt that he *had* killed his own father; that he *had* gone to bed with his own mother. When all hope was gone, stamped out like a beetle. When it was absolutely certain that nothing, nothing could save him. Then he was at peace; then he could smile, almost; then he became beautiful . . . [27]

By communicating the word of the Lord in the language of tragic lament the prophets were calling into play that power of transference by which tragedy works, moving their audience to identify themselves with the pain of God's baffled purposes and unrequited love. They were attempting to stir to life those long-forgotten 'loyalties in the blood' that might respond to God's *ḥesed*-loyalty towards his people. They were enabling their hearers to perceive in the humiliation and endurance of their God, as we perceive in the heroes of great tragedy, a splendour surpassing all the usual notions of sovereign power.

During the devastations of the Second World War a Japanese Christian theologian recognized the same truth in the basic principle in Japanese tragic literature. The technical term for it is *tsurasa*, the ultimate, hidden truth of human nature which is revealed 'when one suffers and dies, or makes his beloved son suffer and die, for the sake of loving and making others live'. On the strength of his realization of this, Kazoh Kitamori wrote his remarkable study, *Theology of the Pain of God*.

> Thus the Japanese mind, which had seen the deepest heart of his fellowman in pain, will come to see the deepest heart of the Absolute God in pain . . . By so doing, one decisive aspect of God's nature, which was overlooked by the Greek churches, will be recovered by the churches of our country.[28]

But the prophets had themselves first been drawn by that strange in-othering empathy to identify themselves with the pain of God. We know that for some of them it was their own human suffering that sparked off the exchange: the infidelities of Hosea's wife, the ostracism and persecution of Jeremiah, the sudden death of Ezekiel's wife, 'the desire of his eyes'. As God made their burden his own, so they made God's burden theirs, and the cry of their personal lamentation became the voice of God.

> The prophet becomes a party to the divine story; the heart and mind of God pass over into that of the prophet to such an extent that the prophet becomes a veritable embodiment of God.[29]

The images, human and divine, overlap and fuse in a quite unsystematic but profoundly evocative series of patterns. From Moses onwards – 'On your account the Lord was angry with me' (Deut.1.37) – the figure of the prophet is that of the Servant, despised and rejected, on whom the iniquity of the faithless people was laid. And because the prophet has so identified himself with the pain of God as well as with the affliction and guilt of his people, the perennial role of this suffering servant reflects the vicarious action of God himself. Though the Old Testament nowhere propounds a doctrine of the Trinity, one can actually discern the trinitarian nature of God, as interpreted in chapter 5,[30] more clearly in this account of God's relationship with Israel and her prophets than in the more commonly cited trio of Yahweh, Word and Wisdom.

It is God as Self-Giver who expresses himself continuously in the spontaneous, uncompelled outflow of love for his people. His is the pure will that at whatever cost to himself they should be there, and a pure delight in their being there whatever the outcome. Because this God fulfils his divinity in inexhaustible self-giving, his delight is the fierce joy of the artist or the mountaineer that persists unabated by any amount of real pain, anger or defeat. His is the bliss that can include and outshine all suffering.

It is the Given Self of God who knows the commitment entailed by such self-abandonment in love. God's Given Self responds to the 'must' and the 'cannot' implied by self-giving, and works out the divine will through all the limitations imposed by creation and covenant, with hands tied by love and love's undertakings. It is the *ḥesed*-faithfulness of God's Given Self that is outraged, with 'the wrath of the Lamb', against human infidelity, that cries, 'How long?', and 'How can I give you up?', and

'What shall I do with you?', and, when retribution falls, suffers the afflictions of God's people with them.

And it is the In-Othered Self of God, whose Being is fulfilled only within the inner experience of God's chosen Other, who 'spake by the prophets' in the manner I have just described. He 'knew' from within them the burning hopes they cherished and the anguish they endured, and, still from within them, he enabled them to 'know' the pain of God, to identify themselves with it and to cry it aloud so that their people, and all humanity, might hear it and understand. So, anticipating St Paul, we may say of this mysterious interchange of sympathy, human and divine, in the Old Testament prophets, that God's In-Othered Self, the Spirit, searching their inmost being, and pleading through their inarticulate groans, not only affirmed to their spirits that they and all God's people were still God's children, but explored for them even the depth of God's own nature (Rom.8.16,26,27; I Cor.2.10,11).

There is more than Christians have generally acknowledged in the designation of Jesus of Nazareth as 'a great prophet'. For in him we can see fully realized the exchange and reciprocity which God had looked for in the people as a community, but which had, for the most part, been manifested only in the special awareness of the prophets. In Jesus, it seems, people could see that mutual intimacy, loyalty and partnership which was a true fulfilment of Moses and the prophets. The new covenant, promised by Jeremiah and claimed by the first Christians, was supposed to have made a corporate reality of that exchange of mutual understanding and trust: 'All of them, high and low alike, will know me, says the Lord.' And Jesus, as we have seen, certainly expected to incorporate others with himself in the obedience of the covenant, the cross and the kingdom. But still there is little evidence that either church or synagogue as such looks like the corporate, this-worldly realization of God's long hope. 'O Lord, how long?'

That question can conjure the spectre of despair, as it did for Isaiah more than twenty-seven centuries ago. As we approach the start of another millennium of Christianity, the church may need to found her fortitude upon a less impatient time-scale. While we live wisely, as we surely must, in the knowledge that humanity could bring the end of the world upon itself, and while we celebrate gratefully, as we ever shall, the completeness of what God accomplished for that same humanity in Jesus Christ, we would do well to recognize more gladly, along with our

Jewish fellow pilgrims, the 'not yet' which is an equally clear-sounding theme in the New Testament. 'We do not yet see everything under human control; what we do see is Jesus.' 'We are now God's children; what we shall be has not yet been disclosed.' 'If we hope for something we do not yet see, then we look forward to it eagerly and with patience' (Heb.2.8,9; I John 3.2; Rom.8.25). God, it seems, had been working his purpose out for a not inconsiderable time before Abraham, or even Adam, appeared upon the scene and, for all we know, it had given God as great delight, and perhaps pain, as the brief history of humanity has done. To that cosmological time-scale and its implications we must now turn our trembling attention.

7

God Saw that it was Good

The Cost of Creation

1. Can this be love?

In the culminating vision of the Creator with which Dante closed his *Divine Comedy* the poet-pilgrim sees deity and humanity conjoined in God, but can find no way of expressing the perfect unity of it, except to say:

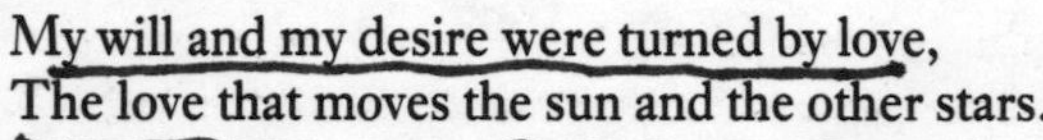

My will and my desire were turned by love,
The love that moves the sun and the other stars.

Dante was too steeped in mediaeval theology and far too great a poet to be capable of ending his masterpiece with such a trivial sentiment as 'It's love that makes the world go round.' He was actually affirming in all seriousness that the impulse which set this vast universe in being and still sustains it in existence is the energy of divine love, which is the very being of God. And like all others who have hazarded the same claim, he based it upon the only part of the universe of which he had any inside knowledge, which was himself – 'my will and my desire'.

The truth of that claim can have been no more self-evident to the fourteenth-century Dante than it is to us at the end of the twentieth; it only seems more impossible to make sense of it in relation to the scale of space and time that we are talking about. For it now appears that Dante's sun, and ours, is an average-sized star, almost a hundred times the volume of all its nine planets combined. Its energy, travelling at the speed of light, takes eight minutes to reach us, which puts it about ninety-three million miles away. The light of the next nearest star-sun in our galaxy takes four years to reach us. That galaxy of ours, straddling our night sky as the Milky Way, is a slowly rotating spiral consisting of a hundred thousand million such suns. The light of the farthest flung stars on one edge of the spiral takes roughly 100,000 years to reach those upon the opposite edge. (To state how wide that is in miles requires the figure 575 followed by fifteen zeros!) So much for the home galaxy, which is only one of a hundred billion others that are visible to modern telescopes. And, according to the 'big bang' hypothesis which many cosmologists now accept, all that matter was formerly compressed within a point of infinite density, immeasurably small and hot, so that neither time nor space existed and none of the known laws of physics could operate. The theory is that fifteen billion years ago this exploded into an unthinkable expansion of energy, and we are joy-riding on a speck of dust amid what Teilhard de Chardin called 'a cyclone of stars' on the continuing outrush of that explosion. If it seems impossible to relate such a scenario to the action of creative love, it is no simpler to relate it to anything else, since it defies all imagination. If we have lost track of the Creator in the face of such immensities, we have greater grounds than ever for awe and overwhelming wonder. The parade of natural marvels that reduced Job to silence and self-abhorrence, or the apocalyptic visions that felled John of Patmos to the ground in wordless reverence, shrink into domesticity compared to the beginning and the projected ending of this universe which scientists are asking us to accept as probable facts.

It does seem almost meaningless to say that it was love that was acting upon the slow coagulations of fiery gas and the gradually cooling elements on this headlong eruption through space. It can make sense only if we accept a huge enlargement of our normal concept of love – such an enlargement of meaning as that enchanting child, Anna, grasped intuitively quite early in her relationship with Fynn, the author of her story.

> 'Fynn, Mister God doesn't love us.' She hesitated. 'He doesn't really, you know, only people can love. I love Bossy (the cat) but Bossy don't love me. I love the pollywogs, but they don't love me. I love you, Fynn, and you love me, don't you?'
>
> I tightened my arm about her.

'You love me because you are people. I love Mister God truly, but he don't love me.'

It sounded like a death-knell. 'Damn and blast,' I thought. 'Why does this have to happen to people? Now she's lost everything.' But I was wrong. She had got both feet planted firmly on the next stepping-stone.

'No,' she went on, 'no, he don't love me, not like you do, it's different, it's millions of times bigger.'[1]

A necessary step towards realizing that difference between God's bigger love and ours is to recall that the essence of any love that is more than sentiment is an ardent will that the other should *be* and a disinterested delight in the other's being there. Every passing wish that the other were not there, and every lapse of delight into indifference, is a cessation of love. To talk of God's love for the universe holding it in being during the vast unfolding of its physical form is to speak of the divine self-giving that wills, and delights in, the existence of this other.

But the self-giving and self-giveness of God is not simply extraneous to his other; it carries God to the point of in-othering. God wills and delights in each detail of the universe *from within its being*. He is the Beyond at the heart of the music. As Anna went on to say in the same conversation:

'You see, Fynn, people can only love outside, and can only kiss outside, but Mister God can love you right inside, and Mister God can kiss you right inside, so it's different. Mister God ain't like us; we are a little bit like Mister God, but not much yet.'[2]

The ardent will and delight of the Beyond that is at the heart of all things is what we mean by the immanence of the Creator. In the Bushmen's myth of Creation, according to Laurens van der Post, God created by becoming each thing in turn, one species of wild flower after another, each kind of tree, each creature, finally becoming the tears of mankind; yet after each day of new becoming, when night falls, God is simply God.[3] With an equally clear avoidance of pantheism, which merely identifies God with the All, Austin Farrer, in terms clearly derived from what Aquinas had written in the *Summa* (1a. Q8. art.2), propounded in very similar terms the 'within-ness' of God's creative activity, which is God's love.

> The shape, the idiom of the Creator's thought is the very shape and idiom of his creature's existence. God's thought of man is human, for he thinks man as he is . . . God's thought of lions is lionlike, and of sparrows sparrow-like; and elementary things that have neither life nor sense are thought and willed by him exactly as they are or as they go.[4]

We might say, then, that God is Being itself which gives itself, gives *being*, for each distinct existent to possess *in its own way*. Without that love-gift there is no reason why there should be anything at all, rather than just nothing. But before pursuing that thought it is necessary to recognize that more has been deduced about the nature of God from the fact that he is the Creator and Sustainer of all things than logic actually warrants.

2. *The seamless fabric of being*

That God is good, for example, is not the only conclusion that can be argued from his being our Creator. This interlocking hierarchy of living creatures devouring other living creatures might denote a creator who is cruel or morally indifferent, and there have been philosophers who held the world to be the handiwork not of God but of the Demiurge, the originator of evil.

By the same token it is perfectly logical to hold that God is the continual source of all being without necessarily concluding that this gives him absolute power and control over all that issues from their existence. In order to be the perpetual *fons et origo* from which everything derives its being moment by moment, what God has to be is not all-powerful but inexhaustible. It is significant as a physical analogy that when a certain spring first broke surface, no one knows how long ago, and welled out upon a level plateau in northern Zambia, had the foot of a passing elephant depressed the swampy soil on one side rather than the other at that time, the River Congo would today be flowing into the Indian instead of the Atlantic Ocean. Yet that trickle of water, so at the mercy of external circumstance, will none the less find a way around or through every obstacle and somewhere reach the sea, so irrepressible is its gentle flow: not power but persistence.

It is even questionable whether our believing that God is the Creator of the universe justifies our calling him the First Cause in a chain of causation. Just as God should not be imagined as the supreme being among other beings, so God should not be described as the first cause of all subsequent causes. Whether causation is ever a true synonym for creation or not, God's act as Creator is not to be looked for in the same framework of reference as the interactions of beings upon each other within the created order, which is what both philosophers and scientists mean by causation. An analogy from the creative activity of a novelist may clarify this. Readers of Emily Brontë's *Wuthering Heights* can legitimately argue whether Heathcliff's tormented personality was chiefly due to the actions of old Mr Earnshaw, the behaviour of his daughter Cathy, or to the boy's own unknown heredity. It is just as reasonable for anyone to say that only Emily Brontë made Heathcliff what he was. But it would be nonsensical to debate whether Emily Brontë or Cathy Earnshaw was the more responsible, for the parts they played in 'causing' Heathcliff to become the man he was belong to two different frames of reference and it is misleading to use the same word to describe their respective influence upon the story.

It was natural, perhaps, to deduce divine omnipotence from the act of creation when the creatures, whether sun and moon or worms and feathered fowl, were supposed to have been fixed unchanging phenomena from the start. A universe of ready-made objects, like a child's Noah's ark, might be likened to the products of a carpenter's bench or a potter's kiln or a draughtsman's board, and all such models suggest the maker's unlimited power to manipulate his handiwork at will. But when our own model of the universe became an organic one with the emphasis on process and growth, *a creatio continua*, we were bound to pay more attention to the autonomy and responsiveness of each object and to think of the relationship of God and the world in terms of immanence and interaction. As this more dynamic model began to win the assent of human imagination, religious folk feared that it contradicted their scriptures. But most of them soon found that it only stimulated them to reappraise the various metaphors and images in holy writ, seeing some of them as more fanciful than they had previously appeared, while others rang true with a new illuminating aptness.

The idea of a progressive creation by stages, which is expressed in many of the world's myths about the origin of things, including the first chapter of Genesis, accords well with the reductionist methodology of modern scientific investigation. Unlike the science of ancient Greece and mediaeval Europe which was content to observe and classify phenomena just as they were, and thereby favoured a static, once-for-all view of things, the science of the past five centuries has proceeded by analysis to explain the more complex wholes by finding out the structures and functions of their component parts, and this predisposes us to see the world as a hierarchy of systems. The simpler and lowlier systems are the units of which the more complex systems are built – the atom is a structure of energy particles, the molecule a structure of atoms, each chemical a structure of molecules, the living cell a highly complex structure of chemicals, and so on.

The ladder of advancing complexity ascends in unbroken continuity from the elementary particles to the emergence of life, of consciousness and of the capacity for spiritual response. Human beings, as we have seen in earlier chapters, have always sensed from time to time the essential unity of all created things, and their myths, without pretending to express scientific truths, embody this purely intuitive conviction. So the first chapter of Genesis presents in its own way a progression, phase by phase, from the original energy of light to the inanimate matter of water and air, earth and the heavenly bodies, and so to the living creatures inhabiting sea, sky and land, and humanity not as a seventh day wonder but firmly included in the animal creation, though with a difference. The poets, like the myth-makers, have often reminded us that the cosmos is not merely the stage on which the human drama is played out but that we too are part of the fabric,

> Rolled round in earth's diurnal course
> With rocks, and stones, and trees.[5]

But it has taken the dispassionate voice of twentieth-century biochemistry to bring that perspective home to us.

> Our familiar environments of stone, water, air, earth, grass, birds, animals and so on are seen both to share with us common molecular structures and to be phases in a common development in time. The

> very stuff of which we are made and the way it has become organized as ourselves is an inherent part of the ongoing development of the physical cosmos which we survey. We with all other living creatures have emerged in time out of the non-living world of water, air and rocks which seem so distinct and different from us.[6]

The fact that every living creature from bacteria to humans shares the same mechanism for storing and using energy, or that the same code serves to translate the base sequence in their DNA into the amino-acid sequence in protein, has naturally tempted some scientists into thinking that the more complex systems can be fully explained in the terms of their simpler constituent elements. There are many among them who would like to claim that all moral decisions and mental responses can be accounted for in the terms of neurophysiology, which can likewise be reduced to biochemical processes, which are themselves explainable in terms of chemistry and physics. That kind of reductionism is a dominant feature in popular fantasies about contemporary scientists, but in reality it is a dangerous half-truth.

It is true that there are no material discontinuities between one rung of the ladder and the next. Nothing extraneous, no new ingredient, has been added at any point to the primordial matter of which this living whole has built itself up. What have occurred all the way along are new ways of organizing what was already there, so creating new conditions and unprecedented possibilities, as, for example, when chemical molecules that have no power of reproduction become reorganized to form a living cell which has that capacity. Then the language of pure chemistry is no longer adequate to describe what is there. The investigations of a group of scientists in Brussels in the 1970s has shown that, throughout the whole hierarchy of physical processes, stable systems that are obeying known laws with deterministic regularity become, under new conditions, suddenly unstable and begin to manifest new ordered patterns in space and/or time. This occurs in such a commonplace occurrence as the heating of a column of liquid from below when the upward transmission of heat by conduction alone reaches a point at which stability breaks down, after which a new stable molecular state is established wherein transmission by convection plays a part. A more readily understandable example is found in the behaviour of certain amoebic slime molds:

When the environment in which these amoebas live and multiply becomes poor in nutrients, they undergo a spectacular transformation. Starting as a population of isolated cells, they join to form a mass composed of some tens of thousands of cells. This 'pseudoplasmodium' then undergoes differentiation, all the while changing shape. A 'foot' forms, consisting of about one third of the cells and containing abundant cellulose. This 'foot' supports a round mass of spores which will detach themselves and spread, multiplying as soon as they come in contact with a suitable nutrient medium and thus forming a new colony of amoebas.[7]

Whenever in nature the stability of a system breaks down into chaos a 'bifurcation point' is reached which is more like a fork in the road than a simple change of direction, and which of the possible alternatives will be taken is not predetermined.

3. *The power of potentiality*

At every stage in the continuous, self-generating process by which things have come to be and are still coming to be we find diversity and complexity emerging out of homogeneity and simplicity. New forms of organization with unprecedented properties and ways of behaviour occur which would have been unpredictable before they appeared but are subsequently seen as inherently potential in the substances and mechanisms that were there already. 'Emergence' is an appropriate word to describe these moments of re-ordering because it suggests the birth of a child from its parents, something totally new out of the givenness of what they already are, involving no extraneous addition yet going beyond, or transcending them. And since it often happens that the emergence is preceded by a breaking down of a stable system into the chaos of indeterminacy, it also resembles a dying – the death that precedes a resurrection. For indeterminacy, or the surrender of absolute predictability, opens the door for unrealized potentiality.

It was this indeterminacy in the universe which the theory of quantum mechanics established. It requires that investigation, instead of anticipating a single certain result from an observation, predict all possible outcomes and calculate how likely each one of them is. This so affronted Einstein as to evoke the famous dictum: 'God does not throw dice.' Yet it now appears that that is exactly what God does do; that the entire evolution of matter from the first inconceivable explosion of energy to the emergence of moral self-awareness on at least this planet of ours, has been brought about by an interplay between what we might call the rules of the game and the fall of the dice. In any game of chance, and in many aspects of life, this interplay of law and pure accident can be surprisingly one-directional if the rules are such as to exploit chance in a certain way.

> A God who only played dice would be a gambler. None of his products would have any meaning. That is what disturbed Einstein. But a God who never played dice would have constructed a machine and none of his products would be free. 'Does God play dice, then?' asks Manfred Eigen. 'Certainly. But he also follows his rules for the game.' And only the gap between the two provides both meaning and freedom.[8]

Despite the immense randomness of the story of the universe the 'laws' of physics and chemistry, the stable behaviour of the elements, have from the beginning been such that out of matter and pure chance there could emerge, against astronomical odds, life, consciousness and spiritual response. The possibility was there. And to explain that the Archbishop of Canterbury is 59% water is not so much reductionism as a tribute to the remarkable potentialities of water.

It appears, then, that potentiality rather than necessity has been the formative factor in the extraordinary history of the universe. Which is only another way of saying that God has used the inherent capacity of all things and their open-endedness as the two main tools in his workshop. Austin Farrer saw this as the principle of creation whereby God, the giver of being, makes his creation the agent of its own development, letting each creature be itself and fulfil its potential within a co-ordinating purpose.

> It is no matter of regret to God that the universe is not a piece of streamlined engineering. It is meant to be what it is – a free-for-all of self-moving forces, each being itself with all its might, and yet (wonder of wonders!) by their free interaction settling into the

balanced systems we know, and into the complexities whereby we exist.[9]

It was pointed out in chapter five that Aristotle had recognized that potentiality is the middle term or, one might say, the bridge whereby what is may pass over into becoming, and what is becoming may arrive at being. He also regarded potentiality as a cause – not the nudge of antecedent causation but the pull of future possibility. All things, he taught, are constant and predictable because they remain true to their actuality and the laws that determine it, yet everything is also in process of becoming, drawn by its own potentiality. Potentiality is something no scientist can put his finger on. It does not exist as an additional element in an entity to be identified along with its other components. It presents no evidence of itself until its hour of revelation is come, yet it is there, inherent and undefined, for uncertainty is its nature. It is the undetermined future latent in the present. Potentiality has many affinities with the immanent God.

Quite properly the integrity of the scientific approach shrinks from describing the unfolding story of the universe as progress or recognizing purpose as a causative factor. Talk of progress, after all, is a value-judgment that reflects the interest of the speaker: progress in the fight against malaria was a set-back for the anopheles parasite, and the emergence of *homo sapiens* may yet prove to have been the ultimate disaster for life on this planet. The human species, considered as a system, is certainly in a state of chaotic instability from which we may only hope that a new unrealized level of being may emerge. So science rightly sticks to the neutral ground of antecedent causes and finds in the interplay of random occurrence and the laws of nature all the explanation it needs of the way things have so far turned out.

And yet there are exceptions to this principle; there are some anomalies and flukes that seem to thrust beneath the most objective noses the possibility that the unrealized future *is* a force exercising some pull over the direction that the development is taking. Morpho-genesis, the process whereby mutilated structures in some living organisms are replaced or, as in the brain, have their function taken over by other parts, raises this thought. So does the obvious but rarely asked question: why should simple systems tend to develop into more and more complex ones and not in the other direction? There is also the remarkably specific series of staggeringly improbable coincidences in the development of the universe which have lent credence to what cosmologists call the anthropic principle – the notion that the cosmos is oriented towards the emergence of humanity. The odds against this outcome have been immeasurably great. According to Stephen Hawking's best-seller *A Brief History of Time*, if the 'big bang' was the physical start of it all, within the first hundredth of a second the ratio of nuclear particles to photons, electrons and neutrons was precisely right for the eventual emergence of proteins, and so of life, twelve billion years later. Had the ratio been fractionally different in that first split second the cosmos would have been for ever devoid of any form of life. No less specific has been the formation of our solar system. If our planet had not come to rotate about the sun in nearly circular orbits – had the orbiting been much more elliptical, resulting in greater extremes of temperature – life could never have evolved. And the process whereby the various living species have emerged, the survival of the fittest, tends inevitably towards greater sensitivity, responsiveness, adaptation and, eventually, consciousness, rather than greater brute strength.

All of this does undeniably look as though human thought, moral responsibility and spiritual awareness, or something comparable to these in other forms elsewhere within the universe, were the end-product which the vast process had been designed to bring forth. Flattering though that is to our self-esteem, we must also admit that the picture would look exactly the same if human life had been a quite fortuitous result within the process, not the crowning glory but an incidental and freakish spin-off of the cosmic explosion. It is not for science to decide. What science appears to be saying is that, if on other grounds we do choose to read the facts as an adventure with a purpose, the facts do not refute us. We can believe that God has an end in view which is never abandoned, but no predetermined route for getting there. There is no grieving over what might have been. The principle of potentiality, of openness to the possibilities, means that God's action within the cosmic process resembles the habitual response that we have seen demonstrated on the human scale in the career of Jesus. It is always *ad hoc*: 'Where shall we go from here? What shall we make of this?'

4. *The hazard of letting be*

But possibilities and spontaneity do not guarantee that a particular end will be reached. Potentiality is by definition uncertain. Its promise is provisional. There are negative capabilities in every situation that is open to the future as well as creative ones. God is playing dice, and even though the rules of the game may give it a bias in one direction, the history of the universe appears to be a saga of accidents, reverses and prodigious waste. Anything that is allowed to develop by trial and error entails such risks.

> God not only makes the world, he makes it make itself; or rather, he causes its innumerable constituents to make it. And this in spite of the fact that the constituents are not for the most part intelligent. They cannot enter into the creative purposes they serve. They cannot see beyond the tip of their noses, they have, indeed, no noses not to see beyond, nor any eyes with which to fail in the attempt. All they can do is blind away at being themselves, and fulfil the repetitive pattern of their existence. When you contemplate this amazing structure, do you wonder that it should be full of flaws, breaks, accidents, collisions and disasters? Will you not be more inclined to wonder why chaos does not triumph . . . ?[10]

If it is indeed the divine love, God's delighted will that this universe should be, which, immanent within all things, gives them the coherence and interchange that prevails against chaos, then it is the same love which not only lets all things have their being but lets them in their own way become more perfectly what they are. For, in the relationship of love, letting *be* means letting go, even to the point of letting Adam and Eve go out of paradise. In a touching poem, C. Day Lewis recalled just such a parting from his first-born son Sean and saw that significance in it.

> It is eighteen years ago, almost to the day –
> A sunny day with the leaves just turning,
> The touch-lines new-ruled – since I watched you play
> Your first game of football, then, like a satellite
> Wrenched from its orbit, go drifting away

Behind a scatter of boys. I can see
You walking away from me towards the school
With the pathos of a half-fledged thing set free
Into a wilderness, the gait of one
Who finds no path where the path should be.

That hesitant figure, eddying away
Like a winged seed loosened from its parent stem,
Has something I never quite grasp to convey
About nature's give-and-take – the small, the scorching
Ordeals which fire one's irresolute clay.

I have had worse partings, but none that so
Gnaws at my mind still. Perhaps it is roughly
Saying what God alone could perfectly show –
How selfhood begins with a walking away,
And love is proved in the letting go.[11]

The bewilderment is greater for the one who is walking away but the pain is almost certainly worse for the one who, out of love and knowing the hazards, lets go.

With a profound spiritual insight inspired by their great prophets the Jews perceived a similarity between God's long-suffering commitment to his people Israel, and his relationship to the whole creation. Towards both God cherishes an unchanging purpose, and in both it is at risk. They expressed this truth by the way in which they spoke of the creation of the world as a reflection on a vast scale of God's covenant with Israel. The opening chapter of Genesis describes the creation of the world as a series of acts of separation or setting apart: God separated light from darkness, the water below from the water above, day from night. It is the same word that is used of the election of Israel for the covenant: 'I am Yahweh your God; I have made a clear separation between you and the nations' (Lev. 20.24; I Kings 8.53). Furthermore, just as the covenant with Israel presumed a conflict with Egypt, and later with the Canaanite tribes that were to be replaced, so the creation of a world presumed a conflict with the chaos of non-being, the *tohu va bohu* or formless emptiness of Genesis 1–2. This state of nothingness was symbolized in the twin image of darkness and ocean, which remained always in the

Jewish consciousness as symbols of ultimate menace, never to be completely absent until the new heaven and the new earth. The priestly author of Genesis 1 envisaged God vanquishing chaos to set free and to set apart the world of living beings which was in his eyes very good. Election and deliverance are the elements in this story of the Creation just as much as in the story of the Exodus. The psalmist saw the passage of the Red Sea and the crossing of Jordan as a re-enactment of God's primordial triumph in the creation of the world. 'The waters saw you, God, they saw you and writhed in anguish, the ocean was troubled to its depths . . . Your path was through the sea, your way through mighty waters; you guided your people like a flock shepherded by Moses and Aaron' (Ps. 77.16–20). The significance of these parallels, of course, lay in the conclusion that God has bound himself up in a covenant kinship with what he has created just as he bound himself to Israel. God is committed to the universe by his free and sovereign choice, inspired by a gratuitous movement of desire and love. For better or worse, God seeks a shared and reciprocal relationship with his creation by which he not only affects but is affected. The *ḥesed*-faithfulness of God towards the creation was affirmed in the story of Noah. 'Whenever the bow appears in the cloud I shall see it and remember the everlasting covenant which I have established with all that lives on earth' (Gen. 9.16). The Babylonian Isaiah saw the link also. 'As I swore that the waters of Noah's flood' – the symbol of nothingness again – 'should never again pour over the earth, so now I swear to you never again to be angry with you or rebuke you. Though the mountains may move and the hills shake, my love will be immovable and never fail, and my covenant promising peace will not be shaken, says Yahweh in his pity, his womb-yearning, for you' (Isa. 54.9,10).

That last poignant phrase of the passage from Isaiah points to the inescapable implication of this comparison of God's commitment to the whole creation with God's commitment to Israel: it has exposed God to the risk of uncertain contingencies and to the pain of love that may meet with no response. Creation entails for God a degree of self-limitation and vulnerability. This truth was grasped with the greatest theological seriousness in the sixteenth century of our era by a Jewish mystic of the Kabbalah tradition called Isaac Luria. He started from the question of nothingness which later fascinated the philosopher Leibnitz. But instead of asking why there is anything at all rather than just nothing, Luria pushed the question, as it were, further back still: How can God create a world out of nothing when there is no nothing, God being omnipresent? Since God is all in all, all there is, how can there be any place for what is not God? Luria's full answer was complicated and more than a little fanciful, but basic to it was the doctrine of *tsimtsum* or contraction. According to him God makes room for a world of beings that are other than God by an inward self-withdrawal, abandoning a space within himself and leaving a primordial emptiness and darkness, the non-God, the Void, within which God can 'let be' some Other which is not God, bestowing his gift of being upon that which is not himself.

The concept affords two most valuable insights. First it enables us to think of the created order not as something outside God but as something within, yet other than, God. So it retains St Paul's understanding of God as the one in whom we live and move and have our being. Jürgen Moltmann makes the same point.

> Has God not therefore created the world 'in himself', giving it time *in* his eternity, finitude *in* his infinity, space *in* his omnipresence and freedom *in* his selfless love?[12]

Two analogies come readily to mind of a created 'other' which is nonetheless within – the freely acting characters of *Wuthering Heights* that are within the mind of their author, and the real otherness of an unborn child whom the mother 'lets be' within the surrendered space of her womb – and both have theological implications.

The second important insight yielded by the *tsimtsum* doctrine is that of the cost of creation to God. It brings to the theology of creation something similar to what the doctrine of *kenosis* or self-emptying brought to the theology of incarnation. Simone Weil must have been familiar with Luria's thought when she wrote of the renunciation and sacrifice that God's 'letting be' entails.

> God has created, that is, not that he has produced something outside himself, but that he has withdrawn himself, permitting a part of being to be other than God.[13]

So the self-limiting and suffering of God with regard to the world, the *passio Dei*, is not to be attributed to the Fall, the disobedience of humanity, as it often has been, nor even to the creation's independence from God which is built into the structure of the universe, but to the very desire of God to be given away, the predisposition of Being itself to 'let be', which is the outpouring of divine love. Simone Weil put it in characteristically startling terms.

> Because he is the creator God is not all-powerful. Creation is abdication. But he is all-powerful in this sense, that his abdication is voluntary. He knows its effects and wills them.[14]

This is the truth enshrined in that evocative phrase in the Book of Revelation, 'The Lamb slain from the foundation of the world'.[15] The Jewish theologian Gershom Scholem stresses the continuous nature of the divine self-withdrawal: 'Every new act of emanation and manifestation', he says, 'is preceded by one of concentration and retraction.'[16] In Jewish spirituality the virtue of human negation-of-self, *billul ha yesh*, is always modelled on God, not contrasted with God's pre-eminence. Therefore, like God's self-renunciation, it serves an ultimate fulfilment. So Scholem says of the creation.

> The first act of all is not an act of Revelation but of limitation. Only in the second act does God send out a ray of his light and begin his Revelation, or rather his unfolding as God the Creator, in the primordial space of his own creation . . . But for this perpetual tension, this ever-repeated effort, with which God holds himself back, nothing in the world would exist.[17]

God's purpose in his divine withdrawal is to regain what has been surrendered, not by direct re-possession but by achieving an ultimate communion and co-inherence with his 'Other' through mutual love and interchange.

5. *The passion story of creation*

For the interim the effect of God's voluntary abdication, in Simone Weil's term, is uncertainty, unpredictability and risk, since the outcome cannot be guaranteed. The letting-be of particular autonomous beings exposes God to risk in a new condition of change and possibility. One might venture to say that the stable state of eternal Being has committed itself to the openness of becoming. God faces the original risk and pain of making nothingness and godlessness as real possibilities. God faces the risk that, as particular beings grow towards freedom and self-determination they may turn the grace and gift of 'being with' into a hoarded 'being for oneself', the very antithesis of Being which gives itself away, and thereby fall back into the nothingness which is the ever-threatening alternative surrounding them. It is purely a matter of faith that this uncertain interim will not last for ever, faith in the drawing power of the eternal love. Believing in God is believing in God's gamble with no guarantee that it will come off.

The story of Christ's walking on the water presents problems for contemporary minds,[18] but it furnishes a vivid image of the God who invites us to leave our already storm-tossed certainties and join him in his divine precariousness with the void of ultimate nothingness beneath our feet. Insecurity is the place where God's presence becomes convincing reality, not because God looks for our abject dependence but simply because insecurity is the condition in which God has placed himself. A God who relies on the risks of potentiality for making and sustaining the universe and who copes with every reverse and disappointment with an unwearying *ad hoc* 'Where shall we go from here?' is not a God of all certainty but of all hope. Karl Rahner has well said that 'hope is the name of an attitude in which we dare to commit ourselves to that which is radically beyond all human control',[19] – which is a fair description of walking on the waves and fits the divine hope as well as our own.

What then, once more, is this purpose of it all on which God's hope is set? The parallel of the call of Israel to the creation of the world must provide the clue. As an act of spontaneous, unconditioned delight and desire the self-giving God has sought some other-than-himself on which to lavish his love and with which to share himself in mutual exchange. Being itself, which is in itself an eternal interflow and exchange of self-giving, out of the very abundance and generosity of that love, seeks to overflow in communion with that which is not itself but its image.

> From eternity God has desired not only himself but the world too, for he did not merely want to communicate himself to himself; he wanted to communicate himself to the one who is other than himself as well.[20]

In its over-solicitous concern for God's good name Western philosophy has been at great pains to avoid any statement that might suggest that God ever needed the world. God must be seen to be perfectly fulfilled and all-sufficient within himself. But if we take that to mean that there need never have been a creation and God's decision to make a universe was purely arbitrary we debase the value of existence and reduce God's love to a divine whim. To say that God is love is to say that God is *far more* than self-sufficient. It is an error to describe loving as needing. God *had* to create a universe, it was in the nature of things that God should do so, not because God *needed* anything beyond God, but because love is more than satisfying need, more than necessity. Love means giving ultimate significance to some other; it is bestowing the gift of indispensability upon another. God's freedom does not lie in having an infinite number of choices but in having no choice except to be true to his own nature. God is free to act all that he wills and to will all that he is. And what God *is* eternally is limitless self-giving love. For no other reason than that, this universe and, for all we can know, an infinite succession of universes, has received its being. And in every act of letting-be God's will has been voluntarily subjected to becoming God's precarious hope.

For how else does Being whose essence is self-giving love set about creating beings who are other than himself and can give back and give forth an answering love? Love cannot be commanded, or it is not love. It cannot be conjured up fully grown like Athene from the head of Zeus, or it is an automaton's reaction, not a true 'other' giving an authentic response. Love is love only when consciously and freely given, and a world of particular beings can only attain the capacity to give back love by being set free to grow towards that far off point. They must develop out of their own givenness, not by external manipulation; so they must learn, as it were, by trial and error. I say 'as it were' because I am thinking of inanimate molecules and chemical compounds no less than rats and monkeys. All growth, all learning by trial and error, requires a condition of both freedom and constancy, randomness and law, such as we see throughout the universe. There must be constant parameters – fire must always burn and burning hurt, since no creature could learn to avoid or handle it safely if it sometimes burned and sometimes was miraculously extinguished. And within that constancy there must be freedom, either to go blindly into destruction or creatively on a new advance along the road. And to constancy and freedom must be added the capacity to feel. Over millions of years living organisms have developed a more and more complex nervous system and with that came pleasure and pain. Their gradual evolution towards sensitivity, responsiveness, consciousness, entailed more sophisticated pleasure and much higher levels of pain. In his book *Freedom, Suffering and Love* Andrew Elphinstone showed that pain has been one of the most creative forces in the whole process, as a protection, a warning and a stimulus to discovery.

> Pain may be overwhelmingly the preserve and the plaything of evil, the enemy and the destroyer, but it is also the thing required by God in creation, capable of being ally and creator, even though, to our frail feelings, unwelcome ally and unwelcome creator.[21]

So there will be accidents and casualties by the million every step of the way. Yet with all the risks, its agonies and tragedies, there is no other conceivable environment in which responsive self-giving love, to say nothing of courage, compassion or self-sacrifice, could have evolved. To speak in crudely human terms, the choice before God has been this or nothing. And, in a sense, that is the ultimate choice each one of us has to come to, for, as I have already said, 'I believe in God' is a vote of confidence in the Creator and in the bloodstained enterprise in which willy-nilly he has involved us and himself.

Not that there is nothing else to say about the suffering than that the as yet unrealized end will justify the means of getting there. That is a Marxist, not a Christian consolation and it shows scant respect for those dying in the ditches while the survivors march on. There is more real comfort, even for those who have had the cruellest of raw deals, in remembering the joy of living, the moments of intense beauty, the riches of human goodness and eccentricity, the glimpses of the Beyond in the midst of things, which are the bright assets of that capacity for feeling which also condemns us to pain.

> Some of you say, 'Joy is greater than sorrow', and others say, 'Nay, sorrow is the greater.' But I say unto you, they are inseparable. Together they come, and when one sits alone with you at your board, remember that the other is asleep upon your bed.[22]

That is no superficial wisdom. Other living creatures that are hunted and hurt in the struggle for survival spend at least as much of their time contentedly, even ecstatically, 'blinding away at being themselves'. Their satisfactions in simply being and the delight or wonder they evoke in us are pale reflections of the joy of God at their very existence which is his gift and which he knows from within them. The Creator is neither bland nor unaware when he looks upon what he has made and sees that it is very good.

For in all our afflictions he is afflicted. That is the strongest source of consolation in the Judaeo-Christian tradition. The tragic accidents that befall us and those we love, the natural disasters that blindly strike down thousands, the bacilli innocently thrown up by the onward surge of evolution yet so deadly to human life, so far from being willed or planned by God are simply a fortuitous part of the monstrous price of this adventure, this precious world; and God the self-giver who for love lets it be, with all its risk, is also the in-othered God who pays that price with and within each suffering creature. Though God knows his own purpose and the hoped-for outcome as we cannot, the same God also feels more keenly than ever we can do every incidental agony along the way, each frustration of his will for life and fulfilment, and gives himself to us in fortitude and, yes, in joy, asking, 'What shall we make of this?'

The Baron von Hügel excluded all possibility of suffering from the being of God on the grounds of an absolute polarity between suffering and joy. Because God is, and knows, absolute bliss, and because suffering, according to him, is intrinsically evil, there is no place for pain in the Creator.[23] But such exclusive definitions betray a very simplistic view of joy. Even in our limited human experience we know that the joy of loving and the joy of creating is not diminished but actually intensified by the pain that is also entailed, so that we can at least partly understand how God's joy in creating what is not God, and in giving his very self to the 'other', is suffused with pain. The Creator's transcendent gladness includes within its intensity the pain of *tsimtsum* self-withdrawal, the pain of a hazardous letting go, and the pain of all the victims of the enterprise which God makes his own through love's in-othering. So, too, we have grounds for believing that in Christ's endurance of the crucifixion the joy that was set before him was not simply subsequent to the ordeal but was undergirding the agony and abandonment itself.

6. *The problem of evil*

None of this alleviates the outrage we feel at the suffering of the innocent and the brutal arbitrariness of a creation that throws up disastrously malfunctioning children and obliterates living communities under rubble, flood-water or mud. No specific reason can be found for these events because they are the product of pure chance and pure chance is inherently irrational. As ill-chance we naturally hate it, whomsoever it befalls, just as we would welcome good luck, but chance itself is strictly neutral, there is no ill-will in it.

Some condemn as inherently evil the whole divine initiative that set about creating life and consciousness by means of the potentiality of chance and the stimulus of pain. If that is the necessary cost, as it seems to be, they would have preferred God to have called off the whole expedition. Like Ivan in *The Brothers Karamazov*, they would accept God but most respectfully return him the ticket. Whatever God's ultimate designs may be, they consider the means can never be justified, even though there are those who miraculously turn the worst disasters to good account, even though there are those who learn from them, and even though it is this monstrously unjust creation that has ironically brought forth beings with such an ingrained idea of fairness and of a God who ought to be just.

Many more thinkers have faith in God's purpose and in the essential goodness of the creation, but are affronted by the unfairness of life and the torments of its innocent victims which they feel bound to describe not as incidental but as positive evil. Without defining how the natural order might behave differently, they conclude that it has in some way been spoiled and that, quite apart from human sin, evil has entered the universe as a force opposed to God. Since the Bible as a whole is opposed to any kind of dualism this view could never have gained credence were it not for one factor, namely the universal human recognition that the wrong we are aware of in ourselves and, even more, in society appears to have an autonomous dynamic of its own. In order to do and be what we consider as right we find that we have to resist a contrary bias in the way things are. Moreover, on examination, we find that it is a bias towards negating, undoing, denying what is positively good and alive.

Some have seen this as another aspect of the risk to which God was exposed by the adventure of giving being to his 'other'. As Luria was saying by means of his image of *tsimtsum* or divine contraction, in order that what is not God may come to be, non-God becomes possible; in order that things may come to be, the Void of non-being is there. The risk is taken: nothingness and godlessness are potentialities. Now, as the biblical myth brilliantly portrays it, human creatures desire to 'know', to enter into intimate experience of good and evil as genuine options instead of knowing God as the only possible way. By actualizing those options the human mind and spirit has turned non-God into anti-God and non-being into anti-being. A real slipping back towards the void has become a possibility. The mystery of evil is actually the mystery of human responsibility in relation to God and to the rest of creation when it turns away from God to unmake what he is doing.

We are on much more certain ground when we reserve the word 'evil' for the suffering caused by human beings. We are not responsible for earthquakes, hurricanes, or avalanches, nor are all diseases our fault, though many are. The fact is, however, that selfishness and sin account for more of the misery and the spoiling of the world that all other causes. *Homo sapiens* is the most destructively rapacious of all earth's creatures. No other inflicts such deliberate cruelty upon its own kind as we do. The Nazi Holocaust stands as an indisputable sign of the human capacity for evil. The systematic extermination was accompanied by a calculated degradation and destruction of the humanity of its victims in a hell of brutalization, fear and lovelessness. But that has not deterred others from inflicting mass killings in subsequent wars, always preceded by the dehumanizing of the enemy's image by political rhetoric and cartoons. It is our very self-transcendence, our capacity to give ourselves away to that which lies beyond our horizon, which, if it is not directed towards its true fulfilment in God, is handed over to infinite possibilities of evil. Evil is the deformed product of our higher nature, not the residual habit of some sub-human or animal past.

> It was in the highest ranges of the spiritual and not in the shallows of the material world that evil first showed itself. Evil in its origin is spiritual by nature and belongs to the spiritual world . . . The myth of Satan is a symbolic reflection of an event belonging to the highest levels of the spiritual world. It was there that the clouds first gathered and that for the first time freedom gave a negative response to the appeal of God and to God's need to experience the love of His other

> self. It is at this point that creation by a process of self-affirmation began to enter upon the path of isolation, division and hatred.[24]

To recognize that evil grows from the topmost branch of our evolution and is a corruption of the best capacities we have negates all easy-going dreams of spiritual development. It is dangerously misleading to teach young people, as is often done in confirmation classes, that evil resides in our 'lower nature'. Evil springs from that element in ourselves that relates consciously to God, the human spirit. So it is the wound God receives in the house of his friends, the disappointment of God's highest hopes. That is why none but God can forgive sin since God is the one primarily injured. If individually we should ever see all that might have been had we got things right the burden would be intolerable.

Sin, as we normally think of it (though not as St Paul did) is individual and particular; evil is more comprehensive and more autonomous, as though it had a life and a will of its own. This does not necessarily signify that the Devil or Evil One is anything more than a personification, and it certainly does not relieve us of our human and personal responsibility for evil. What gives evil its independent power and reduces us to slavery is the fact that it has rooted itself like a parasite upon the very instruments which the Creator has used to make us what we are: freedom and pain.

Because God's will is set upon a free response to his freely given love the letting be of creation has been a letting go. Freedom has been a necessary condition. Even at the lowliest levels the separate beings are presented with states of indeterminacy so that latent potentiality is free to emerge. The degree of independence increases all the way until the freedom of the human spirit is attained. But there is such a thing as negative potential, and the power of self-transcendence, which is the image of God in humanity, deludes us into behaving as though our own 'infinite horizon' rather than God's were the be-all and end-all of reality – 'Ye shall become as gods.' We have already seen, especially through the teaching of Karl Rahner, that the ultimate potential of our human nature lies on the farther side of some radical experience of, and acceptance of, our finitude and mortality, at the point where we find ourselves by abandoning ourselves to the incomprehensible mystery of the love of God. Evil arises from a distortion of this truth whereby we prefer to believe that our self-fulfilment lies within the reach of our own powers; and because it feeds upon the very freedom and openness to the future which have made us what we are, the delusion has infected us, as a species, with a spiritual hypertrophy of over-growth and excess. The fruits from this parasitic root are the particular sins of aggressive hunger for power over others and a discontented need for possession which together breed vanity, avarice, jealousy, hatred, tyranny and oppression at every level. History, like the moon, has its phases: at the moment, since becoming a global village, humanity seems to be heading towards a world society in which the few overweening predators try by more and more desperate means to secure the non-proliferation of their power and wealth.

The negative potential of our human nature has gained its strength by exploiting also that other instrument of our creation, pain and the fear of pain. It was Andrew Elphinstone who developed this theme most convincingly some sixteen years ago.

> It is pain, in one form or another, which deters man from taking the morally higher course (when he perceives that course) in human relations and duty because the way of it is strait and narrow, because it is the line of most resistance, most effort, most self-giving, most risk of rebuff, most fear of failure, most threat of ridicule or a thousand other hurts to pride, body or estate. Equally, it is the dread of pain by which man is lured to take the morally lower course, dictated by inclination or self-interest because it is the way of least resistance, least sacrifice, least discomfort, least cost to self and least confrontation with pain.[25]

If the evil that battens upon freedom induces us to ignore the limitations of human existence and imagine ourselves superhuman, the evil that feeds on our avoidance of pain makes us succumb abjectly to those limitations and devalue ourselves as subhuman. And this breeds not only the sins of self-indulgence but the more deadly lethargy of spirit which shrinks from the pain of being fully alive, retreats from responsibility, grows a protective shell and turns down the invitation, the high calling of God. Such a deliberate preference for being only half alive, relieved by bouts of substitute stimulation of one kind or another, throws the whole creative venture back in God's face. This is the evil which now threatens the human family with a slow atrophy of its capacity to sustain truly personalized relationships within living communities.

People everywhere are shrinking more and more from the pain and joy of exposure to one another as persons; 'I – It' is predominating over 'I – You'. The technological revolution is the global circumstance that encourages this regression, but the cause of it is our evil perversion of that other elemental instrument of creation, the avoidance of pain.

Evil, then, gains its semblance of self-directing energy from its insinuation into these creative forces. But it provides no alibi for us since it is itself the product of our spiritual powers when these are divorced from their natural fulfilment in God. We who have ears attuned to the divine voice refuse to listen and, to coin C. S. Lewis's phrase, we who have faces have turned them away from God's gaze. The problem of evil is pre-eminently the problem of humankind. During the past century we have looked into the darkest depths of hell on the Somme, in the Gulag, at Dachau and Auschwitz. There we have seen that the human spirit, made in the image of God but turning freedom into nihilism, could systematically dehumanize women and men before herding them to the gas chambers and throw children alive on to the open fires; while as many other human spirits, knowing or partly knowing this, could choose to look the other way because avoidance of pain has become their dominant impulse. In the face of these facts the true, the fitting question is not 'Why does God,' but 'Why do we, do or permit this?'

7. *The cross at the heart of creation*

It is hard for anyone who makes a principle of avoiding pain or reactively paying it back on someone else to understand what forgiveness means, and aggressively independent natures cannot conceive of the miracle whereby one who pardons an injury contains the sting and outrage of it in the hope of preserving the relationship at any cost and turning an evil act into an occasion of greater good. Yet that is what the self-giving God has always done and is committed to doing for so long as evil negates the divine purpose and people fail to respond to that love. Forgiveness has been there unchangeably in the will and the disposition and the pain of God in face of human sin. But the will and disposition and pain of forgiveness must needs be manifest in action if it is to be known and received. When the moment comes the father has to run and embrace and kiss before the wayward son can realize how little his prepared speech of contrition matters since it is enough that he has come home.

So, when the right moment came, God's given self, ever obedient to the unchanging purpose, embodied the will and disposition and pain of love's eternal forgiveness in the manifest act of Calvary. There all can see the running to meet us, the embrace, the kiss.

There is, however, more to the cross than an act of pardon and reconciliation. The self-givenness of the Son in the self-surrender of Jesus broke the power of evil, entrenched as it was in the highest, human level of the creative process, and freed us from the slavery of sin. We are indebted to Gustaf Aulen for reinstating this early Christian interpretation of Christ's passion and resurrection, though it is Elphinstone's treatment of the theme that I have found most illuminating. Because the Creator, for the achievement of his purpose, has chosen to 'make the world by making it make itself', and furthermore, because it is at the level of the human spirit that evil has been established in the creative process, its power could be confronted and overcome, says Elphinstone, only when the incarnation had 'made the uncreated love of God an indigenous part of the createdness of humanity'.[26] Then the man whom God's given self had become laid hold of his birthright of freedom and lived out the fullest potentiality of a human being made in the image of God with breathtaking spontaneity, yet with no abuse of power to serve his own self-aggrandizement or self-protection, and finally used that perfect liberty to lay down his life in self-abandonment to God. And in that dying especially, that man, with his human vulnerability, endured the price of divine forgiveness which is the confrontation of pain by love.

> What we know to have gone on during the hours of crucifixion was the battle between the intent of divine creative love and the retrogressive pull goaded by pain to cease, let go, despair, wash the hands, regard the task as impossible, at times perhaps to let the creation sink back into non-being.[27]

Evil – which in truth we have to acknowledge and confess as our own, our corporate human evil – still works upon us through the freedom and the fear of pain which are agents of our on-going creation. Evil is still inescapable, but no longer invincible, since love's supremacy has once been demonstrated and made accessible to any who will make bold to arm themselves with it.

Elphinstone ventures a further startling suggestion as a possible element in the inexhaustible significance of the cross. He asks at the end of his book:

> Dare we discern anything so outrageous as the idea that here God is making an atonement towards man for all that his desired creation costs man in the making: that he was making love's amends to all those who feel, and have felt, that they cannot forgive God for all the pains which life has foisted, unwanted, upon them?[28]

To the ears of strict orthodoxy the question smacks of impiety. Yet it does not at all echo the sceptical *lèse majesté* of Omar Khayyam's famous quatrain.[29] God alone, presumably, knows how many there have been in the history of humankind who, having worshipped and trusted God, have at some time been so appalled at the suffering, usually of others, and at God's non-intervention, as to become bitterly alienated from the Creator of such a world. The declaration that God does care, like the declaration that God forgives, calls for some demonstration, either of divine rescue or, if that is more often than not ruled out, of divine fellow suffering. The God who in Christ was reconciling the alienated uncomprehending world to himself is perhaps more ready than his defence counsel to admit responsibility and show that he is sharing the consequences.

There is, I find, an eloquent parable of this in Act IV of Shakespeare's *Henry V*. Before the Battle of Agincourt the king moves incognito among the common soldiers of the different nationalities of his realm. He hears the honest Michael Williams going on about the heavy reckoning the king will have to make on the day of judgment when the hacked and broken bodies of all the casualties of the war will rise and accuse the king of having brought sudden death upon them – 'some swearing, some crying for a surgeon, some upon their wives left poor behind them, some upon the debts they owe, some upon their children rawly left' and all through the reckless adventure of his own designs. And those who have to pay the price had better keep their mouths shut for 'that's a perilous shot out of an elder-gun, that a poor and a private displeasure can do against a monarch'. Henry knows only too well his responsibility and what he is asking of them. He knows too the burden this lays upon him:

Upon the king! let us our lives, our souls,
Our debts, our careful wives,
Our children, and our sins lay on the king!
We must bear all.

Yet he still believes it will prove worthwhile and, as morning breaks, he rallies his small force to believe in it with him, just as he will share the risks and the wounds with them. So he instils into them his own hope, his faith in the value of the enterprise.

Shorn of the splendid rhetoric of Elizabethan patriotism and the half-truths of all war talk, and whispered, as it were, out of the dark ambiguity of the crucifixion, I believe it was something of that kind that was being said by our Creator through the human faith of the dying Jesus. God does know more intimately than any the price his creatures have been paying for his huge adventure of making this universe of accident and freedom and pain as the only environment in which love could one day emerge to receive and delight in and respond to his joyous love. He still believes the outcome will outweigh the immense waste and agony, not least the agony of his seeming indifference and inaction. So, knowing we cannot understand, cannot forgive, what he is doing, God has come among us as a fellow-being and fellow-sufferer to make amends and to win back trust. Through his own abandonment and death that Given Self of our Creator calls us to share his hope as he shares our pain, to believe in his staggering, costly venture even while there is little evidence of it ever succeeding.

We few, we happy few, we band of brothers;
For he today who sheds his blood with me
Shall be my brother.

8

Where is Now thy God?

The Problem of Providence

1. Does 'Thank God!' make sense?

Thinking about God seems at times to lead one to the brink of some very bleak questions. If the gift of existence, God's letting be, must entail letting go for the sake of a genuinely free, autonomous other-than-God, are we actually driven back to the deists' concept of an absentee God who once wound up the universe and then left it alone to tick its way through time? Or if God, in a continuing process of creation, is making the world make itself by obeying the laws inherent in its own elements, can there be any place for a divine hand or mind controlling and guiding events, or must that reassuring image go? In any case, since 'action' as we understand it, even the act of thinking, requires some physical agent and material causation, is it not a misuse of words to speak of divine action at all? What do we imagine is the nature of God's point of contact with any part of creation? Can God, does God, intervene? How can God be in control? Those who allow themselves to think about God and God's relation to the universe find sooner or later that their feet are no longer on solid rock but walking on water with five fathom of uncertainty beneath them.

Should we never have started the exploration? Can we turn back to an unquestioning faith and a simpler love? To leave the frightening questions unasked would be a denial of love and a surrender of all claim to faith, seeing that these are the questions which multitudes of people have been asking ever since they discovered that everything is *not* all right and wondered whether 'mother' had been lying.

A part of the difficulty arises from the wider problem of language about God which is always present. The point has already been made several times that language can perfectly well be metaphorical, anthropomorphic and mythological without thereby becoming a fabrication. The only means we have for speaking about God are the words and images we normally use to describe an experience of the world around us, and we use them by analogy to indicate what we believe is something equivalent in God and his relation to the world. God's 'thoughts' are not what we know as thinking, and God's 'acts' do not apply our kind of causation, but this does not amount to saying that God makes no difference to the course of events. Our recognition that whatever we say or think about God is necessarily metaphorical does, however, lay upon us a double discipline. It obliges us constantly to ask ourselves what we are referring to, what point in the course of events we have in mind, when we speak of God's hand, God's control, God's action; it also compels us to realize that we can never understand *how* God acts upon created beings, since this would involve knowing what it means to be God, which is impenetrable to us.

It is not meaningless to thank God for a particular event or for the course of a lifetime despite being unable to explain the way in which God gave it that form. It is in any case probably nearer the truth to think of God as the giver rather than the cause, since causes are essentially this-worldly factors, and God cannot be just another of those. If we eliminate this sense of certain happenings being a special gift, an intended event, we are left not with God but with fate. It is helpful to approach the question of divine providence from this starting-point of a universal human instinct to feel grateful, rather than merely glad, when things go well. What is more significant is that this gratitude is generally considered wise and good, in that it is better that a mature person should learn to feel grateful for whatever happens rather than merely acquiescing. Starting from the phenomenon of thankfulness also brings out the fact that providence is perceived in retrospect. Hans Küng writes delightfully about the account in Exodus 33 of Moses' desire to see the full glory of God, and God's answer: 'You shall see my back but my face shall not be seen.'

It is only afterward that I can see what had been the deeper meaning from the beginning. I do not see God from the front, but I do not

> need to see him from the front. I rely on his promise and do not expect any spectacular demonstrations. He is too great for me to be able to make such demands on him.[1]

Gratitude for events seen in retrospect may, however, encourage us to expect 'spectacular demonstrations' in the future, and such naive belief in divine providence is basic to all primitive religion. A parent whose child is sick or whose crop has been flattened by hailstones asks, Who caused it? If the child recovers or the harvest is after all a good one the question becomes, Whom have I to thank? In everyone there is a natural instinct to feel, when things go particularly well, that the universe is on their side and, when badly, that some malign force is against them. All basic paganism looks for supernatural interventions, but does not expect them to conform to any consistent pattern or betray a steady purpose. A time of prosperity may be overturned by sudden disaster or a superior enemy unexpectedly vanquished, but no underlying objective is sought to explain these arbitrary miracles. Paganism reflects in supernatural terms the accidental nature of all existence.

The faith of the early Hebrews was established on a different foundation. The recollection of Yahweh's special intervention in the deliverance from Egypt encouraged them to see their one God playing an active role in the history of their nation and to think of their history as a consistent outworking of the divine purpose towards a promised fulfilment. Providence, therefore, was not seen in terms of individual good or bad luck so much as in the fortunes of the people as a whole; it was in their *corporate* history that the Hebrews perceived the revelation of God. In the earliest narrative material of the Old Testament God's active participation in Israel's history is presented as entirely unilateral action. The people are simply spectators and beneficiaries. God does it alone. The means that God is thought to employ are forces of nature over which human beings have no control – flood or fire from heaven, wind and storm, plague and pestilence, even the movement of the sun. What God has promised to undertake, God will perform: that provides the outline for all the narratives. God promises Abraham that his descendants will possess the land in which he dwells as an alien: the book of Joshua sees the occupation completed. Within that broad sweep several sub-plots mirror the same pattern. At Bethel the fugitive Jacob is promised safe return, and at Bethel the pledge is fulfilled. The undertaking implicit in Joseph's two dreams of ascendancy is completed against all likelihood with that classic enunciation of the doctrine of divine overruling: 'Do not be distressed or blame yourselves for selling me into slavery here . . . God sent me on ahead of you to ensure that you will have descendants on earth, and to preserve for you a host of survivors. It is clear it was not you who sent me here, but God' (Gen. 45–5–8). The emphasis is again on the long-term corporate purpose more than on the individual well-being. The Exodus story starts with the undertaking given to Moses at Horeb, the mountain of God, and is brought to fulfilment at the same mountain with the covenant ritual. As soon as King David establishes Jerusalem as his capital, God, through the prophet Nathan, promises that his dynasty will remain upon the throne, and after all the struggles over the succession, the story reaches a climax with Solomon's prayer at the dedication of his temple: 'Lord God of Israel, no God like you keeps covenant and faithfulness with your servants.'

2. God's fellow workers

Such a categorical and predetermined picture of God's providential control over the world, however, is not typical of the Old Testament as a whole. It was the genius of Hebrew religion to perceive quite soon, and certainly by the eighth century BC, that, whatever was the nature of God's action upon events, it was not purely unilateral but was contingent upon creaturely response and co-operation. Though the Bible applies this insight mainly to God's reliance on human agents, the principle has implications for God's relationship with the whole of creation, as Aquinas saw.

> God is at work in all creaturely activity, but not on his own without intermediaries, as if creatures were powerless to do anything themselves: as if fire did not make things hot, but only God acting in the fire. That would deprive creation of all causal order and derogate the creator's power; for part of any agent's power is its ability to pass on power to act in its effects . . . So we must understand God to act in things in such a way that the things act themselves.[2]

This insight in the Old Testament vastly enriched the concept of divine providence; it also set limits to the concept of divine power.

A school of biblical interpretation calling itself 'narrative theology' lays its emphasis very helpfully on the fact that the central actor in the Old Testament stories is God, and the narrative is unfolded not because the Hebrews were a race of historians but because the story itself reveals what manner of God this is and what may be expected of him. That observation, however, should be qualified. Though the protagonist in Israel's history is always God himself, the stories follow the career of the woman or the man God is using as agent. So to Moses God says 'I have come down to rescue them . . . Come now; I will send you to Pharaoh' (Ex. 3.7–10). And Gideon's dialogue with God runs: 'If the Lord really is with us, why has all this happened to us? What has become of all those wonderful deeds of his?' 'Go and use this strength of yours to free Israel from the power of the Midianites' (Judg. 6.13, 14). God was seen to have a preference for working with a human partner, and this was for an educational purpose; God's human partners were to be like apprentices who learn their master's ways and come to reflect their master's character by working with him. Chapter 6 has already touched upon this theme of reciprocity and co-operation which is vital for an understanding of God's action in the world.[3]

The role that Moses plays in the epic of God's deliverance of the people from Egypt, the giving of the law and the journeyings in the desert, is a model of human participation as an element in divine providence. The affinity between God's action and God's agent is epitomized in the oft-repeated 'I am with you' (Ex. 3.12; 4.12.15) which in turn echoes the sacred name, 'I am present,' and is picked up again in the reciprocal 'I will put forth my hand.' 'Put forth your hand' (*shalah*, Ex. 3.20; 4.4) and again 'I stretch out my hand.' 'Stretch out your hand' (*natah*, Ex. 7.5, 19). The interplay of action and agency appears clearly in the last verse of psalm 77: 'You led your people like a flock of sheep by the hand of Moses and Aaron.'

If it is true that God acts upon events through the agency of a human partner or any other created being, the providential occurrence must be open to different interpretations, some that see it almost exclusively as a divine action, others that stress in varying degrees the role of the human or other agent. The three strands of story telling which have been woven into those chapters (Ex. 7–12) which tell of the plagues of

Egypt illustrate these differences. The earliest strand, which contributes the largest amount of the material, presents God as the sole bringer of the various calamities, the first six of which are natural disasters – the fish in the Nile die, frogs swarm the river, flies plague the houses, pestilence strikes the livestock, hail destroys the standing crops, and a wind brings locusts from the eastern desert. In each case Moses speaks in God's name to warn Pharoah what to expect, and at his request, when the plague has struck, prays God to remove it; but he is not instrumental either in summoning or removing the disaster. A later strand, which appears only here and there, heightens the miraculous nature of the plague and gives Moses a more active role as God's agent: with his rod he turns the water of the Nile to blood, and calls up a hailstorm and the locusts, and also a thick darkness. The latest strand emphasizes the role of Aaron as the worker of wonders in competition with the magicians of Egypt. His staff changes into a serpent which devours theirs, turns all the water in the land into blood, calls up the frogs and turns the dust of the ground into maggots. It is significant that this account, by so labouring the human element in the events, trivializes them.

Even more significant is the part played by Moses as God's human partner in the events at Mount Sinai as the go-between in the giving of the law, the celebrant in the covenant ritual, the intercessor for the faithless people, the agent of divine wrath, the mystic who, for the nation's sake, desires a more direct vision of God and the perfect apprentice who, without knowing it, has acquired a recognizable likeness to the master he serves.[4] The reciprocity between the God of providence and the agent through which that providence operates is brought out in a moving passage (Ex. 33.1–3, 12–17) in which Moses confesses that the special relationship in which he stands before Yahweh can be of use only so long as Yahweh remains actively present. Divine action cannot be delegated: it can only be channelled. Yet it is contingent upon the readiness and response of the channel. This necessary co-inherence of God with God's agent is a theme that runs through the stories of so many other characters of the Old Testament and reaches its peak in the emergence of the great prophets. But they are only a paradigm of what God intended for his people as a whole: Israel was called to be the human partner with whom and in whom God would bless all humanity. Humanity in its turn is to be blessed by becoming the partner, the agent, of God towards the world.

Co-inherence is the mode of God's loving, the objective for which God desires an 'other'. As the Father loves the Son by making the Son the free agent of the Father's self-expression, so the blessed Trinity loves the creation by calling it to be the agent of the divine action. This principle was consummated in the incarnation whereby the Son, God's Given Self, became the human partner through whom the only kind of intervention open to God might be perfectly realized. Reflecting the divine strategy, Jesus chose partnership and co-inherence as his mode of action, first calling disciples to become what St Paul dared to call 'fellow workers with God' and 'joint heirs with Christ', to share his mission, drink his cup and undergo his baptism, and then gathering the church to become his own bodily agent animated by the Spirit. Jesus' prayer, 'I in them and thou in me', epitomizes the principle of co-inherence as the mode of divine providence.

Because God loves by sharing, he wills to act upon his creation, his 'other', only in and through the processes of the creation, making it make itself. God's providence depends upon finding a channel, a partner. It also depends on that partner's response and co-operation. This is the second way in which the Old Testament declares God's action upon events to be contingent, and the tragic aspect of Israel's special relationship with God and, by implication, of all humanity's relationship with God, derives from this uncertain factor. God and the world may be kept waiting a long time before divine promises can be kept. Jesus also revealed in his own experience that he could do no miracle where there was unbelief and was powerless to save those who would not have it. This understanding of God's providence did not eliminate the confidence of the biblical writers in God's sovereignty and initiative. God could still, they thought, summon the forces of nature and the might of nations to punish or restore his fickle people. Above all, God's Spirit could tirelessly strive with man through the mouths of the prophets. Yet they saw in a deepening pessimism that human resistance and sin is a powerful factor that can decide the course of events in opposition to the determinative promises of God. God's hands are tied by God's pre-eminent will to love.

3. An in-built providence

To discern in the Bible the principle of co-inherence – God's preference for working through a creaturely channel or agent – is one thing. It is another thing to exemplify this principle in the world as we experience it or even in our own lives. And that we must try to do if we are to fulfil the obligation to know what we mean when we use metaphorical or mythological language.

The paramount activity of divine providence is simply the letting be, the ceaseless self-giving whereby all things are held in existence. The basic question, Why is there anything rather than just nothing?, is answered, if at all, not by the doctrine of creation alone but also by the doctrine of providence. God holds the world in being. So it is reasonable to look for the primary instruments of God's action upon the world in the very constancy of some of the processes by which the universe is sustained.

One of these is the ecological principle of redress whereby every serious imbalance is corrected and excess is curbed. Just as the laws of nature, combining with pure chance, have produced a steady movement towards greater sensitivity, responsiveness and consciousness, so too the very inter-relatedness of things brings about a restoration of the balance whenever a particular phenomenon increases itself to an inordinate degree. Plague may sweep across a continent but will eventually burn itself out or stimulate the antibodies for its own elimination. One species may for a while dominate over all others in an environment but ends in exhausting its own food supply. There is a rough and ready justice built into the fabric of the world which extends to the dynamics of human history also. The classical world called it nemesis and revered it as a goddess. The Bible calls it judgment. Such personification may strike our age as superstitious, yet it is grimly reassuring, for if this is God's world it is natural to see the Creator's intention to preserve it by means of this in-built system of redress. Tyranny may seem impregnable, yet the rhythm of history will bring a turn of the tide as retribution and purgation sweep back over the corrupted land. A few nations may grasp and defend an overweening proportion of the world's wealth-production only until the imbalance undermines their economy or the weapons they have arrogantly abrogated to their sole control start inevitably to proliferate. There is a limit to the spread of evil because it overreaches itself, provokes reaction and brings about its own destruction. The ancient motto, 'Nothing in excess', is written into the fabric of the world. Prophets at all periods of history have been gifted with a specially acute sense of nemesis. An Amos or Jeremiah could see approaching events not merely as a punishment for national disobedience and folly, but as their direct outcome. With the same prophet's clarity, it seems, Jesus could see more clearly than many of his contemporaries that, unless the new high priestly aristocracy abandoned their reliance on power politics and submitted the nation to the rule and the relationships of God's universal Kingdom, their policies would so provoke the incipient revolutionaries as to make a more serious revolt inevitable and bring down Rome's final solution upon the Jewish state. 'Would that even today you knew the things that bring peace! But now they are hidden from your eyes.' The blindness and self-seeking of a minority in power can bring about the destruction of a whole people.

It is no less reasonable to marvel at the way in which the threads of existence spun by innumerable entities at all levels of being, each pursuing its individual self-interest, are woven together into a web of interdependence, and to see in this also the immanent activity of God. A poem by John Wain presents this at the simple human level.

This above all is precious and remarkable
How we put ourselves in one another's care,
How in spite of everything, we trust each other.

Fishermen at whatever point they are dipping and lifting
On the dark green swell they partly think of as home
Hear the gale warnings that fly to them like gulls.

The scientists study the weather for love of studying it,
And not specially for love of the fishermen,
And the wireless engineers do the transmission for love of wireless,

But how it adds up is that when the terrible white malice
Of the waves high as cliffs is let loose to seek a victim
The fishermen are somewhere else and so not drowned.

And why should this chain of miracles be easier to believe

Than that my darling should come to me as naturally
As she trusts a restaurant not to poison her?

They are simply examples of well-known types of miracle,
The two of them,
That can happen at any time of the day or night.[5]

Austin Farrer perceived the infinitely more complex interlocking of sub-human and inanimate units which constitute this living world and likened it to the work of a supreme novelist who allows all the characters to be true to their own natures and yet combines them into a satisfying story. He maintained that the Creator

> thinks all the natural processes at any level into being themselves and into running themselves true to type. And yet without faking the story or defying probability at any point he pulls the history together into the patterns we observe . . . A thought living at once on every level of natural process and thinking all levels into a single story is to believers the wonder of omnipotence and to sceptics the height of absurdity.[6]

Another constant feature built into the universe from the start which may be regarded as an agent of divine control is that interplay of chance and 'the rules of the game' which was noted in the last chapter. By this means the Creator seems to have established from the outset a bias towards the emergence of more complex systems out of simpler ones, but the element of spontaneity in the development suggests a continuous extemporizing rather than an automatic outgrowth. The physical bio-chemist, Arthur Peacocke, has likened it to the improvisation of a supreme musician who begins almost tentatively with a sequence of a few notes which are tried out and explored in a variety of arrangements until a distinct tune emerges. This is then elaborated and expanded into a fugue whereby every repetition and modulation of the original theme generates new surprises and fresh beginnings.[7] In such a way is the complex profusion of a world or of an individual life story being created out of the interplay between the constancy of a theme and the openness towards new invention: 'Where do we go from here?'

That analogy points to the positive role that potentiality has played and continues to play in the processes of creation. We know now that causation does not have to take the form of a single antecedent cause producing a single predictable result, but may often be, even at the level of the molecular structure, an actualizing of one out of a number of possibilities. What calls for further cautious exploration is the idea that one of the latent possibilities may exercise a particular attraction, as though it already possessed a quasi-existence of its own.

The thought would deserve a summary dismissal were it not a fair statement of what seems actually to occur in a different sphere of creative development, namely the growth of a work of art. A striking example can be seen in the composition of Wilfred Owen's war poem, *Anthem for Dead Youth*, later included most memorably in Britten's *War Requiem*. The British Museum has four successive drafts which reveal the evolution of the verse.[8] The opening line of the final draft

What passing-bells for these who die as cattle?

is melodically so perfect with the sharp detonation of its final word that it is hard to believe that it existed in any other form. Yet in the first draft it ended lamely: 'die so fast?' In the second draft Owen was working on the rhymes: to 'the monstrous anger of the guns' which he had already in his second line, he added for contrast in the third 'the stuttering rifles' rattled words' and this suggested 'died in herds?' to end his first line. With the image of 'herds' and the sound of 'rattled' together on the page it is hard to avoid the impression that 'die as cattle?' was at hand all along, calling to be noticed. Owen heard it in time for his third draft but spoilt the simplicity with the over-loaded 'dumb-dying cattle?', and this he pruned out in the final version. The evolution of that peerless opening line can be paralleled throughout the entire sonnet. A study of the four drafts reveals Owen stumbling in pursuit of this beckoning potentiality like Michelangelo releasing from a block of marble the fully-formed sculpture imprisoned within. Since our introspective observation of the working of our own creativity is the only clue we possess to the inwardness of any other part of creation, it would be presumptuous to rule out the possibility that a particular unrealized potentiality may be one of the influences determining the direction of a new advance even at the inanimate levels in the hierarchy of being.

These elemental principles of interdependence, improvisation, potentiality, and nemesis, together constitute an in-built providence, an auto-pilot, to keep this self-generating unpredictable universe on course.

4. Special providences

A self-giving Creator's continual care for his creation, however, cannot be limited to the general set of the universe and its bias towards some distant fulfilment. It must also entail an immediate and active presence of God bearing upon specific events. We have seen how the biblical narratives of God acting with and through some human partner point to the principle of what Austin Farrer used to call 'double agency' and earlier philosophers designated as first and secondary causation. The God who is not of this world, not part of its web of inter-related forces, works upon the world through the agency of its processes and events. We should also notice that the biblical stories find this principle illustrated in specific and remarkable instances. For while it is the theist's belief, and an important belief, that every detail of the world process is happening by virtue of God's ubiquitous letting-be, to say that God pollinates the flower by getting the bee to pollinate the flower is a pious truism which, applied as a general principle, equates God with nature and robs the word 'providence' of its meaning. In this century theologians have quite properly tended to avoid speaking of divine 'intervention' because the word suggests that God is only occasionally present and at work in the world; but this caution should not blind us to the biblical insight that there is a particularity in God's providence which gives certain occurrences a revelatory significance for the people concerned.

'Providence,' says T. J. Gorringe, 'is not another physical factor to be placed alongside gravity, wind, temperature and so on but speaks of God's use of such factors.'[9] When God desires to affect the course of events he does not supersede or suspend the natural causes of those events, but works with them as they are. It is illogical to suppose that God's trademark is the supernatural, seeing that the natural processes are the ones he made. Nor have we any reason to be more ready to discern God at work in the exotic fringes of the natural world – faith healing, psychic experience, extra-sensory perception – merely because we know less about them. God's providence bears upon the world as it is, accepting the conditions of its laws as well as the opportunities of its openness. Immanent within the world, God makes himself one with its ordinariness, as he did in his incarnation, so that everyone who wishes can marvel at the facts without attributing them to God and only the eye of faith discerns who is present.

Any attempt to guess how God acts upon things at specific points must be limited, as has already been said, by the impossibility of imagining what it is to be God. Yet it is necessary to search for some analogy if talk of divine action is to have any meaning. There are two kinds of causation, from without and from within. If I wish to rid the lawn of moss I can either apply moss killer and rake it out or, recognizing that moss has evolved to flourish on water-logged terrain and grass on drier uplands, I can drain the lawn. The first method is an external attack, the latter, by changing the environment, uses the inner propensity of the two plants. Similarly, for some cases of mental illness a doctor can either prescribe electric shock or drug treatment or, alternatively, recommend the patient to a psychiatrist, whose skill consists in helping the patient to achieve his/her own next steps towards relief. (Doctor and gardener may, of course, use both approaches to be doubly sure.) Without intending any pat on the back of psychiatry or organic gardening, it has to be said that internal causation is the truer analogy of the way God acts upon the world.

The moss is discouraged by a well-drained lawn, having become the kind of plant it is through innumerable tiny adaptations to a spongy environment. On a far shorter time-scale the patient may win through to release from mental illness by becoming, little by little, the kind of person who can face and accept more self-understanding and compassion towards others. Although it has been that patient's own achievement, she or he may truly say, 'If it were not for my psychiatrist I wouldn't have become what I am.' The decisions I freely take today, as well as all my unthinking reactions, arise from the person I have become. Looking back over the lifetime's evolution of my own personhood I have to say 'If it were not for many people and innumerable events and influences I wouldn't be what I am.' And they in turn were to me what they were as a result of their own histories of episode and influence. The mind boggles at such an intricacy of random interactions and freely made decisions; but not the mind of God. God sees this network of influences in its entirety, holds it all together and integrates his own gentle orientation into it by awakening the awareness, the responsiveness of his creatures towards what is there and what might be.

By contributing to the network of influences that condition our actions, God can continuously shape the possibilities toward which we live and so can aim our self-creative activity toward the fulfilment God intends for us. In this way God affects us not as an alien power that disrupts or compels but rather as an intimate contributor to our own creative activity.[10]

That quotation clearly refers to the *human* experience of divine influence. I would wish to add that, while it is impossible for us to envisage the inwardness of non-human beings, we should think of God bearing upon their existence in the same way, taking into account their lesser degree of free choice and awareness/response.

Various writers have offered other analogies that may make it easier to visualize divine action upon individual creaturely existence. The good teacher's stimulation of a pupil's capacity to learn, and the process whereby one person induces another to change her mind, are variations upon the model of psychiatrist and patient. The way in which the entire gamut of antecedent causality in a given situation may be made to affect a subject differently without altering any of the facts can be observed in the cinema industry where the same sequence can be rendered darkly sinister or hilariously funny by the musical sound track. By instilling the mood music of hope into an occurrence God can bring new possibilities to birth without changing anything else. The power of an evil can be disarmed, without being removed, by the simple conviction that one is infinitely loved – a conviction which is purely the gift of God.

T. J. Gorringe has recently come up with a 'marvellous parable of God's activity' which he discovered in *The Empty Space*, Peter Brook's account of his own experiences as a director with the Royal Shakespeare Company. Gorringe draws from this analogy the truth that God is not imposing his own interpretation of the play nor has he worked out a plan of the moves the actors should make. He does not shout direction from the auditorium but is in amongst the actors, though not one of them. He does, however, actively direct.

If you just let a play speak, it may not make a sound. If what you want is for the play to be heard, then you must conjure its sound from it. This demands many deliberate actions.[11]

So in what Brook calls 'a dialogue and a dance between director and player' God demands that his actors find the inner impulse of the play and of their parts in it. Sometimes God seems to do nothing for them except, like Brook, 'drumming out a rhythm'. Yet all the time, with infinite inventiveness, he is stimulating them to discover together where they are making for and in what ways they are failing to get there. The Christlike God is with us always, directing his world through stimulation, persuasion, mutual exchange and joint discovery.

No human analogy can convey the whole truth of our relationship with God, and the image of the theatre director at work does not do full justice to the absolute otherness of the invisible God. In his provident direction of the world God uses creaturely agents, the influence of one actor upon others; but his own action belongs to a different frame of reference from that of the interactions of created beings. To impart this we need the image of authorship and the relationship, touched upon earlier, between Emily Brontë and her characters. She is their creator, not a person in their story. They exist in her mind, she does not exist in theirs. Indeed she is at such pains to distance herself from them that the reader hears their story not directly from her but from the lips of two participants in the tale, Mr Lockwood, the new tenant of Thrushcross Grange, and Mrs Dean his housekeeper. This deliberate self-distancing by the author enhances the autonomy of the main characters by leaving the reader free to recognize that there is more to them than the two narrators could have known. They are Emily Brontë's creatures but not her puppets. Her act of creation is a true letting be. Not once does she ask any of them to behave contrary to the law of their being for the sake of the plot. They are, each one, what their own nature and their situation have made them, and the situation is largely what their idiosyncracies have made it. She foists no incongruous turn of events upon them: there are no miracles. Yet the story reflects the inner being of Emily Brontë as it is expressed in her poems, and it could have been no one else's. It is her craftsmanship that has integrated these truly living creatures and the events that befall them into a coherent and rounded work of art. Another name for craftsmanship of this quality and integrity is love. Out of herself and her imagination she has loved them into life. Spiteful, capricious Catherine shines with vitality, Heathcliff, for all his vengeful cruelties, is magnificent with tragic irony, and even the detestable Hindley Earnshaw is to be pitied for the damage inflicted by a father's whim. In somewhat the same way all of us, like every other thing that is, are responsible for what we make of ourselves, yet the author of our lives is God who has not finished yet and hates nothing that he has made. We know not the end of the story, nor even its next page. We can still only vaguely surmise what it is about. It has already contained one episode, however, to which, as Dorothy L. Sayers put it, Christianity draws our attention. 'The leading part of this was played, it is alleged, by the Author, who presents it as a brief epitome of the plan of the whole work.'[12]

5. *Expectation of miracles*

Dorothy L. Sayers, who was both novelist and no mean theologian, also pointed out that the good writer refrains not only from unduly manipulating the characters but also from unnaturally rigging the plot.

> Whatever we may think of the possibilities of direct divine intervention in the affairs of the universe, it is quite evident that the writer can – and often does – intervene at any moment in the development of his own story; he is absolute master, able to perform any miracle he likes . . . He can slay inconvenient characters, effect abrupt conversions, or bring about accidents or convulsions of nature to rescue the characters from the consequences of their own conduct. He can, in fact, behave exactly as, in our more egotistical and unenlightened petitions, we try to persuade God to behave . . . but if we examine more closely the implications of our analogy, we may be driven to ask ourselves how far it is really *desirable* that he should do anything of the kind.[13]

Should we then expect no miracles? If we use the word in its strict, broad sense, then we are surrounded by miracles. For its literal meaning is a marvel, something worthy of wonder. In the Old Testament the plagues of Egypt and the healing of Hezekiah are called 'marvels', so too are Jonathan's love for David, Solomon's temple, the way of an eagle in the air or a serpent over rock, and the way of a man with a maid. The other term denoting a miracle in the Bible is 'sign' – a sign of God's greatness. The skill whereby a swallow navigates a six thousand mile flight from its winter quarters in a reed bed in South Africa to arrive at the same English cottage under the eaves of which it nested the previous year is but one of the breathtaking marvels of our 'ordinary' world. So too are the powers of self-healing and recuperation latent in the human body upon which medical practice relies and which can also be activated by mental reorientation through prayer and other forms of 'spiritual' therapy. 'God', said Francis Bacon, 'never wrought miracle to convince atheism, because his ordinary works convince it'.[14]

We draw unwarranted distinctions between explicable marvels, like the migration of birds, remarkable coincidences which are the purest form of chance, and marvels which are inexplicable unless attributed to some supernatural agency. These last are what we normally mean by 'miracles'. In earlier times so many common experiences were unexplained, including such phenomena as the migration of birds (Jer. 8.7), that it was natural to attribute large areas of life to the sole activity of God: God gave the rain, sent the pestilence and blessed the harvest with no intermediate cause. All the time, however, more of the 'natural' explanations were being recognized. The farmer learned what he had to do besides trusting in God; the doctor also: 'Honour the physician according to your need of him for the Lord created him, for healing comes from the Most High . . . The Lord created medicines from the earth and a sensible man will not despise them' (Ecclus. 38.1–4). So the concept of 'double agency', of God's human partner, took form, and with it the realization that many phenomena, like spiritual healing, are only at present inexplicable, as was the navigation of migratory birds until recently. This does not imply that God's side of the partnership can be ignored in such cases, but it does remove the need to assume any suspension of the laws of nature. Events that, without an appeal to supernatural causation, are only currently inexplicable are marvels but not miracles in the narrower sense. Only the inherently inexplicable, which are out of kilter with the created world, are pure miracles. I do not say they are impossible. I say in all reverence that we should not expect them or pray for them.

When the vagaries of our climate were more of a mystery than they are today it was a sound religious instinct for whole congregations to petition God for rain or fair weather. Forecasting has now made us well aware that the force of winds and ocean currents thousands of miles away have already dealt out next week's weather for us. In this context my prayer for a fine day for the church fête is a kind of frivolity, the frivolity of expecting a God, who so greatly respects the integrity of the world as he has made it and the responsibility of the characters in the story, to take liberties with his standards of authorship. It is conceivable that God might on occasion indulge in the frivolity of something like *The Comedy of Errors* by foisting absurd coincidences and improbabilities on his plot. In that event the proper response should be laughter. In that spirit I have, I confess, sometimes prayed such a trivial prayer, knowing it to be laughable, and once in a while, as if someone were keeping up the joke, I have got what I wanted. But if that kind of expectation of God is entertained seriously in a serious situation it distorts our image of God, as when a nation at war discerns divine providence in a storm that has destroyed the enemy fleet. When people wonder why God does not strike tyrants dead or prosper a virtuous man's business they are actually asking for another universe with a different purpose. They resemble David Garrick who improved *Hamlet* with a happy ending!

It is not that God is without points of entry to the course of events. 'Points of entry' is, in fact, the wrong image, since God is within the flow of events, as we have seen, working through the in-built principles of nemesis and potentiality, and by interior influence in particular instances. Our mistake lies in thinking of miracles as extraneous intervention. Forty years ago my wife, Peggy, and I were climbing a mountain in East Africa with four friends. After a night in a mountain hut the others set out to make for the summit while we prepared food and water for the evening meal; then we went after them. We got up without encountering them but this did not surprise us as they had been gone some time. When we started back I made a reckless blunder. Forgetting that the summit had been a constant landmark and the return would be without one, I suggested a short cut across the wide arc we had come by. We lost our bearings, got into very rough terrain and had to cringe under an overhanging cliff while a black thunderstorm drenched us. When it passed I looked in all directions with no idea where the hut lay, and an appalled realization of what I had done. In a very small voice Peggy said, 'We're lost, aren't we?'

I said, 'Yes. I'm dreadfully sorry, it's my fault.'

She said, her voice quite steady, 'I'm frightened, John.'

'So am I,' was all I could answer.

And then she said, 'Well. It is Whitsunday,' and at that instant a beam of sunlight struck through the cloud and shone for a few seconds on the hut about two miles away, reflected dazzlingly from its aluminium roof, giving us our bearings. It was the most direct act of God I have personally experienced, but the miracle did not happen up there in the grey sky. The break in the cloud was going to happen anyway. What I know for certain is that, had I characteristically been protesting that we could still find our way, and had Peggy retorted, with justice, 'How could you be such a fool?', we would have been glaring at each other and would never have seen that pointing shaft of light. The miracle was in us, as they almost always are.

6. *Jesus and providence*

God's interaction with the world and his pressure upon events, then, is to be found at the point of the inwardness of things, our individual and corporate interiority. God is, as has been reiterated almost *ad nauseam*, the Beyond in the midst. God shapes what we call history through the inward response made to him by the leaders, the prophets and poets, and the holy and humble people, within the contingency of events. The difference between the false and the true expectation of divine help emerges clearly from a comparison of the old and the new English tradition of the claim St Paul made towards the end of his letter to the church at Philippi (Phil. 4.13). The King James, the Revised and the Revised Standard versions all say: 'I can do all things in him who strengthens me', suggesting a participation through Christ in the divine omnipotence as traditionally perceived. The NEB and REB are more faithful in rendering the main verb *ischuo* (I am strong to endure), and the latter translates the verse: 'I am able to face anything through him who gives me strength.' This accords better with the previous verse in which Paul says he has been thoroughly initiated into good times and bad. If we are still worrying about the weather for the church fête, we should remember that we pray to a God who does not allow himself to switch on a fine day at will but can give us cheerful and resourceful minds whatever comes.

The Christ in whose name we adjust and present our prayers was not powerless. At his word men, women and children were restored to health and demonic powers, as they understood them, were overcome. What stands out from the Gospel narratives is the regularity with which Jesus involved people in their own healing: Stand up. Stretch out your arm.

Go and wash. Something within themselves had to be reached. Even more significant for our expectations is the fact that Jesus worked no miracle for his own well-being, convenience or safety. Intensely aware of a divinely appointed task, he did not on that account expect life to work out to his advantage. He knew that this is not that kind of world. Towers do not fall on pre-selected victims, they fall by accident or from sinful carelessness, so they may fall on anyone. His intimate trust in God did not depend upon special interventions but upon the inner communion of his prayers and his gift of seeing such ordinary things as sunrise and rainfall, the quiet blossoming of flowers and the foraging of birds as evidence of God's care. Consequently he took responsibility for events in such practical ways as having a donkey standing by ready for his ride into the capital and a pre-arranged guide to the room he had booked for the last supper – a characteristic which shamed the disciples when they had forgotten to bring along enough bread for the day, but not one usually found in people who expect angels to look after them. Nor did he. 'Do you suppose that I could not appeal to my Father and at once be sent more than twelve legions of angels?' Do *we* suppose it even thinkable that he would, he who had just been crying, 'If it be possible, let this cup pass me by,' but always adding, 'Not what I will but what you *will*, your age-long purpose'? If there was intervention now, 'how then could the scriptures be fulfilled that it must be so' – not some particular texts about the death and the atoning sacrifice, but the *whole witness* of God's eternal *will* to raise up an 'other' to be the object and heir of his love, and to return love for love in freedom? To pray for angels then would have been calling for a different world and the abandonment of the whole universe just as it was on the brink of fulfilment. 'We may ask ourselves', wrote Dorothy L. Sayers, 'how much power would be left in the story of the crucifixion, as a story, if Christ had come down from the cross.'[15] It was as Jesus was lifted up on the cross between earth and heaven and there was no intervention from beyond that God's total self-giving was perfectly reflected, and perfectly returned in the self-giving of man.

That much of God's withholding we can see and understand. We can forgo the adventitious miracles, the bolt from the blue, the angelic rescue, in the light of Christ's experience. In any case this relieves us of the painful question, Why did God do it for your child and not for mine?

We can learn to recognize the divine hand within the action of the human partner, the double agency, God in the bee. We can find the courage, if called on, to become agents of providence ourselves: 'Come, now I will send you.' We can seek to grow more aware, more open to the God whose special point of entry into events is ''neath the low lintel of the human heart'. We can even accept as his greatest miracle the inner strengthening that enables us to endure his non-intervention and inaction, the inner consolation that does not remit the pain. All this we can, perhaps, face up to because it was the kind of providence Christ could trust and call *Ab'ba*.

But there remains a darkness which we cannot penetrate, the one question for the asking of which Jesus could not say *Ab'ba*: 'My God, why has thou forsaken me?' That the God who so cherishes the world's autonomy and whose hands are tied by love, cannot miraculous intervene, we can with difficulty grant. But that the God who can *inwardly* strengthen and reassure the one who looks to him in suffering, who frequently does, should ever withdraw that last evidence of love is inexplicable. This is the absence, the blank silence that annihilates belief. It murdered Elie Wiesel's faith as a teenager in Auschwitz.[16] It confounded the fifteen-year-old Bridget Spufford whose life was painfully constricted and, at twenty-two ended, by a rare congenital disease. Following the distressful death of a boy in the next cubicle to hers in the hospital ward, she wrote out the rage she felt towards the God she did not then believe in: 'If "you" exist, then why in blazes didn't you stick out a hand to help him fight his way through?'[17]

To that 'why?', which is Christ's 'why?' there is no answer, only darkness and silence. A great many people have been in that darkness, a great many are there now, yet each of them is alone, for they have gone out of reach. Those who want to help can do no more than the prophet Ezekiel could do for his fellow Jews in their detention camp: 'I went in bitterness, in the heat of my spirit and the hand of the Lord was strong upon me. Then I came to them of the captivity of Tel Abib, who sat by the Chebar river; and I sat where they sat, desolate and dumb' (Ezek. 3.14,15). To attempt an explanation of God's inaction is to become totally estranged from that silence, and also from God himself, because the silence and the absence has something to do with the ultimate mystery of God, of Being and non-being. At the end of seven days of merely being there the word of the Lord came to Ezekiel. It may be so for others who wait in the same bitterness of spirit; but while the Word has died, let there be no words.

7. Justifying the ways of God

There is another aspect of faith in divine providence on which the Bible has expended an enormous number of words: rewards and punishments and the justice of God. It is still a problem for popular religion, and again it calls for a sense of the development of ideas.

The early Hebrews learned the lesson of history in very simplistic terms: God protected and advanced the nation when it followed his righteous ways, but permitted disasters of one kind or another to bring it to repentance when disobedient. For a long time the doctrine of rewards and punishments was understood in these strictly corporate terms – 'the fathers have eaten sour grapes and the children's teeth are set on edge' – and was accepted as entirely just and natural so long as the innocent sufferers were involved closely enough in the offending group – 'to the third and fourth generation'. The prophet who warned his people of impending doom expected to share the disaster in solidarity with them if his words were not heeded (Jer. 45).

After the Deuteronomic reforms under King Josiah a new note of individual answerability began to infiltrate the doctrine. There were protests at the injustice of communal retribution: 'Our fathers have sinned and are not; and we have borne their iniquities' (Lam. 5.7). Jeremiah and Ezekiel propounded a new ethic of individual rewards and punishments: 'The one who eats the sour grapes is the one whose teeth will be set on edge' (Jer. 31.29,30; Ezek. 18.1–4). This sounds so eminently just that it was at once recognized as the way God ought to behave and this view has persisted in the Jewish and Christian traditions to this day. It is the simple nursery ethic of fair play. Unfortunately it is based on the assumption that God who is just is also directly responsible for everything that happens in the world apart from human naughtiness. It was to be many centuries before believers began to comprehend that divine omnipotence is qualified by the primacy of divine love. They had not come to terms with the necessary randomness of God's world and frequently cried out against it.

My feet had almost slipped
my foothold had all but given way,
because boasters roused my envy
when I saw how the wicked prosper.
No painful suffering for them!
They are sleek and sound in body,
not in trouble like ordinary mortals,
nor afflicted like other folk (Ps.73.2–5).

One way of answering such complaints and justifying the ways of God to man was to postpone individual rewards and punishments, together with the fulfilment of all God's other promises, to some new age beyond history. This seemed to offer an easy way out of the central problem of the doctrine of divine providence, but it laid the doctrine itself open to serious attack on two fronts.

On the one hand there was the charge that such an interpretation of God's purposes abandoned this world to a completely amoral wilderness. The writer of Ecclesiastes is the spokesman of their criticism.

> Here are upright men and wise; and it is a drudge's task they do; all in God's keeping, and yet men have no means of telling whether they have earned his love or his displeasure! This remains yet uncertain, and meanwhile all have the same lot, upright and godless, good and wicked, clean and unclean alike. Brought they offerings or brought they none, well did they or ill, true swore they or false, it is all one. Of all that goes amiss here under the sun, nothing does more hurt than this equality of fortunes; what wonder if men's hearts, while yet they live, are full of malice and defiance? (Eccles. 9.1–3, tr. R. Knox).

On the other hand the deeply rooted idea of punishment and rewards in this world or the next was open to denunciation on the grounds that it encouraged a merely prudential morality. If it pays to be good, how good is goodness? This imputation was put into the mouth of Satan, the devil's advocate, in the opening two chapters of Job, that work which, by seeming to endorse the traditional concept of divine providence, acutely questions it.

> Has not Job good reason to be god-fearing? Have you not hedged him

> round on every side with your protection? But stretch out your hand and touch all that he has, and he will curse you to your face (Job. 1.9–11).

Determined to vindicate both his human partner and his wise providence, God hands Job over to the test. After the total loss of children and possessions, Job bows to his fate with no surrender of his piety. The devil's advocate presses his point more cynically.

> Skin for skin. There is nothing a man will not relinquish to save himself. But stretch out your hand to touch his own bone, his own flesh, and he will curse you to your face (Job 2.5).

God again takes on the wager, as it were, demanding only that Job be kept alive to vindicate God's faith in him. Job is miserably afflicted but, despite his wife's persuasion to renounce this unjust God and accept death, he transcends all anxiety to establish either divine justice or human deserts with an unquestioning faith: 'If we accept good from God, shall we not accept evil?'

Now Job has to defend that unconditional trust against the champions of the dogma of a morally inspired providence – virtue will be rewarded and sin punished – and we observe that teaching being turned into the most subtle of all the weapons in Satan's armoury. In his first agonized outpouring of despair Job curses the day he was born but he brings no complaint against God. It is the three traditionalists who introduce the insidious question, Why?, and it is this which starts the train of thought that undermines Job's trust. When they first insinuate and then impatiently insist upon Job's guilt, he who would not impugn God's goodness cannot impugn his own. If the dogma is true, then God's justice has gone awry and Job will not be silenced. That dogma has been the foundation of the prophets' teaching about God's hand in history and upon individual lives, and Job has to be handed over to his passion of doubt and indignation to expose the flaw in it.

8. *God justified or revealed?*

In spite of that magnificently courageous book, the expectation has lived on none the less that God sees to it that people get their deserts in this life or the next, and that this is what divine providence is all about. Job is not the last to have his faith undermined by it. There are two appalling sayings in the Fourth Gospel.

> It was not that this man sinned nor his parents, but that the works of God might be made manifest in him (John 9.3).

> This illness is not unto death, it is for the glory of God, that the Son of God may be glorified by means of it (John 11.4).

Those words are appalling because of the misinterpretation which can be, and has been, put upon them. Is a man to suffer half a lifetime of blindness, is a friend to succumb to fatal illness and his family be plunged into mourning, in order that Jesus may work a miracle and win greater credit for God? That is what the words seem to mean. Can we respect a Creator who fixes things at our expense for his own glorification? This is the awkward question we overlook in reading the opening chapters of Job, but we do not expect it to arise in the Gospels.

When we react in this manner, or, worse still, when we produce dutiful justifications for such a God, we are making the same unwarrantable assumption as the disciples did that somebody caused the sickness. We, in fact, with our fixation on antecedent causation, are more prone than Jesus would have been to suppose that if something serves a purpose it must have been made for that purpose. If we look more carefully at both these narratives we can see that Jesus said nothing to imply that God sent or allowed the affliction. On the contrary, he repudiated the search for any deliberate personal responsibility for it, which is always a hunt for a scapegoat. Rather than looking back for explanations he confronted each situation by looking forward. He had the gift of fitting out a bad situation with a new reason – which is not a bad definition of a miracle, or of providence itself. It was the potential that appealed to him. 'What shall we make of this?' This illness is not unto death; that is not the direction it has to take. Even the death of this friend and the reproachful grief of the sisters was playing not into the hands of death but into the hands of God. Jesus was inviting them all to share in that victory, even though he could foresee better than they that the spectacular raising of Lazarus could be the direct cause of the Sanhedrin's decision to seek his own death – 'so that the Son of Man may be glorified by means of it'. (The Johannine use of 'glorifying' suggests that sequence of ideas.) That ultimate outcome also was not 'unto death', but for the glory, the outward shining, of God.

What, then, was the outcome of Job's crucifixion at the hands of the traditional moralists? He, too, was tormented by the question 'Why?' and the darkness of God. But instead of the silence of heaven he was engulfed in a storm of argumentative explanation. Where God's action or inaction has become inexplicable to any sufferer, attempts to justify God are cruel as well as futile. That is not where faith will be found. The true triumph of Job lies in the fact that, although undermined, his trust in God was never extinguished. It was as though he succumbed to an embittered belief in their God who had condemned him unjustly yet continued to trust that his God, the God of *ḥesed*-trustworthiness, would plead his cause.

> I know that my *go'el*, my kinsman vindicator, lives, and that he will rise last to stand forth in the dust of the court. I shall discern my witness standing at my side and see my defending counsel, even God himself, whom I shall see with my own eyes, I myself and no other (Job 19.25–27).[18]

Again Job dares to hope that it is his God, not theirs, who sits in judgment over all.

> If only I knew how to reach him, how to enter his court. I should state my case before him and set out my arguments in full. Then I should learn what answer *he* would give and understand what he would say to me. Would he exert his great power to browbeat me? No; God himself would never set his face against me (Job 23.3–6).

When at last God breaks his silence it seems at first sight that browbeating is exactly what he does do in an overwhelming demonstration of omnipotence, and Job appears to take it in that sense. But there is no trace of hostility or umbrage in God's address to Job as he unfolds the great pageant of creation, nor is God seeking merely to humble his servant and silence his presumption. On the contrary God rallies Job: 'Brace yourself and stand up like a man. I will ask the questions and you will answer.' Twice is that challenge given by God, and the same words occur surprisingly in Job's last response. The Hebrew text is exasperatingly confused at that critical point, and the words may be misplaced. As they stand they suggest that, abased as he is, Job is being called to stand on a frightening and infinitely more daring footing with God.

> I have spoken of things I did not understand, things too wonderful for me to grasp. Yet listen, and let me speak. I shall put questions to you and you shall answer. I knew of you only by hearsay, but now I see you with my own eyes, therefore I melt away, repentant in dust and ashes (Job 42.3–6).

Be that as it may, the core of that final avowal is 'I have seen you.' This is the climax to which this great drama converges. The whale and the crocodile, even under the grandiloquent names, Behemoth and Leviathan, are no answer to anyone betrayed by life's injustice or God's withdrawal. Nothing but a gift of the presence of God can meet that person's need. That is what the stupendous array of God's workmanship is actually intended to convey. The pillars of the world, the dwelling place of darkness, the storehouses of the snow, the calving of the wild doe and the soaring of the eagle, these are only metaphors of the ineffable: 'I have seen *you*.' What was given to Job was a numinous experience of the nearness of God, like the similar gift bestowed upon Moses when Yahweh passed before him, pronouncing his own name. The answer to Job's long battle of words is not a theodicy or justification of God, but a theophany, a revelation of God. To most people who receive such revelation it comes not as a vision but as the quiet, unlooked-for gift of absolute certainty that God loves them. When someone has been unmanned by the darkness of an inscrutable providence, this gift does not answer the questions; it effaces them.

It also replaces them. Encounter with the living God presents us with new questions. 'Brace yourself and stand up like a man' is a reminder that while we question God about unjust suffering and rampant evil, he has other questions in mind, of which the first is, 'Where were you?' That is an uncomfortable question to face when we have been wondering why God allowed Auschwitz. When we ask why he has done nothing about some particular suffering, God's response is to call upon his human partner. 'I have seen the misery, I have heard the cry, I have known the suffering, I am come down to rescue. Come now, I will send you.' Unless we are ready for that, our complaints at God's injustice or our attempts to prove God just are equally hollow protestations. We who would like to say, and rightly, that God suffers with and in the victims must validate the claim by being, if possible, the agent, the body, in whom God does that sharing. Despite the annihilation of trust and compassion, there were those in Auschwitz who gave their lives for others. They had the right to say that God was with them still.

God's fellow workers and partners in salvation should have no triumphalist pretensions about their power to put the world to rights. Three duties only are laid upon them when they are brought face to face with human affliction: to stay with the victims where the suffering is, without backing off or hoping it will be a one-off encounter; to see through the confusion and untruth in which the evil in the situation conceals itself and call it by its right name, not in order to occupy the moral high ground but because only those who see their human capacity for evil can take in the miracle of God's unchanged and costly involvement; to do all possible to alleviate the suffering and abolish the conditions that are causing it. For providence's proper name is Immanuel, God with us.

9

Dwell in Me, I in You

The Co-Inherence of Love

1. Giving and receiving

The mystery that is God, the ocean in which all things are sustained and from which they receive their being, the unimaginable Beyond which makes people aware of itself in sudden glimpses of another dimension of glory and meaning in ordinary phenomena and events, this sea of joy which is, within itself, the timeless exchange of love given and received, this self-renouncing Christlike power, in the weakness of self-chosen limitation, is set upon the venture of opening out that love into a relationship with what is not God but a true Other, raised up within God to be the object and heir of that love and joy, returning love for love and sharing the eternal bliss.

All love is potentially mutual. It implies relationship and exchange. The Latin phrase, *Amor Dei*, can mean God's love or love for God. This ambiguity is not a looseness of language but a reflection of the truth – like another Latin word, *hospes*, which can mean either guest or host, since the roles are transferable. Love may often be unreciprocated or rejected and yet remain steadfast, but whenever that happens the love is unfulfilled and to that extent incomplete inasmuch as aspects of love are not brought into play. One of the conditions of loving is that whoever gives love has accepted the possibility of being forever unnoticed and disappointed. The other condition of loving, the counterpart of the first, is that whoever loves knows that a response is possible and that what is given could in some measure be given back. As the Japanese theologian, Kazoh Kitamori, has said, 'Love cannot help becoming hope.' The subject of the verb 'love' must recognize that it could be the object, and the object could become subject. Love is essentially reciprocal, though often not so in the event. God, in loving the world as his other, waits for the world's responsive love for his fulfilment. When Christians speak of *Amor Dei* they should always be thinking of a love and its mirror image. Whatever may be said about God's love for the world, for humanity, for me, may also in principle though not in scale be said about human love, my love, for God, and also about my love for others and the love I receive from them. The only difference, other than the immeasurable difference of scale and inclusion, is that God's love is always the prior love, always there, always the source. 'We love because he first loved.'

People have not always or universally been able to think of such mutuality of love between humanity and God. Generally speaking, the Old Testament writers would have considered the idea inappropriate. The words *ahab* and *ahabah*, as was mentioned in chapter 6, are most frequently used of the loves and desires of human beings for one another and less often of human love for God or God's for his people, and, in the latter, almost never of God's love for individuals. The term which most typifies God's relation to humanity throughout the Old Testament is *ḥesed*, merciful fidelity, and that could not easily be regarded as mutual between God and people. So the virtual coining of the word *agapē* by the New Testament writers represented a breakthrough to a new understanding since the same noun or verb can denote God's love for people, corporate or individual, their love for God, or one person's love for another. It could well be that the idea of a flow and counter-flow of the same quality of love between God and humanity arose directly from the disciples' observation of Jesus of Nazareth's communion with God, his *Ab'ba*, and thereafter from their experience of their own prayer and their communion with one another in the Holy Spirit.

Granted that the divine love is 'millions of times bigger', yet a reciprocal love between God and his created 'Other' is the outcome towards which the vast purposed process has moved from the beginning. It is in order to win our human capacity for love, the tiny reflection of his blazing *agapē* that we *can* return, that God empties himself to accommodate the otherness of a creation within himself, and has translated the fullness of that divine love, which is God's being, into the human love of Jesus of Nazareth. Because of that 'translation', because of the incarnation, human love and the divine love have become 'univocal'

– i.e. they have the same meaning – and constitute the common ground of our relationship with God. 'Ground', however, is not the best image for this reality which is more like a flow and counterflow.

Flow and counterflow, giving and receiving – those are the terms in which we have learned to describe the most basic processes by which this physical world is constituted. God has certainly set the pattern of his own being upon the substance of his creation.[1] Energy is in continuous flux from where it is concentrated to where it is not. At the lowliest level of physical existence primary particles fuse, losing something of themselves to others, gaining something from others, to form more complete elements. This is the law of existence that has determined the movement from simplicity to complexity rather than in the opposite direction. Through an exchange of heat and cold vast masses of incandescence cooled and broke apart into solid identities. The original rocks of this planet were eroded, surrendering their dust to the rivers and the seas where by further exchanges it was re-ordered to form our sandstones and marbles, our limestones and chalk. As life emerged it depended for its development and its very survival upon the variations afforded by the giving and receiving of genes through the process of reproduction and the continual exchange across the dividing walls of separate cells. This universal process of mutuality and interdependence, which reflects the nature of the triune God, is no less essential for human life as well. Human sexuality is simply the essential incompleteness of the self alone which lies at the core of every person. No man alone and no woman alone can produce a child. Every person's very existence begins within another, literally inhering in the mother. And of the growing up of a man or woman Austin Farrer has written:

> We need others to be human ourselves. What is our mind, but a dialogue with the thought of our contemporaries or predecessors? And what is our moral being, but a complex of relationships? You would be another man if your friends, relations, and *bêtes noires* were different: and your personal being is profoundly altered if you deeply love a woman and go on in that companionship.[2]

The interdependence of human work and the mysterious ways in which the different trades and professions, each following its own bent, interlock in the manner described in John Wain's poem in the previous chapter, should be seen as an aspect of providence built into the structure of creation itself. The glory of human nature, properly understood, is to depend on one another for everything and to be responsible for one another in everything. To learn that lesson and to practise it is the one sure way by which we may become capable of accepting the same kind of mutual exchange in our relationship with God. The founder of Christian monasticism, St Antony, after long years of solitary communion with God in the deserts of Upper Egypt, summed up what he had learnt in the words: 'My life and my death are in my neighbour.'

2. *A medium of exchange*

Austin Farrer drew from the fact of our indebtedness to others for all that we are as individuals this startling conclusion:

> But have you reflected that Jesus was that Jesus because of Mary and Joseph and the village rabbi, a man to us unknown; above all because of the disciples to whom he gave himself and the poor people to whose need he ministered? But for these people he would have been another Jesus. To be a man, he must have them, and to continue a man (as he still indeed is) he must retain them. So the life of God, incarnate in Jesus, cannot be locked within his breast; it becomes a spreading complex of personal being, centred in Jesus, and annexing his companions. Though we are each but a minute cell in the social body of Christ, yet, taking us in the lump and in the gross, he is what he humanly is by his relation to us.[3]

The individual Christian's relationship to Jesus Christ is formed and nourished through her or his relationship with other believers. And the depth of that relationship to Christ grows in proportion to the depth of that person's relationship with other people. By accepting and living to the full our mutual dependence upon, and responsibility for, one another we would grow naturally into the same reciprocal relationship with God. Doing what comes naturally should be the easy way to heaven! Yet we fear and resist it. We are not ready for love. Much depends on our grasping the reasons for this.

Our own development as individual persons is one reason. When I was still an infant, the whole world, including my own limbs and sensations, presented itself to me, was present to me, was addressing itself to me, as the ultimate Mystery, the Other. I did not explore or possess or control, I was literally nothing but awareness and receptivity and response. I was probably taking in more impressions, learning more experiences, each waking minute than I have ever done since that beginning-time. Vague memories of that way of relating to everything are built into our myth of paradise. In Martin Buber's words, that Other, each thing that was there, said 'You' to me, and gave itself to me, thereby creating this '*me*' as a person able to say 'You' to it and give myself to it. That is what Buber meant whenever he used the word 'relationship' – that, and nothing less. I was involved then in *relationship* with everything else.

But gradually I came to distinguish more sharply between the 'I', the self, that was receiving all this, and the other, all the rest, to which I said 'You'. Becoming aware of my separate self, I began analysing and ordering all these impressions, learning to handle and control what was there. Instead of being the Mystery, the Other, it became my environment, the object of my reflection, the source of my pleasure or discomfort. The more distinctly I set myself apart as the centre, the observer, the subject, the less it addressed me or gave itself to me. I ceased saying 'You' to what was there and started to see everything as 'It'. Buber refused to describe that as 'relationship' and referred to it instead as 'experience'. I experience everything as 'It'; I only relate to anything as 'You'.[4]

For so long the church has seemed to foster individual salvation, individual devotion, that today politicians never tire of proclaiming that the supreme dogma of Christianity is the value of the individual. It is not. Christianity, like its parent Judaism, teaches that human life achieves its transcendent potential in the exchange and interflow between persons in community. Because we started our lives by detaching ourselves from the Other and standing alone, we can realize this human potential only through a reversal, by 'unknowing' or unlearning. This psychological and spiritual change of direction is like a 'bifurcation point' in the realm of physics when a stable system becomes, under new conditions, suddenly unstable until a new ordered pattern takes over. In our case, painfully, the change has to be conscious and partly deliberate.

It is important to understand that Buber did *not* disparage our 'I-It' experiences of the world. He knew quite well that it is an essential mode of knowing the world if we are to live in it and communicate with others about it. He understood that the individuation is necessary for our human maturity. But he perceived that during the recent history of the human race, and especially since the rapid advance of technology, we are becoming 'stuck' in the 'I-It' experience of reality, and actually losing our capacity to recognize and receive an 'I-You' relationship with any part of reality.[5]

The most explicit and insistent teacher of this doctrine of exchange in this century was that prophetic novelist, theologian and poet, Charles Williams, the friend of C. S. Lewis and J. R. R. Tolkien. He returned to it again and again in one form or another. He, like Buber who was writing at the same time, understood how the advance of technology, while it offers new opportunities for enhancing human interdependence, like the radioed gale warnings in John Wain's poem, also conceals the reality of that interdependence by supplanting the more basic and obvious forms of it. In the earlier of his two cycles of poems based on the Arthurian legends, Williams takes the introduction of coinage in place of the direct barter of goods for goods as symbol both of technological advance and of the principle of exchange.[6] In the debate which he describes, Sir Kay, the king's steward and treasurer, naturally sees the advantages of circulating throughout the realm this new currency, stamped with the dragon of Wales.

> Kay, the King's steward, wise in economics, said:
> 'Good; these cover the years and the miles
> and talk one style's dialects to London and Omsk.
> Traffic can hold now and treasure be held,
> streams are bridged and mountains of ridged space
> tunnelled; gold dances deftly over frontiers.
> The poor have choice of purchase, the rich of rents,
> and events move now in a smoother control
> than the swords of lords or the orisons of nuns.
> Money is the medium of exchange.'

The next to speak is the poet, Taliessin. As a craftsman in words he knows how readily language can be carried along by its own momentum in a direction quite different from that demanded by the meaning and the logic it is intended to communicate. Any symbol functions at one remove from what it is standing for and can serve to widen that gap if it becomes such common currency, such a dead metaphor that everyone forgets the reality behind it. When wealth no longer signifies goods or services but something which begets more wealth of its own accord, it works against human interdependence and mutual exchange instead of enhancing it. The very convenience of technology makes us more prone to see one another as 'It'.

> Taliessin's look darkened; his hand shook
> while he touched the dragons: he said, 'We had a good thought.
> Sir, if you made verse, you would doubt symbols.
> I am afraid of the little loosed dragons.
> When the means are autonomous, they are deadly; when words
> escape from verse they hurry to rape souls;
> when sensation slips from intellect, expect the tyrant;
> the brood of carriers levels the goods they carry.
> We have taught our images to be free; are ye glad?
> Are we glad to have brought convenient heresy to Logres?'

The strength and soundness of Charles Williams lay in his constant ability to look beyond his own intuitive fears or enthusiasms and see a greater potentiality. He seemed to be ever ready to take the divine perspective of 'What shall we make of this?' even when it entailed taking also the divine risk. In the Arthurian poems the Archbishop represents the spiritual vision which sees, beyond immediate advantage or danger, the abiding truth embodied and concealed within the innovation. Since truth about God and God's ways is always wrapped in parable, his speech makes subtle use of the words of that most difficult of Jesus' parables, the tale of the Unjust Steward, to disclose the doctrine of exchange.

> The Archbishop answered the Lords:
> his words went up through a slope of calm air:
> 'Might may take symbols and folly make treasure,
> and greed bid God, who hides himself for man's pleasure
> by occasion, hide himself essentially: this abides –
> that the everlasting house the soul discovers
> is always another's; we must lose our own ends,

we must always live in the habitation of our lovers,
my friend's shelter for me, mine for him.
This is the day of this world in the day of that other's;
make yourselves friends by means of the riches of iniquity,
for the wealth of the self is the health of the self exchanged.
What saith Heraclitus? – and what is the City's breath? –
dying each other's life, living each other's death.
Money is a medium of exchange.'

It is no more possible to put technological advance back into Pandora's box than it is to return to the barter of goods for goods in order to rediscover the true meaning of a market economy. By examining the reasons why we fear and resist the mutual dependence and responsibility that should come so naturally, we may yet be able to restore the way of real exchange to our common life.

3. *No self-made men*

Another reason for our refusal of exchange is simple pride. In a small pamphlet which Charles Williams wrote in 1941 when he was very conscious of the realities of the war, he pointed out that most human beings in the highly individualized Western countries resent the truth that 'we are always in the condition that we are because of others'. We would prefer to see ourselves as self-made. Most of us have sense enough to make the effort to tolerate what others are doing to us, but few can make the effort to realize that others are having to tolerate us! After developing the theme of exchange to the point of a disturbing vision of mutual burden-bearing (as we shall see), Williams concluded:

> Our chief temptation is to limit its operation. We can believe it happily of ourselves as regards our lovers and our friends . . . We find it as an outrage that we should be intimately inter-related, physically and spiritually, to others who have offended our pride or our principles.[7]

This cherished self-sufficiency of ours makes it peculiarly hard for us to take the first step of the way of exchange by recognizing how much of ourselves we receive from other people – 'the everlasting house the soul discovers is always another's'. St Paul was patently indebted to

Greeks and non-Greeks, to both learned and simple folk, by virtue of his background and training, as his writings bear witness, and one likes to think that he was acknowledging this as well as declaring the obligation he felt to bring them the gospel when he said as much at the start of his letter to the church in Rome (Rom. 1.14). If so it can have been no easier for him than it is for most of us. For, as Williams said in his pamphlet:

> It is regarded as Christian to live 'for' others; it is not so often regarded as Christian doctrine that we live 'from' others – except certainly in rare experiences. There has been, everywhere, a doctrine of unselfishness, but that the self everywhere lives only within others has been less familiar.[8]

In the previous year Williams had presented this idea in an entertaining poem for *Time and Tide*. Every nuance in it illuminates Williams' perception of the doctrine so that it needs to be quoted in full. He called it *Apologue on the Parable of the Wedding Guest*.[9]

The Prince Immanual gave a ball:
cards, adequately sent to all
who by the smallest kind of claim
were known to royalty by name,
held, red on white, the neat, express
instruction printed: *Fancy Dress*.

Within Earth's town there chanced to be
a gentleman of quality,
whose table, delicately decked,
centred at times the Court's elect;
there Under-Secretaries dined,
Gold Sticks in waiting spoke their mind
or, through the smoke of their cigars,
discussed the taxes and the wars,
and ran administrations down;
but always blessed the triune Crown.

The ball drew near; the evening came.
Our lordling, conscious of his name,

retained particular distaste
for dressing up, and half-effaced,
by a subjective sleight of eye –
objectionable objectivity –
the card's direction. 'I long since
have been familiar with the Prince
at public meetings and bazaars,
and even ridden in his cars',
he thought; 'His Highness will excuse
a freedom, knowing that I use
always my motto to obey:
"Egomet semper: I alway".'

Neatly and shiningly achieved
in evening dress, his car received
his figure, masked, but otherwise
completely in his usual guise.
Behold thc Palace; and the Guest
approached the door among the rest.
The Great Hall opened; at his side
a voice breathed: 'Pardon, sir.' He spied,
half turned, a footman. 'Sir, your card –
dare I request? This door is barred
to all if not in fancy dress.'

'Nonsense.' 'Your card, sir!' 'I confess
I have not strictly . . . an old friend . . .
His Highness . . . Come, let me ascend.
My family has always been
in its own exquisite habit seen.
What, argue?' Dropping rays of light,
the footman uttered: 'Sir, tonight
is strictly kept as strictly given;
the fair equivalents of heaven
exhibit, at our Lord's desire,
their other selves, and all require
virtues and beauties not their own

ere genuflecting to the Throne.
Sir, by your leave.' 'But – ' 'Look and see!'

The footman's blazing livery
in half-withdrawal left the throng
clear to his eyes. He saw along
the Great Hall and the heavenly Stair
one blaze of glorious changes there,
cloaks, brooches, decorations, swords,
jewels – every virtue that affords
(by dispensation of the Throne)
beauty to wearers not their own.
This guest his brother's courage wore;
that, his wife's zeal, while, just before,
she in his steady patience shone;
there a young lover had put on
the fine integrity of sense
his mistress used; magnificence
a father borrowed from his son,
who was not there, ashamed to don
his father's wise economy.
No he or she was he or she
merely; no single being dared,
except the Angels of the Guard,
come without other kind of dress
than his poor life had to profess,
and yet those very robes were shown,
when from preserval as his own
into another's glory given,
bright ambiguities of heaven.
Below each change was manifest;
above, the Prince received each guest
smiling. Our lordling gazed; in vain
he at the footman glanced again.
He had his own; his own was all
but that permitted at the Ball.

The darkness creeping down the street
received his virtuous shining feet;
and, courteous as such beings are,
the Angels bowed him to his car.

4. The eclipse of God

Egotism is inherently lonely, and it is not good that man should be alone, not merely because we need company but because we need substance, the substance we can receive only as a gift from other people. Martin Buber maintained that the 'I' of our familiar 'I-It' experiences is not the same as the 'I' that responds to an 'I-You' relationship. The one is what we call our ego; the other 'I', and only the other, is a person. 'Egos appear', said Buber, 'by setting themselves apart from other egos. Persons appear by entering into relation to other persons.'[10] And he seriously proposed that that fact explains what he called 'the eclipse of God in the modern world'.

When humanity becomes stuck in the realm of 'I-It', and sees everything as an object, we can think of God only as another object, a super-object, maybe, but an object nonetheless which we can find, which we try to prove, which we want to use. But the living God can never be known as an object among the other objects I experience; and my ego, in its self-absorbed individualism, is not open or silent enough to know when God addresses himself to me. Only the 'I' that is a person relating to other persons is capable of becoming aware of God as the mystery, the Other, giving himself to me, saying 'You' to me, and enabling me to say 'You' to him. This was why Yahweh, as we saw in chapter 6, desired, as a response to his love, not the mystical devotion of individual saints, but the harmony of a whole community infused by the same quality of love for one another.

It is the almost universal loss of the sense of being in relationship with the otherness of other persons and answerable to them as part of one body, the almost total loss, in a word, of community, which renders our present society and nation so inimical to a sense of God, and so incapable of prayer. Restoring the realities of genuine relationship wherever and however that may be achieved is possibly the one valid form of evangelism left to us.

The world in which only the 'I-It' experience of reality is known offers two alternative anthropologies and the social structures corresponding to them, namely individualism and collectivism. Buber saw that both spring from the same root, the inward isolation of the human person who has lost the capacity for making any 'I-You' relationship with reality. He called this 'an existential constitution of solitude such as has probably never existed before to the same extent'. In a lecture he gave in Jerusalem in 1938, he showed that in modern individualism the human being actually affirms this position and glorifies his solitary state to save himself from the despair with which it threatens him. In collectivism he tries to escape his personal isolation by surrendering his small ego to the embrace of the whole, the general will. Each of these alternatives, said Buber, 'is a mighty abstraction. The individual is a fact of existence in so far as he steps into a living relation with other individuals. The aggregate is a fact of existence in so far as it is built up of living units of relation. The fundamental fact of human existence is *man with man*.'[11]

Without that the two illusory systems will more and more plague our world with the sickness of the one and the demons of the other. The tragedy of this moment of history lies in the fact that the catastrophic collapse of collectivism finds us with nothing to offer in its place but the grievous sickness of Western individualism. We have failed to discover, or even to look for, a third way.

Sickness and demons – it was for the healing of such a world that Jesus called to himself and to one another twelve men with much in common and much that differentiated them, and set about welding them into a communion, a community of mutual presence, and shared with them his authority to drive out unclean spirits and to cure every kind of sickness. And we, the church, are that same communion, that community of mutual presence, learning, if we will, to say 'You' to one another and to all others, and to give ourselves to one another in obedience to the law of mutual exchange. These are fine sounding words. But we are almost fatally disillusioned. We have heard them before, have been challenged before, we have been renewed before; but where has it got us after two thousand years? The wind is against us and Christ is not here. Yet it has always been in an hour of terror and despair, between three and six in the morning, that the Lord of potentiality, the God of hope, comes, precarious as ever, to ask, 'What shall we make of this? Where shall we go from here?'

Where shall we go? The answer must be, 'to one another'. Anything else, anything more 'religious', must lack concreteness if Buber's and Williams' diagnosis of our malaise is correct. The secret power of the Kingdom of Heaven starts to work when Peter and Matthew and John and Judas look into each other and know that they are all in the same boat, that they are all, in a sense, in one another. This is not the evasive fellowship of stirring hymns or study groups. It is something far more fundamental, yet more natural and ready to hand. It is what Buber called 'Presence' or again, 'man with man'.

> What is peculiarly characteristic of the human world is above all that something takes place between one being and another the like of which can be found nowhere in nature . . . It is rooted in one being turning to another as another, as this particular other being, in order to communicate with it in a sphere which is common to them but which reaches out beyond the special sphere of each. I call this sphere, which is established with the existence of man as man, but which is conceptually still uncomprehended, the sphere of 'between'. Though being realized in very different degrees, it is a primal category of human reality. This is where the genuine third alternative must begin.[12]

Though it is peculiarly applicable to humanity's present need at the start of this new millennium, this theme of exchange and co-inherence is not an innovation, and for all the originality of Buber's and Williams' separate explorations, each of them regarded his work as a re-statement of old truth. In his book on the figure of Beatrice in Dante's *Divine Comedy*, Charles Williams drew attention to the poet's daring syntax at that point in the ninth canto of the *Paradiso* where he encounters the soul of the ardent troubadour, Folco of Marseilles. To convey the interpenetration of two persons, Dante invented verbs formed upon personal pronouns, 'me', 'thee', 'him', just as we form verbs from nouns when we say we 'enrobe' or 'incase' or 'entrain' someone or something. In the poem Dante is aware that Folco knows what he is thinking, and says to him:

> 'Even as God sees all', said I, 'so in such wise,
> Beloved spirit, thy sight in-others itself, that things
> hidden deep in my heart lie open to thine eyes.'

and five lines later he continues:

> 'I would not have so long lingered for thy request
> Had I in-thee'd myself as thou in-meëst thyself.'[13]

Charles Williams comments on this verbal device:

> Something of this is known, on occasion, in the life of lovers; not, perhaps, in many; not, certainly, often. There is some kind of experience which can only be expressed by saying, 'Love you? I *am* you.' This is a natural thing, but then there is the moral duty. It is the moral duty of lovers, as they certainly at moments know, to plunge with love into each other's life – bringing power, power to resist temptation, to affirm, to purify, to pray. 'I will pray for you' is a good saying; a better – 'I will pray *in* you.'[14]

5. *Bearing one another's burdens*

That concept was explored more daringly, some would say fantastically, in Charles Williams' novels. In *Many Dimensions*, Chloe Burnett, the young secretary to the Chief Justice, rescues a man who has become trapped in the past by experiencing his utter desolation within herself. To Williams exchange always includes the possibility of vicarious substitution, since that also is part of the way things are in this world's interrelatedness. He enlarges on that theme in *Descent into Hell* and it is necessary to read the whole novel to appreciate how different aspects of it are explored in connection with nearly every character in the story. In this context two of them must suffice. A local theatrical company is rehearsing a new play in a small but historic country town where, three centuries earlier, a Protestant priest had been martyred. Little was known about him but the story went that, having lost his nerve and almost apostatized while awaiting execution, he had gone to his death with surprising courage. Pauline Anstruther, a young actress in the company that is rehearsing, is terrified of being alone out of doors because, since childhood, she has from time to time seen her double, her spectral Doppelganger, coming towards her down the street. So far she has avoided an actual confrontation, but these occurrences are becoming more frequent. At last she is persuaded to confide her terror to Peter Stanhope, the sensitive playwright. When he has heard it all he says to her:

> 'Listen. When you go from here, when you're alone, when you think you'll be afraid, let me put myself in your place, and be afraid instead of you . . . For what can be simpler than for you to think to yourself that, since I am there to be troubled instead of you, therefore you needn't be troubled . . . Haven't you heard it said that we ought to bear one another's burdens?' . . .
>
> 'And if I could,' she said, 'If I could do – whatever it is you mean, would I? Would I push my burden on to anybody else?'
>
> 'Not if you insist on making a universe for yourself,' he answered. 'If you want to disobey and refuse the laws that are common to us all, if you want to live in pride and division and anger, you can. But if you will be part of the best of us, and live and laugh and be ashamed with us, then you must be content to be helped. You must give your burden up to someone, and you must carry someone else's burden. I haven't made the universe and it isn't my fault. But I'm sure this is a law of the universe, and not to give up your parcel is as much to rebel as not to carry another's . . .'
>
> She stood up. 'I can't imagine not being afraid,' she said.
>
> 'But you will not be,' he answered, also rising, certainty in his voice, 'because you will leave all that to me. Will you please me by remembering that absolutely?'
>
> 'I am to remember,' she said, and almost broke into a little trembling laugh, 'that you are being worried and terrified instead of me?'
>
> 'That I have taken it all over,' he said, 'and there is nothing left for you.'[15]

Towards the end of the novel, when Pauline has been able to meet her spectral double, which is her true self, with no trace of the old fear, she learns through the experience that there is a new terror – new for her – which she is now strong enough to take voluntarily upon herself. Mysteriously there is laid upon her 'across the intervening centuries' the dark horror of the sixteenth-century martyr, thus enabling him to walk triumphantly to the stake.

Peter Stanhope in that novel is in many respects Christ-like, but Charles Williams did not intend him to stand as a symbol. He is a fallible human being and the thrust of the story is that such bearing of another's burden, such 'in-othering', is not only possible for ordinary people, it is a law of our existence in this universe, it is our God-given potential, though we generally ignore it and disbelieve and remain undeveloped. 'To refuse the Co-inherence', says Williams in his greatest theological work, 'is to separate oneself from the nature of things.'[16] In the pamphlet already mentioned he argues that the idea of bearing another's burden in such terms is a practical possibility.

> Compacts can be made for the taking over of the suffering of troubles, and worries and distresses, as simply and as effectually as an assent is given to the carrying of a parcel. A man can cease to worry about x because his friend has agreed to be worried by x . . . No doubt the first man may still have to deal directly with x; the point is that his friend may well relieve him of the extra burden.[17]

Williams recommended those who took him seriously to begin with small burdens such as sleeplessness, anxiety and slight pains. He said that to believe in such possibilities encourages humility and gives 'a faint insight' into 'loving from within', which is God's prerogative. And he added:

> We have to avoid portentousness, we have not to promise anything we cannot do. But perhaps there is very little that could not be done.[18]

Throughout this remarkable essay phrases from the New Testament resound with new profundity which, once heard, can never again be absent from their meaning. 'Members – limbs – one of another' becomes a more vivid image, and Williams himself claims that 'He saved others, himself he cannot save' is the definition of Christ's Kingdom, since it sums up the relation of each of its citizens to his fellows.

Co-inherence, exchange, 'in-othering' are, says Williams, 'a natural fact as well as a supernatural truth'.[19] It is the nature of things because it is the nature of God as Trinity, as Love: the Self-Giver, the Self-Given and the in-othered Spirit. Since this is the mystery of God's own being it has been also the means whereby God saves the world. The incarnation, or the Flesh-taking, as he preferred to call it, was an interpenetration of divine and human being. The atonement was the supreme substitution, God bearing the burden of his Other's self-destruction. The gift of the Holy Spirit is the mutual indwelling of disciples and Lord. Charles Williams propounded this in his major theological books, *He came down from Heaven* and *The Descent of the Dove*. He considered the words, 'Abide in my and I in you' to be the supreme expression of the doctrine of exchange, and he finds it exemplified in the story of the slave-girl martyred with her mistress under the edict of the emperor Severus in the year 203.

> Her name was Felicitas; she was Carthaginian; she lay in prison; there she bore a child. In her pain she screamed. The jailers asked her how, if she shrieked at *that*, she expected to endure death by the beasts. She said: 'Now *I* suffer what *I* suffer; then another will be in me who will suffer for me, as I shall suffer for him.'[20]

Williams' theology was built upon his recognizing in the cry of Felicitas the voice of the incomprehensible Alone, 'Another is in Me.'

6. *Towards a greater in-othering*

God's love for the world is an overflow of the eternal exchange within the Trinity. The response that God waits for from his creation must be in the form of a similar co-inherence. This is the climax of the prayer of Jesus in the Fourth Gospel: 'As you, Father, are in me and I in you, so also may they be in us . . . I in them and you in me' (John 17. 21, 22). And it is on the mundane earth of our relations with one another that we develop that openness to exchange which is the kind of love God gives and looks for. Our response to God cannot exist independently of our mutual response to one another. God has shown us the nature of the divine love through the in-othering of the incarnation: 'This is how he showed his love among us: he sent his only Son into the world that we might live through him. This is what love really is' – not the kind of love we have offered to God, but the love that is seen in the substitution of atonement – 'sent as a sacrifice to atone for our sins'. In-othering, then, must be the mode of our love for one another: 'If God *thus* loved us, my dear friends, we also must love one another.' For if we are refusing the mutuality of dependence and responsibility, the 'I-You' of giving and receiving, in our human intercourse, then we do not have it in us to make that kind of relationship with God. 'Whoever fails to love the fellow-being he has seen is incapable of loving the invisible God' (I John 4. 9–11, 20).

If these ideas of a more profound and intimate mutual dependence and mutual responsibility are to become more than playing with 'exciting' ideas like coloured balloons, they need to be embodied in actual behaviour. In his second cycle of Arthurian poems, Charles Williams included one which he called *The Founding of the Company* in which he describes a human community which, in varying degrees, recognized and practised the doctrine of exchange in the daily intercourse of living. At the simplest level people just affirmed more consciously the 'precious and remarkable' interlocking of their several callings and interests in the one community.

> . . . At the first station
> were those who lived by a frankness of honourable exchange,
> labour in the kingdom, devotion in the Church, the need
> each had of other.

What distinguishes the ethos of this society as imagined by Williams from the normal experience of life seems to be the shared awareness of what is taking place between each and all, and the joy in generosity which springs from it.

> . . . nay, servitude itself
> was sweetly fee'd and freed by the willing proffer
> of itself to another, the taking of another to itself
> in degree, the making of a mutual beauty in exchange,
> be this exchange dutiful or freely debonair.[21]

That does sound a little folksy in the style of William Morris, though with a stronger blend of theology infusing it. Charles Williams himself considered that it was the necessary context in which the next level of more intimate mutual responsibility comes to be regarded as natural and normal.

> The Company's second mode bore farther
> the labour and fruition; it exchanged the proper self,

and wherever need was drew breath daily
in another's place, according to the grace of the Spirit
'dying each other's life, living each other's death.'
Terrible and lovely is the substitution of souls
the Flesh-taking ordained for its mortal images
. . . since it deigned to be dead in the stead of each man.[22]

There Williams is once again describing the more mysterious possibilities of mutual dependence and burden-bearing which he portrayed in his novels and discussed in his pamphlet. The third level of exchange, which 'few – and that hardly – entered' from among the members of the Company in this poem, is attained by those who, like the Virgin Mary, are raised into such a sharing in the active love of God, 'bearing and being borne', that in them the original purpose of God for all humanity is realized. Achievement is entirely the wrong word for this since, paradoxically, the price – or is it reward? – of such oneness with God is the adoring acceptance of being superfluous to God, created and enfolded entirely out of love.

. . . the God-bearer
is the prime and sublime image of entire superfluity.[23]

The whole of this poem is a declaration of Williams' belief that human beings can and, for their salvation, must come to a conscious living out of this doctrine of exchange in mutual dependence and burden-bearing and that this calls for some deliberate planning. Rosemary Haughton, writing in 1980, believed that this was already beginning to take place as people, in many different ways and circumstances, had for some time been forming groups, communities or protest movements to reach after a more human future for our world. What she says is impressive because she was writing from within such experience and had thrown herself unreservedly into it.

'What is happening', she wrote, 'is world-wide, and it is growing as much in the secular as in the "religious" world, indeed, what Christians are doing is simply to live out more consciously the inner meaning of what is happening to many others.'[24] She had in mind the base communities of the very poor in Latin and Central America, the various experiments in communal living in North America, the anti-nuclear movement, and the house churches in Europe. She would no doubt have included under the same head organizations like Jean Vanier's L'Arche, the Carr-Gomm housing association for the victims of loneliness, the rapidly expanding house churches in China – in fact the proliferation is too wide and varied to be categorized.

> If they come to pray, as so many do even if they are not Christians and have no religious background at all, then the common experience of this adventure, the support they give each other, the discoveries they confide to each other, also deepen and widen the scope of their human awareness, first of each other and then of themselves as part of a greater whole, many of whose members suffer dumbly and remediably. So, often and often, just as the groups that have gathered for 'social action' end up praying, so the group that is gathered to pray ends up giving service to those in need.[25]

With a passionate optimism Rosemary Haughton said ten years ago, 'This is how the Church is happening now.' I wish I could believe that. I hesitate, not because many of those who make up the broad movement are shy of such commitment but because groups that are so open can easily fall prey to leaders that are over-committed to some crankiness or power-seeking of their own. Part of the house church movement has become a highly manipulative structure controlling its individual members, and the New Age movement is becoming a happy hunting ground for those who are more interested in grinding eccentric axes than exploring new paths.

The significance of this vast variety of experiment and dissatisfaction lies in the hunger that is being expressed. It is a hunger for human mutuality, for bearing one another's burdens, for what Buber called 'the sphere of between' which is our true home and the place of our meeting with God. All the obscure longing and abortive experimentation is pointing towards that goal and may be preparing the way for a break-through. In the meantime those who have been given glimpses of the way of exchange and are prepared to live in that openness and vulnerability towards others, depending and responding without fear, do recognize one another when their paths cross, no matter what religious or cultural labels they are wearing. The Company has been founded and can never be dissolved, though it is misleading to identify it with any group. Its members are trying to take seriously this basic law of all existence, the exchange and interflow of all things, and, without romanticizing what is a sober and arduous truth, to raise it to the fullest degree of willing awareness in themselves and in the way they live with others. Every opening of one's whole self towards some other, every taking upon oneself the burden and the gift of some other, contributes a little to that quiet tide which is flowing back and forth, carrying us with it into the very being of God, sweeping us back with him into the life of the world.

10

Whose I Am, Whom I Serve

Power and Prayer

1. Implications of an image

Belief in the Christlike God has wide-ranging implications for the believer's personal lifestyle and the style of society she or he thinks is worth striving for. Many assumptions, ideals and objectives are called in question if divine omnipotence is qualified by the divine will for freely given response and communion, if God's unchanging purpose, like that of a supreme chess player, is being achieved by precarious opportunism – Where do we go from here? – and if providence works not by external interventions but from within the interplay of created beings and the response of the human partner. The worshippers of a God who is essentially and eternally Self-Giver, Self-Given and In-othered are committed to much rigorous re-assessment and self-examination.

For example, this understanding of God touches upon our own exercise of power, and this is brought home to us with added force in our present situation of inter-faith contacts. In this world of pluralist societies in which the adherents of many faiths live together as neighbours and share responsibility for the future of the planet, it is a matter of enormous importance that believers of all kinds should speak to one another across the religious divides as people who know that what they have in common is their sense of the reality of God. This wider ecumenism means that we no longer meet as people who consider other faiths than their own to be wholly wrong, but as God-fearers who would like to share with one another those insights of their own religion which seem to them most precious and universally significant. To say 'Jesus

Christ is divine' is in that context a take-it-or-leave-it statement which, at best, invites the response, 'So you believe'; whereas to say 'Whatever else God is, I believe he is Christlike,' is to suggest something of immense import yet not patently unacceptable to followers of other faiths, something which does at least invite the question, 'What do you mean by Christlike?' More importantly it is a statement that stands or falls according to the lifestyle of the speaker and the community she or he represents. The Mahatma Gandhi could have said it and carried conviction. The Persian poet Hafiz almost said as much. Many of the saints and multitudes of humble unnamed servants of God have demonstrated it. But crusaders, inquisitors and conquistadors of all periods, who no doubt proclaimed Jesus as divine, could not have brought one soul to believe in the Christlike God, neither will those whose image in the eyes of the world today is one of economic and political domination. In this day of pluralism the witness of one faith to another is more than ever before dependent upon the lives of the witnesses. 'By their fruits shall ye know them.'

St Paul could convince his hearers at Corinth that the folly of God was wiser than human wisdom, that the weakness of God was stronger than human strength, and that Christ nailed to the cross was the world's salvation, because he had himself come among them in weakness, fear and trepidation with no pretension of eloquence or wisdom. If the gospel is ever to redeem humanity from its obsession with militarism and domination by showing that Jesus' voluntary surrender of himself into hostile hands, his rejection, suffering and degrading death actually challenges all previous ideas of God and God's relation to the world, the church will have to reflect this truer image of God in a more distinctive lifestyle and a clearer grasp of the nature of power.

Quite apart from all such deliberate changes as the church or the individual believer may make in obedience to the vision of the Christlike God, the simple act of holding to that vision is likely, sooner or later, to influence thought outside the religious sphere. David Nicholls who is both theologian and historian of political economy has written about the respective images or analogies of religion and politics.

> God's rule in the universe is often seen as a model for the government's function in the economy, and economic institutions and assumptions in turn influence human images of God.[1]

It is not always clear whether the one is determining the other or whether both are willy nilly marching to the tune of the *Zeitgeist*. From the late nineteenth century onwards liberal theology made much use of the image of God as a patriarchal father actively involved in providing for the wellbeing and security of his children, and this went hand in hand with an image of an autocratic state benignly pursuing a highly interventionist policy of state welfare. The 'enterprise culture' pioneered in Britain by Margaret Thatcher in opposition to the proliferation of state-sponsored welfare has also had its theological counterpart in a strong reaction against the God of special interventions and direct experience in favour of a more austere concept of divine transcendence and ultimate mystery. The Tories of the 1980s may not have been much aware of this contemporary parallel but were consciously repeating a reaction of exactly the same kind that took place two centuries before. Adam Smith, followed by Thomas Chalmers and Robert Malthus, rejected the paternalism of the poor laws and state bounties and revolutionized the economic theory. Drawing upon the rational naturalism of some of the leading thinkers in the Established Church, they visualized God as an infinitely far-seeing Contriver of the universe who had set it up in such a way that each creature in it, by pursuing its own ends, contributed to the integration of a harmonious whole. Divine intervention was scarcely needed. From this model they concluded that the state also should limit its role to guidance and regulation, without attempting to curb individual self-interest or soften the consequences of individual failure.

There is no reason to be either dismayed or elated by such parallels since a close similarity of images need not imply an all round concurrence of ideas. Nicholls has pointed out that the English Puritans used the image of God as the supreme monarch over all to refute the use James I made of it to support his own divine right, just as Karl Barth's dismissal of natural theology and his stress on God's absolute sovereignty was intended not to provide support but to condemn the German state's rejection of natural law and Hitler's totalitarian claims. Moreover history shows that as often as politics and religion have spoken the same language in response to the spirit of the age, some dissenting religious voice has been raised in protest. Such were the Evangelicals who believed in God's interventions and campaigned for state action in social affairs just when Adam Smith's *Wealth of Nations* was having its greatest effect.

Affirming and challenging the *Zeitgeist* at the same time is, in fact, the proper stance for true religion. This issue became central for Dietrich Bonhoeffer. He was acutely aware of the tension between being fully immersed in the world and its dynamics while deriving one's ways of seeing and judging from another point of reference altogether. He saw this tension as the necessary corollary of God's reconciliation of the world to himself. For that reason a responsible follower of Christ should not strive to extricate his thoughts and actions from the pressures of the spirit of the age or to avoid images of God merely because they are common currency.

> The responsible man does not have to impose upon reality a law which is alien to it, but his action is in the true sense 'in accordance with reality'.[2]

The spirit of the age is an expression of the vitality of the given moment, growing by development from, and reaction against, the immediate past. It is the mainstream of a people's thought, and those who would challenge it can do so only from within it. Where there is no correspondence there is no communication. So Bonhoeffer proceeds, referring to the world's reality as 'the factual':

> The true meaning of correspondence with reality lies neither in this servility towards the factual nor yet in a principle of opposition to the factual, a principle of revolt against the factual in the name of some higher reality. Both extremes alike are very far removed from the essence of the matter. In action which is genuinely in accordance with reality there is an indissoluble link between the acknowledgment and the contradiction of the factual.[3]

2. *Power on trial*

In the dilemma we are considering with regard to power the tension between what Bonhoeffer called the 'acknowledgment and the contradiction of the factual' must be sustained. Acknowledgment means that the responsible Christian community accepts the realities of power: power is necessary at all levels, but by definition it entails coercion and inequality; it tends to become self-perpetuating and to corrupt; and it can be corrected only by counterbalancing power. The responsible Christian community embraces the necessity of working within that structure. But acknowledgment must be given in harness with contradiction, which means, for example, withstanding the pretensions and self-interest of power, the close hoarding of power and the false hope that power's corruption may be contained and sterilized by being channelled into boards and councils.

All decisions in the real world are provisional and have to be taken in the light of particular circumstance. That is why Jesus sometimes seemed to renounce power and yet at certain moments staged a forceful demonstration. Consistency lies *below* the surface. So Bonhoeffer characteristically adds:

> Action which is in accordance with Christ is in accordance with reality because it allows the world to be the world; it reckons with the world as the world; and yet it never forgets that in Jesus Christ the world is loved, condemned and reconciled by God. This does not mean that a 'secular principle' and a 'Christian principle' are set up in opposition to one another. On the contrary . . . any such attempt to provide a theoretical basis for Christian action in the world leads . . . to the ruin and destruction of the world which in Christ is reconciled with God.[+]

Making ethical decisions in response to particular situations rather than by rule of thumb is not an easy option but in practice is far more exacting because the mental and moral struggle has to be undergone afresh on each occasion. We are given a profound insight into just such a struggle, undergone in the light of an intimate understanding of God's use of power, in the story of Christ's temptation in the wilderness.

The *context* of that withdrawal into the desert was political, the mounting hostility towards John the Baptist which was soon to culminate in his arrest. The *content* of the spiritual struggle which took place there was the right use of power.

Politics is the arena of the struggle of power against power, the 'angels' and the 'wild beasts', which is going on all around us at every level of society. Out of the struggle emerges government which is the arbiter between the conflicting interests, setting bounds and balances. By participating in the politics of daily life, as we all do, each of us is contributing to his own or someone else's power. Even our passivity or our surrender is an act of collusion with someone else's power. Power is not a function limited to the obvious possessors of wealth or authority, control or status, 'the captains and the kings'. Every parent, every teacher, every ticket collector on the railways, every hospital nurse, janitor, or post office clerk, the strongest boy on the playground or the cutest girl in the class, has an element of power. Every committee and board and pressure group is dealing with power and asserting it in various ways. Somewhere down the line, even in the most small-scale sphere of work team or family unit, everyone is bringing some degree of power to bear on others, playing the power game to some degree.

And power, unless there is an antidote, corrupts. It corrupts by distorting people's perception, especially one's perception of oneself, by confusing people's motives, by creating irresistible pressures and paralysing fears of the loss of power. The exercise of power, on whatever scale, by anyone who has become corrupted, confused and distorted by it, adds one more stone to the structure of alienation, unreality and violence that despoils God's world.

The antidote to power's corruption is not abdication but prayer. That is not as pietistic as it sounds. For prayer is not asking God to get things done in the way we think best: that amounts merely to another trick in the power game. Nor is true prayer a petition for special guidance, which can often be a form of one-upmanship. And prayer most certainly does not consist of 'worrying on my knees' which usually only makes me more confused. To pray is to place oneself in the silent presence of the Eternal Beyond, the God of Truth and Love, and letting the flow of communication between that and one's truest self clarify the distorted vision, purify the motives, countervail the pressures and set one free from dependence upon any other power except the care for others which holds on, trusting, hoping and enduring, until in the long term it wins through.

During the interior conflict of his forty days' withdrawal Jesus contemplated three kinds of power: the power of the provider – 'Tell these stones to become bread'; the power of the possessor – 'I will give you all the kingdoms of the world'; and the power of the performer – 'Throw yourself down from the parapet of the temple.'

The power of the provider. But is this not our heavenly Father's power? Indeed it is, and Jesus exercised it when he fed the multitudes and healed the sick. It is the power of the welfare state, the power of international aid. It is the power of every responsible mother and father, like the parent in the parable of the prodigal son: 'All that I have is yours.' But this can all too easily slide into, 'They who provide know what's best for you,' or 'I'll cook the meals you like, but not for friends of that sort,' or 'You can have a loan but not if you are getting technicians from China.' The acid test of our sincerity in offering resources of renewal to our deprived inner-city areas lies in whether the people who actually live there are encouraged to decide what their community most needs and are given responsibility in managing the new developments. The answer Jesus gave to the corruption inherent in the power of the provider was, 'Man cannot live on bread alone, he needs all the words that God addresses to him,' including what his heart tells him about his own potential humanity. So when Jesus Christ set about feeding the helpless crowd of poor folk, he turned to those about him saying, 'Give them something to eat yourselves. How many loaves have you got? Go and see.' What mattered to him was not the self-esteem of the provider but the self-respect of those provided for. In Jean Anouilh's dialogue for the film about St Vincent de Paul, the saint says to one of his helpers, 'The more unattractive and dirty they are, the more rude and unfair they are, the more you must lavish your love upon them. It is only by feeling your love that the poor will forgive you for your gifts of bread.'

The power of the possessor. Ownership is not wrong, nor proprietorship, nor sovereignty, nor the rights and powers that these confer. Jesus loved his land and his national heritage, nor was he unaware of some mysterious sovereignty which was his, which the church has been trying to define satisfactorily ever since. The stories that he told show that he could understand the satisfaction of having enough to be able to give it away with extravagant generosity. 'I choose to give the workers I hired most recently the same as you. Surely I am free to do what I want with my own money.' Possession can be good.

But just below the surface of every instinct of possession lurks the predator. It is no accident that the word 'possessive' denotes a devouring grasp of other people, or that many of the sufferers that were brought to Jesus were 'possessed' by the devil. The devil, we read, had led him up to some mountain top and shown him in imagination all the kingdoms of the world in a moment of time. To see the world as one whole, to take what we call a global view and know truly how we relate to it, is a Godlike grace. But when the devil gives us a global view it is not as a beloved responsibility for which one might lay down one's life, but as a glittering prize to be captured. An advertisement in a colour supplement many years ago showed a globe constructed of packing cases stamped with the trade name of an air freight company, over the caption 'Now the world is ours.' The supreme military and financial strength of one nation, or the ubiquitous influence of a multinational commercial empire, or the absolute power of decision enjoyed by the banking community, does almost inevitably convince its possessors that they also have a superior wisdom and a more trustworthy stature than the rest of the human race.

Here is the source of power's corruption. It tempts us to play God towards other people – parents towards children, politicians towards their electorate, the great powers towards the destinies of smaller states, as though the world is our chessboard. At any level we human creatures can exercise the power of possessors without becoming predators only so long as we genuinely acknowledge God as the true owner and ourselves, at most, his stewards. 'You shall worship the Lord your God, and him only you shall serve.'

The power of the performer. Many who serve God and humanity well, individuals in whom others put their trust and from whom they draw strength, are essentially performers. Their greatest gift is a kind of stagecraft and they know how to communicate and persuade. This does not make them hypocrites: Dr Billy Graham is no phoney, nor Brother Roger of Taizé, nor was Churchill nor Gandhi. But in each case their power was the power of the performer. Every good teacher and many a GP is gifted with it. The performer is always to some degree a miracle-man, eliciting faith.

Jesus certainly had this power too. His parables are masterly performances. So were his improvisations under pressure, like that play with the coin: 'Whose portrait is this?' You almost expect it to vanish up his sleeve! So why not some dramatic display like the one which suggested itself to him during the prolonged inner conflict in the desert, 'Throw yourself off that pinnacle of the temple and into the angels' arms.' That was in line with the miraculous signs that other would-be messiahs were promising in those days. I cannot believe that anyone as naturally sensitive as Jesus could have entertained the idea for more than a moment, but I do know how subtly corrupting the power of the performer can be. The more one loves the truth, the more one longs to convince others of it; and the more one longs to persuade, the more one hopes they will love the persuader.

> The last temptation is the greatest treason:
> To do the right deed for the wrong reason.

Those who know in themselves that they have something of the performer in them and who want to escape the corruption of its power would do well to consider again that performance by which Jesus most wanted to be remembered. It was, you might say, a private showing before a select audience of twelve of what was going to be a very public performance on the next day. We readily recall how it went. 'This is my body which is for you. This is my blood shed for the many.' Here was the secret of his uncorrupted power. Here was the demonstration of God's kind of power which he had learnt to understand through prayer, through long communion with his Father. He did not abdicate the power of the provider but it was used always for others. 'My body which is for you' – neither profit nor credit sought for himself; not a single miracle or angel invoked for his own protection. Here was a provider who, like God, met human need by giving himself with no strings or conditions, though he knew there was a traitor among them. Here was a possessor who enjoyed his power to give away all that he had, a god-king who must die for his people as the pagan myths had foretold: 'My blood which is shed for the many.' Here was a performer divinely innocent of self-concern who in one unforgettable demonstration did indeed throw himself down as a challenge to the world's values and to every distorted and devouring power, and presented to the eyes of all humanity the helpless yet invincible endurance of God's truth and love. 'Thanks be to God,' we say, but that is not enough. We have our own small exercise of power, as providers, or possessors, or performers, to bring into line with his, lest we add to the corruption and the despair in the world.

3. *Doves or serpents*

So, out of his understanding of the nature of God's power, Jesus challenged and rejected the common assumptions about power. 'Among the nations, kings lord it over their subjects; and those in authority are given the title "Benefactor". Not so with you; on the contrary, the greatest among you must bear himself like the youngest, the one who rules like one who serves . . . I am among you like a servant.' Apply that to family relationships and business management as well as the strategies of great powers and you will feel the force of the challenge.

How then are the followers of Jesus Christ to respond to this topsy-turvy reversal? That is the moot question, and it is crucial for our proper understanding of the way our knowledge of God should shape our ethical decisions.

In this matter of power there are those who conclude that the stark contradiction that Jesus set up constitutes a call to think and live in the terms of ultimate eternal realities regardless of whether this seems to 'work' in the world as it is or not. They do this primarily out of obedience to the way of the cross, which is God's way, but also as a witness against the way of the world. They abandon, as they think, all reliance on the forms of power that belong to the world, which they recognize as inherently violent, and are content to await God's eventual vindication of his way by bringing the world's power structures to an end. Theirs is the radical theology of Psalm 73 whose writer was unnerved by the seeming success of the powerful oppressors.

> Had I thought to speak as they do, I should have been false to your people. I set my mind to understand this but I found it too hard for me, until I went into God's sanctuary, where I saw clearly what their destiny would be. Indeed you place them on slippery ground and drive them headlong into utter ruin.

The Christian 'Tolstoys', if I may call them that, would not echo that note of satisfaction at the eventual downfall of the powerful, but their principle of withdrawal from the arena is the same.

At the opposite end of the scale are those Christian activists who make use of the way of the cross precisely because it does work. In their moments of theological reflection they may perceive that this is so because the structure of the world images the nature of its Creator, just as it does in the constant to-and-fro of interdependence and exchange. But 'the strength of weakness' is for them a fact of the real world that can be turned to good account as a matter of tactics. Management skills include the recognition that power-sharing and open lines of communication generate a more responsible participation among the workforce, and a low profile in top management diminishes hostility. Liberation movements have learnt to make the most of the fact that the poor have nothing to lose and so take greater risks, that it is harder to break a strike of underpaid labour, that people with no future can afford to wait and are not afraid of death. They have learnt also that when the oppressed resort to violence it actually justifies the oppressors in the eyes of the world whereas, if they maintain a non-violent resistance, it gives the oppressor a bad press if not a bad conscience. Canon W. H. Vanstone's two classics, *Love's Endeavour, Love's Expense* and *The Stature of Waiting*, have shown from many human analogies how weakness may be power in the 'real' world. So it is not difficult for Christians with an understanding of social processes to put the pattern of cross and resurrection to use for its this-worldly effectiveness.

To quote 'The weakness of God is stronger than men' or 'When I am weak, then I am strong' is ambiguous, and one should always ask: 'Are you saying that as a statement of faith in the things that are ultimate and unseen, or as a surprising but none the less verifiable fact in a worldly sense? Which kind of language are you using?' Does the way of the cross, the way of God's kind of power, stand in total contradiction to the life of this age, or can it be shown to be the true pattern of this world precisely because it *is* God's world, reconciled through Christ, as Bonhoeffer claimed?

There will be times when Christian faithfulness will demand conformity with the way of the cross from no other consideration but that it is true to the nature of God. J. H. Yoder, who in 1985 prepared the prospectus of a study project on Power and Powerlessness for the World Council of Churches, epitomized this attitude very beautifully in these words.

> Taking up the cross is for us to decide, but the time and mode of the Resurrection are not. One can sight down the line of the rifle to see the enemy it can kill, but one can not sight down the line of an act of enemy-love to predict its salvific fruits. We do not 'hold fast' to the cross because of the promise that we shall win in the end. That would be to translate triumphalism through the protestant virtue of delayed gratification.[5]

On the other hand there are many situations already, and will be more in the future as the causal connections between weakness and effectiveness become better understood, when Christians should pursue the apparent absurdity of weakness because they can see why it actually works. God is no less present and active in the explicable processes than in the unexplained.

> If we can see why 'love works' why should we then not use that knowledge, let it guide us in co-operating with Providence. Trusting Providence blindly is fine when one cannot see anyway . . . But where we have knowledge and our strength permits, let us use it.[6]

That is what Bonhoeffer meant by allowing the world to be the world and living the way of Christ within the reality of the world. It is far more ambivalent and puzzling than holding the two realities, temporal and eternal, apart and distinct. If 'love works' the predators and providers will quickly learn to manipulate its processes. Bismarck gave the masses national insurance and state pensions because he recognized that their greater financial dependence upon the government would deter them from revolution.[7] In the last resort altruism is proved only by sacrifice, yet the intention of altruism is not to be proved but to be of benefit.

Our God of unceasing opportunism whose word has always been 'What shall we make of this?' furnished humanity with no immutable principles. The God who knows no generalities but knows every particularity from within does not commit his people to pacifism or class-struggle or even non-violence, though from time to time they may feel that faithfulness to him in the face of a particular form of evil calls for some such bond of unity. We can never substitute a principle for a living and growing knowledge of God in Jesus Christ within the fellowship of the church. By making that the focus of our thought and responding to it by faith in each developing situation we shall avoid a merely arbitrary expedience.

4. *Practical antidotes to corruption*

We have recognized that the God and Father of our Lord Jesus Christ is the God who lets all things be, not in the sense of *laissez-faire*, but by giving them their own autonomous being in a relationship of mutuality. The outflow of his letting-be may be expressed in the words 'that they may have life and have it more abundantly'. Those who set that Lord ever before them within the realities of this world will, without erecting a principle, tend always in their exercise of power, whether in their families or their management of a sphere of work or their political actions, to create space for others to exercise their gifts and realize their potential. Instead of trying to control the process by controlling the people, either in a household or work-sphere or nation, they will be enabling everyone right down the line to deal responsibly with the process, taking initiatives, taking risks and learning by their mistakes. It is in this way above all that leadership becomes service. Christian service should never mean doing everything for the helpless so as to render them dependent. This, surely, is why Jesus, when healing the sick, so often called their action into play: 'Stretch out your shrivelled arm.' 'Get up and carry your bed home.' 'Your faith has done it.'

Liberation theology has grasped the truth rooted in the nature of God, that the deliverance of oppressed and powerless people consists, essentially, not in the overthrow of the tyrants so much as in the inspiriting and quickening of the downtrodden until they can say, 'Change lies in our hands.' But the same insight, rooted in the nature of God, points to the fact that, as the old structures are shaken and some among the powerful recognize the dawning of a new day, they too should be given space to share responsibly in the process and say, 'Change lies in your hands and ours, together.' This also follows from the vision of the God who lets be, freely giving to all the capacity for relationship with others and with himself.

To say that is not to ignore the fact that power entails coercion; this is one of the realities of the world we must reckon with. At every level, whether in the family or the school, in the sphere of employment or of society or of international affairs, the exercise of power may include compulsion, which means over-powering. Jesus Christ used such language to describe his victories over evil spirits, the stronger who binds the strong; but that scarcely helps us in our treatment of fellow human beings. Jesus used physical coercion in his demonstration against the commercial traffic of the Temple, yet few of us would take that as a model for our reaction to cathedral bookshops. His triumphal entry into Jerusalem contrasted strangely with his general avoidance of political action and was certainly coercive in that he judged that the hour had come to force the leaders of his nation to come to a decision regarding himself. Christians can find in this no clear and specific models to guide their own use of coercion and must rely on the inner leaning or mind-set that is formed in them from their reflection upon the nature of the Christlike God.

Precisely because power may entail coercion it tempts and corrupts those who hold it exclusively, either as individuals or as a bureaucratic group. The locus of power has to be thrown open, first by an exposure of all human authority's inherent fallibility, and then by distributing the power more widely.

The Gospels provide an example of countering the pretensions of authority in their narratives of St Peter's special commission. St Matthew records those words of Jesus which are set around the drum under the great dome inside St Peter's basilica at Rome, in black letters nine feet high on a gold ground: 'Thou art Peter and upon this rock I will build my church and the gates of hell shall not prevail against it.' Hans Küng has suggested that in gold letters on a black ground just below that inscription should be set the next words that Jesus spoke to St Peter: 'Get thee behind me, Satan, for thou mindest not the things of God but the things of men.' St Luke tells also how after the Last Supper St Peter was singled out on the way to Gethsemane with the words, 'Simon, Simon, Satan asked to have you all, but I have prayed for thee that thy faith fail not, and when once thou hast turned again, do thou stablish thy brethren.' This was a further repetition of his commission and was followed at once by the warning, 'I tell thee, Peter, the cock shall not crow this day before thou shalt thrice deny that thou knowest me.' Again St John, reporting the charge given to St Peter by the risen Lord to feed his sheep, says that no sooner had the great apostle begun to exercise that special care with regard to a fellow disciple than he was warned, 'What is that to thee; follow thou *me*.' Authority needs such harsh but salutary reminders, and the church is sometimes called to be the Fool, the court jester, who, because he can always be treated as a joke, and sometimes whipped, is often the only one who dare tell the king the truth.

The corrupting effect of power can also be offset when it is distributed as widely as possible. This need not mean a proliferation of petty officials and local cadres, each closed circle hoarding its own tyranny. That has been the flaw in all so-called people's republics. What is required is the deliberate opening of the circle of power so as to enable as many people as possible at all levels of the system to exercise responsible creativity and initiative. Whatever their past failures, local authorities are vital, and need to be reformed, not diminished. Rather than being funded from the centre they should be empowered to raise much of their required revenue locally in order to become more answerable. The sharing and dispersal of power at all levels is a true and significant reflection of the God who opens himself out and gives himself for the sake of a mutual exchange with his Other.

It is easy to recall the occasions on which Jesus employed a coercive power. But it is surely significant that what we see most often in his relationships is not coercion but confrontation. In the parables he told so skilfully, in the questions he threw out so disconcertingly, and above all in his actions, he challenged the assumptions and habits of the status quo. In that way, to take up Bonhoeffer's word, he 'loved, condemned and reconciled' the world in his Father's name. And this must still be the role of Christians who, living in accordance with the realities of the world, both acknowledge and contradict them. They point to an alternative way so that even those who refuse it can never afterwards say with the same conviction that they had no other choice. They pose the problem in a different light so that the impregnable axioms no longer seem as certain or self-evident. They set up visible signs of a future which continue to haunt even those who reject them as unrealistic. In this way their judgment and condemnation is always at the same time a standing invitation, like God's, like that of Jesus. And many of them will suffer crucifixion at the hands of a world that finds itself redemptively undermined.

I have already said, however, that the most reliable antidote to the corruption inherent in all forms of power is prayer – the communion with God which Jesus Christ relied upon when he went into the desert to ponder his vocation and clarify the issues. Because an obedient response to God in the complex affairs of this world raises so many ambiguous questions, some renewal of the sense of God's presence, God's stillness, becomes absolutely necessary.

5. *The God to whom we pray*

What we make of prayer, however, or what prayer makes of us, does depend upon the truth or untruth of the image of God that we have in mind. 'They that make them shall be like unto them,' says the psalmist about the idols of the great powers, and Jesus in gentler, more personal vein said to the Samaritan women, 'You worship you know not what; we know whom we worship.' If we wish to discern truth from falsehood in the world's values and assumptions we need to escape from the popular images of God himself.

As a corrective to the almost irresistible habit of 'placing' and personifying God it is liberating to dwell sometimes upon a totally amorphous image for one's meditation and prayer. The Bible itself offers the thought of air, wind, breath, spirit. 'Come from the four winds, O breath, and breathe upon these slain that they may live.' Ubiquitous, invisible, usually silent and unnoticed, air envelopes the whole globe. It enfolds each living thing on earth's surface and in the sky, and without it, around them and within them, they could not live. It is so yielding the tiniest bird or gnat can pass through it yet without its support they could not fly. It is air alone that enables me to speak or sing. Entering me on every breath, it refreshes and renews my being, and, exhaled, it takes with it my stale impurities, so that breathing itself is a continuous absolution. Yet, like its match, the ocean waters, this gentle, life-giving air can be gathered to such force as will cut swathes through the forest or flatten a home. When thinking of God it is quite often a good exercise to let go that near-human presence which is quite legitimately dear to the mind and to dwell instead on these images of air, one by one, saying in wondering gratitude: Such is God. Such is the faithfulness, patience, humility of God, and the utter mystery. Such is the eternal love.

Another such image with important overtones, to which reference was made in chapter 7, is that of a river's source. With a memory of the garden of Eden and its spring which became the head-waters of four great rivers, the Book of Revelation ends with the river of the water of life, the source of which is the throne of God and of the Lamb, flowing through the city of God. What the old translations of Psalm 65 called 'the river of God' is actually an irrigation runnel, a *peleg*, such as traditional farmers throughout the Middle East still maintain to bring water to their plantations. The psalm calls it godlike because it gives life, yet when the water is needed at a different point in the field the farmer uses his foot to divert the flow into another channel in the network (Deut. 11.10; Prov. 21.1). It is an image that speaks of the assailable nature of that which is life-giving. The river-source is a mere dribble, easily diverted but never ultimately stemmed. Because it trickles ceaselessly, inexhaustibly, it will always gather strength to break through any blockage and find some way round every obstacle. It seems infinitely resourceful and adaptable. I have seen the rivulets of melted ice dripping from the snout of a glacier in Switzerland so slowly that it would take a minute or more to draw a cupful, and I have been taken into the heart of a mountain lower down to see the stream from that same glacier plunging through a smoothly rounded tunnel with all the force of a turbine. Through the millennia the water has seeped through the tiny flaws and fissures in the rock face, building up its pressure until it gouged out this subterranean course to emerge quietly into the valley below, a broad, tree-lined river. Yet all the time its source is the same slow dripping from that, and other glaciers. Its weakness is real, not merely apparent. It has no force except persistence. This also is a picture of the God whose being is self-giving love.

A third figure of the true omnipotence is the couch grass and stubborn weed that prises open the thick concrete of a disused runway or an unkempt street. That anarchic weakness is a fine symbol of the God of all hope at a time when the wilderness has more life in it than a civilization in terminal decline. But better even than finding new images, which are open to the imputation of 'trendiness', would be a more meticulous reading of the parables that Jesus told than they have generally been given. It is far from certain that he intended his hearers to assume that the farmer, the shepherd, the host at the supper were images of God, but since the church has done so from the beginning we should at least re-tell the stories as they stand.

The shepherd, for example, in Matthew's version of the parable which is probably closer to the original, is much less certain of finding the sheep than the loving shepherd in the reassuring children's hymn. What is certain is the peculiar value given to anything that is lost and the consequent anxiety of the search. *If* he finds it, said Jesus, there will be a correspondingly peculiar happiness. To be true to the heart of the story, the image of God we should draw from it would be that of a person searching far and wide.

Likewise the father of the prodigal son is skilfully kept off the scene for the greater part of the time covered by the story, although he is clearly the character around whom the parable revolves. During the younger son's rake's progress we are not told what the father was doing until it is suddenly disclosed by inference in the revealing short sentence: 'While he was still a long way off his father saw him.' The rest is all rejoicing. If the true picture of the shepherd is of a man searching, that of the father is of a man waiting: the parable ends with him waiting again for the elder son's response.

The farm owner waits while the wheat and the tares compete in his fields until harvest time. The vineyard owner, as in the sad song of Isaiah 5, looks in vain for produce as first his servants and then his son are done to death. The host who gives the great supper suffers the discourtesies of those originally invited and hastens to fill the empty places with all and sundry. The forgiving king suffers the loss of an enormous bad debt. The father of the two sons gets a hurtful response from both of them in one way or the other. Each one of these figures of God, if that is what we take them to be, is at the receiving end of some wrong yet is never diminished nor defeated. That is the Christlike God, and we should correct our conventional images accordingly for it is he alone whom we should adore and seek to resemble in the terms of this world's relationships. If God's omnipotence is qualified by God's nature and God's faithfulness to his purpose of love, our exercise of power needs to be re-examined and transformed.

When we pray, then, we are in the presence of a God whose hands are tied by love for us and the world, a God who believes it is worth waiting for that response which fulfils the divine will for communion with his Other. To make our recognition of this concrete the truest image we can have in mind of the God to whom we pray is that of the crucified Jesus. That must make a difference to our prayers. It is bound to inhibit us from making many of the petitions we might have put to the former image of omnipotence, but it will certainly bring us closer to knowing the Father to whom Jesus prayed. Before that silent endurance it becomes almost unthinkable to ask 'What is the use of praying?' The only valid responses are the silence of wonder and incomprehension, an inarticulate penitence, gratitude and love, and a longing to assist the assuagement of such a passionate thirst.

Yet we are bidden to make known our requests. What action is open to such a God as this? There are five blessings he can and does give to those who offer him the opening of self, the opening of the hands, which is prayer.

First, that mutual response which flows between him and the one who prays, which we call the Holy Spirit, bestows the insight, the recognition and greater understanding of the event or the persons that are the focus of that prayer. The in-othered God enables the one who prays to grasp a little more of the inwardness of the other, not so much through conscious analysis as by intuition. Seeing the situation in a new light is his gift.

Second, inasmuch as the suppliant remains receptive and responsible, this God can give the inner resources of steadiness, courage, endurance, creativity, vitality and joy to meet the demand, the set-back, the tragedy, and to stay where the pain is with something of the divine faithfulness. This is the peace that is beyond understanding, the power to cope, of which St Paul speaks, and it is the most truly supernatural experience most of us will ever know.

Third, God does release within those who are open to his presence powers of self-healing, renewal, wholeness which are implanted in every person but so often inhibited and unrealized. They may not result in 'getting better' as we understand it; they will certainly enable 'getting by'.

The fourth gift, if the one who prays will only receive it, is the strength of God's own longsuffering to absorb whatever evil there is in the situation. This is actually the outworking of that principle of exchange which flows from the mutual love of the Blessed Trinity – 'another will be in me'. It 'works' in various ways. If I have been wronged, if there is hurt and estrangement, the gift that I receive in prayer enables me to take it upon myself instead of throwing it back on another, and thereby to transmute it into a strange goodness. This is the blessing of reconciliation. But the same gift of God's endurance may enable me to take another's fear or suffering upon myself, bearing some of the burden through the same principle of substitution.

The fifth outcome of the practice of prayer arises out of the rest. It is God's invitation to the inconceivable honour of sharing some infinitely small part of his burden of waiting, travail and sorrow. It is greatly to be dreaded since it may take the form of a sense of abandonment and the total absence of God, yet it is a sign of love to those who are called to experience it. Bonhoeffer spoke of it in his well-known poem.

> Men go to God when he is sore bestead,
> Find him poor and scorned, without shelter or bread,

> Whelmed under weight of the wicked, the weak, the dead;
> Christians stand by God in his hour of grieving.[8]

6. *Study to be quiet*

The true meaning of prayer, though, is the communion, the mutual delight and exchange of love which is the purpose of God's creation of that which is not God to be his 'other'. To speak of 'the use of praying' is as wide of the mark as explaining the use of loving. What we most need to clarify our perceptions and give us standards of true measurement in the ambiguities of human life is to be present to the presence of God as Moses was when, on the people's behalf, he went alone into the tent of Meeting. Prayer and the search for silence is not nostalgia; the practice of prayer has to do with today. Prayer is a way of living in this world in the last decade of the twentieth century. Prayer is a way of affecting what will happen in the next century. Prayer is protest, silence is our resistance – no, not ours but God's resistance. Not a resistance against the intruding sounds but a resistance against the tyranny of false values, a resistance against the pressures of quick decisions, superficial opinions, unexamined fears, a resistance against the complex web of influences that tightens around us. St Paul said: 'Do not be conformed to this age but be transformed by the renewal of your mind.' The practice of prayer is not a fad, a personal hobby, an improvement to the quality of life. It is a fight for freedom, our own and that of others, an antidote against illusion and escapism and alienation, a struggle for human space and human ways of living. Think of the prayer, think of the silence in those positive terms even though it consists of a deliberate ceasing, letting go and inaction.

Three words in the Psalms speak of this quality of stillness. In Psalm 4.4, 'Commune with your own heart and be still,' the word means, Stand still. Be at rest like a sword returned to its scabbard (cf. Jer. 47.6). In Psalm 46.10, 'Be still and know that I am God,' it means, Let go. Drop it. The one who makes wars to cease, who breaks the bow and snaps the spear, says: Drop it, and know that I, not you, am God. Don't try to play God in this situation. Psalm 8.2 which speaks of 'stilling' the enemy and the avenger, employs an unusual word that means, literally, making them keep Sabbath. It means rest, knocking off.

Cessation of movement.
Cessation of effort and anxiety.
Cessation of busy-ness and noise.

The human frame and the human mind were not made for perpetual motion, yet that is what we are subjecting ourselves to. We have become the treadmill slaves of time and motion, restlessly straining forward from yesterday to tomorrow. We have so many things that have to be done. We are so desperate to keep up to time we never let it flow past us.

Our inner selves, our minds, are racing too. Our European habit of discursive argument which has spread across the world has now so monopolized the human mind that we are almost unable to remember or imagine any other way of using it. Discursive means running, running on from one thing to another: this being so, it follows that, therefore the next. Our thoughts run on – one damn thing after another – so that we find it almost impossible to hold our minds still and steady on one single point of reality. Even while we talk to a friend our minds are partly on something else, and of course the friend has noticed and it is not long before we for our part realize that that friend is not really listening. Neither of us is wholly there, completely present to the other, yet we both continue the conversation in a mutual absence. We have lost the gift of a total personal presence which I sometimes encountered in village Africa, where an adult or even a child might enter the room and squat on the floor with no more than an occasional exchange of words after the initial greeting, while I got on with whatever I was doing, until after half an hour or so of simply being together, the visitor would get up, saying, 'I have seen you,' and go. I can imagine that people who have not outgrown such simplicity would find it quite natural to sit, silent and attentive, in the presence of God for half an hour, saying only 'I have seen you' at the end. 'Blessed are the pure in heart; they shall see God.' We find it so difficult to become inwardly gathered, intent and still, because we are for ever whisking through the present moment, we almost never live in it. We are like champion sprinters in the hundred metres race, leaning forward, pushing our centre of gravity several yards ahead, so that if we suddenly became still we should fall flat on our faces. So the world around us, the reality of this present moment, is blurred, unclear, empty in fact, because we have already left it behind. And such a natural thing as simply being here and now has become incredibly unnatural to us. Yet which of those two ways of being is more like the being of God, whose name is 'I AM present where I am present'?

Simply being present to the presence of God is the basis of all other prayer. It is the form of prayer which we are in the greatest need of in this age, the form of prayer which is the surest resistance we can put up against the clamour of false values and false hopes, the one form of prayer which still makes sense for many people. It is the simplest kind of prayer, so that a child can take to it quite naturally, yet at first it is the hardest for us adults to adjust to because we are strangers to silence and have forgotten how to let go, how to *be*.

Being is not doing. It is not thinking. As a start, then, let go of all the doing; leave it to God. Let go the thinking. This does not mean making your mind a blank; that is merely a technique and a dangerous one at that. This has nothing to do with techniques, nothing to do with human effort. Just let go of your thinking or not thinking. Hand it back to God, and with it all those words. We are deafened with words and deceived by words. We need silence.

Think of Michelangelo's painting of the creation of Adam on the ceiling of the Sistine Chapel: just the two figures apart from a few delectable angel faces. All the energy, all the will is in God's powerful outstretched arm and hand and finger tip. Adam has just awakened from non-existence. His whole being in utter repose, totally receptive, his hand is uplifted in complete dependence as he receives the gift of life. That is how it should be with anyone who becomes present to the presence of God. For the body, Brother Ass, can be a strong ally when anyone sets about finding this inner stillness. Letting the tension go from each limb in turn; sitting or walking in such a posture that no muscle is called on to do all the work; and then breathing just a little more slowly, a little more deeply, but not so much as to become a distraction; all these can help the mind and the inner self to slow down and let go. If the mind insists on pacing from point to point like a caged beast, give it something to focus upon, something to watch rather than to think about: a candle flame, a well-shaped stone or glass bowl of clear water. Or let it dwell on the rhythm of one's own breathing with a few repetitive words to match: '*Ab'ba*-Father' or 'Jesus, Son of the Living God – have mercy on me a sinner.'

As one naturally, easily, becomes aware of the silence, into which the instrusive sounds dart and disappear like fish in a pool, the silence becomes more than an absence of sound. It becomes an enveloping substance, the substance that is always there throughout the entire universe. And in the silence, as close as the silence, is the presence of God.

It does not always come as easily as that suggests. Because we have accustomed ourselves to rely so heavily on our activities to define who we are, doing nothing but simply being brings us an intolerable feeling of emptiness like the boredom of a child of my own generation condemned to that dreadful half-hour's rest on a bed every afternoon.

That inner emptiness can grow to a great anguish of spirit. It can throw us into self-hatred or it can make us run back the way we have come into the familiar unreality and self-deception of noise and busyness and speed. But there is no need for us to take either of those desperate courses if we will only believe what already we intuitively know – that the God at the heart of the silence loves us already as we are. It is our need of that love that draws us to seek him in the silence. It is that love that enfolds us in the silence. It is to that love that we respond without words. Because of that love God longs to make us more real, to change our empty self into authentic being, to see what is boring changed into rich life. But whether we change or not makes no difference to his love for us because that is unconditional. The assurance of that love is what we receive in the silence: it has to be silence because it is beyond words.

What God loves is nothing but the whole – the whole self in the whole situation. That and nothing less is what is present to God: *all* present. Making a present to God of one's whole self, that is love for God. Being all present, all *now*, that is love for God. This entails calling in one's self from the past, the regrets and resentments and scars, and presenting them to the eyes of his love. It entails calling in one's self from the future, the day-dreams, the fears, the ambitions, and presenting them, leaving them with him. It entails calling in the self from beyond the pale, the self that would properly be banned from one's autobiography but is a true part of the one God loves.

Does this make it all sound enormously self-indulgent? In the face of the whole world's need and suffering, perplexity and sin, should not a follower of Christ be doing something more responsible and more caring than fussily concentrating on the cultivation of his or her own spirituality?

Experience gives the answer to this. If I open myself to God, if I can become present to his presence, then whatever I bring with me and whatever attaches itself to me while I am there is held steady before his gaze, open to his love because it is a part of my reality at that moment. I hear Big Ben strike the hour and I am momentarily aware of the Lords and the Commons who will be sitting there again next week. My flicker of anxiety, the tiny sinking of the heart, which is actually an authentic expression of what they mean to me, has not escaped the all-seeing eyes of love before which I stand. God does not need me to inform him about what may be at stake there, and a recitation of the prayer for the High Court of Parliament would not actually say as much as my brief spontaneous reaction. My silence is broken by the siren of an ambulance racing towards the hospital. For an instant the fear, the pain, perhaps the last moments, of an unknown fellow traveller have invaded my heart and are held there before God. People argue whether God allows himself to intervene in the processes of the world. What I do know is that God allows the processes of the world to intervene while I am intent upon him so that I am at least one little door through which they burst straight into his presence. I have also found that when I do, all too seldom, let me say, enter the loving silence of God, all sorts of people, some who are very close, some whom I have long forgotten, steal in uninvited through my memory and sit with us without disturbing the silence. The prayer of silence is a form of intercession with a quality all its own because it is completely spontaneous, and gives God a chance to suggest whom and what we might pray for. But it is also completely incidental. You are there to be with God to receive and to give back love and truth and understanding. Like every real exchange of love, it overflows and others are enfolded in it.

Thinking about God and loving God, thinking further and loving more, is a pendulum of wonder and incomprehension, illumination and darkness, loss and possession, abasement and bliss which, once started, must continue for ever as we move on into the infinity of God. For all eternity we shall be travelling further and further into the knowledge and love of this God who is our home and our rest, and every step forward will bring us closer to everyone and everything that is included in God's love, since the deeper we go into God and God into us the more we share in God's in-othering in all else. To call him the Christlike God is the supremest truth we can ever learn about his nature and it certainly does not reduce him to our human scale or fit him into the small grasp of our finite apprehension. For God is the Beyond whom we recognize in all things but can never see or reach.

Notes

1. When I was a Child

1. *The Cloud of Unknowing* ed. from the British Museum MS with an introduction by Evelyn Underhill, 5th edn, John M. Watkins 1950, p. 77.

2. Ibid., p. 25.

3. Martin Luther, *The Book of Concord*, tr. T. G. Tappert, Fortress Press, Phildelphia 1949, p. 364.

4. Roger Hooker, *Voices of Varanasi*, Church Missionary Society 1979, p. 108.

5. John Macquarrie, *In Search of Deity*, SCM Press and Crossroad Publishing Co., New York 1984, pp. 18f.

6. *Believing in the Church*, SPCK 1981, and *We Believe in God*, Church House Publishing 1987.

7. Louis Jacobs, *A Jewish Theology*, Darton Longman and Todd 1973, p. 211.

8. From the Elucidation in *The Final Report* of the Anglican-Roman Catholic International Commission, SPCK and Catholic Truth Society 1982, pp. 70f.

9. Kenneth Cragg, *Jesus and the Muslim*, George Allen and Unwin 1985, p. 130.

10. Quoted by Gershom Scholem, *The Messianic Idea in Judaism and Other Essays on Jewish Spirituality*, George Allen and Unwin 1971, p. 283.

2. What we have Heard, What we have Seen

1. *We Believe in God – a Report of the Doctrine Commission of the General Synod of the Church of England*, Church House Publishing 1987, pp. 8f.

2. Rowan Williams, from a book review in *The Tablet*, 24 June 1989, p. 730.

3. Barbara Hepworth, 'Sculpture', an article in *Circle* ed. Martin, Nicholson and Gabo, Faber 1937, p. 113.

4. Edith Sitwell, *Collected Poems*, Macmillan 1957, p. 306.

5. Martin Buber, *I and Thou*, T. & T. Clark 1937; paperback edn 1966, p. 32.

6. Quoted by Sir Alister Hardy in *The Spiritual Nature of Man*, OUP 1979 (reprinted 1984), p. 85.

7. Ninian Smart, *The Religious Experience of Mankind*, Collins Fontana 1971, pp. 366f.

8. From an interview reported in *Living the Questions* ed. Edward Robinson, Religious Experience Research Unit, Westminster College, Oxford 1978, p. 113.

9. Ludwig Wittgenstein, *Culture and Value* ed. G. G. Von Wright, ET Blackwell 1980, p. 24.

10. David Hume, *Essays*, xxiii, 'The Standard of Taste', OUP 1963, p. 234.

11. William Blake, 'The Marriage of Heaven and Hell', *The Complete Writings* ed. Geoffrey Keynes, OUP 1966, p. 154.

12. Quoted by Edward Robinson in *The Original Vision*, Religious Experience Research Unit, Westminster College, Oxford 1977, p. 49.

13. William Wordsworth, 'Ode on Intimations of Immortality', *The Poetical Works*, OUP 1928, p. 587.

14. Thomas Traherne, Century iii.3, *Centuries, Poems and Thanksgivings* ed. H. M. Margoliouth, OUP 1958, Vol. I, p. 111.

15. From the transcript of a talk broadcast on the Home Service of the BBC in February 1961, reproduced in *New Fire* (SSJE Oxford) Vol. VIII, No. 60, Autumn 1984, p. 137.

16. Richard Jefferies, *The Story of My Heart*, Longman Green, pocket edition 1907.

17. Quoted in *Living the Questions*, pp. 134f.

18. P. J. Kavanagh, interview transcript in *Revelations – Glimpses of Reality* ed. Ronald S. Lello, Shepheard-Walwyn Ltd and Border Television plc 1985, pp. 49f.

19. Naum Gabo, Letter to Herbert Read, 1942, published in *Horizon* (London) Vol. X, No. 53, July 1944, quoted in *The Image of Life*, Brenda Lealman and Edward Robinson, Christian Education Movement, London 1980, pp. 12, 14.

20. Edwin Muir, *Collected Poems*, Faber and Faber Ltd 1960, pp. 198f.

21. Quoted by David Hay in *Religious Experience Today*, Mowbray 1990, p. 48.

22. C. E. M. Joad, *God and Evil*, Faber 1942, p. 268.

23. From the archives of the Alister Hardy Research Centre, Westminster College, Oxford, account no. 1153.

24. Ibid., account no. 583.

25. Quoted in *The Original Vision*, p. 37.

26. Quoted from the Alister Hardy Research Centre archives (no. 48) by Geoffrey Ahern in *Spiritual/Religious Experience in Modern Society*, a pilot study submitted to the Centre, 1990, p. 35.

27. Quoted by David Hay in *Religious Experience Today*, Mowbray 1990, p. 45.

28. Peter L. Berger, *A Rumour of Angels*, Penguin 1969, p. 72.

29. P. J. Kavanagh, op. cit., p. 48.

30. Ibid., p. 51.

31. Karl Rahner, *Foundations of Christian Faith*, Darton Longman and Todd 1978, p. 32.

32. Sheila Cassidy, interview transcript in *Revelations – Glimpses of Reality*, op. cit., pp. 17–19.

33. William James, '*The Varieties of Religious Experience*, Longmans Green 1919, pp. 470f.

34. In the Mishnah, *Ta'anit* 3.88 and *Aboth* 3.3. The later Midrash (Genesis Rabbah 68–9) explains the term with the words, 'He is the place of the world, but the world is not His place.'

35. Austin Farrer, 'The Christian Apologist' in *Light on C. S. Lewis* ed. J. Gibb, Harcourt, Brace and World, New York 1966, p. 40.

36. Dietrich Bonhoeffer, *Ethics*, SCM Press and the Macmillan Co., New York 1955, p. 1.

37. W. H. Auden, *A Certain World – a commonplace book*, Faber 1971, p. 331.

38. Abhishiktananda, *Saccidananda*, ISPCK, Delhi 1974, pp. 19f.

39. Austin Farrer, *Said or Sung*, Faith Press 1960, p. 139.

40. *The Original Vision*, p. 73.

3. When I Consider

1. The two usages of the syllable *el* or *eil*, either as the name of God or as a more primitive term meaning numinous power, imparts to some phrases in the Old Testament an ambiguity which is reflected in the words into which different English versions of the Bible have translated them. A familiar example is Genesis 1.2, where the phrase *ruach elohim* can mean either the spirit of God or an awesome wind. Similar phrases are: *arzei el* (Ps. 80.10): God's cedars or stupendous cedars; *ke-harerei eil* (Ps. 36.6): the mountains of God or the sublime mountains; *kokh'vei eil* (Isa. 14.13): stars of God or mysterious stars; *machaneh elohim* (I Chron. 12.22): the army of God or an army of gods or an overwhelming host. The probable meaning of *adat el* in Psalm 82.1 is the assembly of gods (see similarly Ps. 29.1), but because such a polytheistic image seems alien to the general teaching of the Bible, some have translated it as the divine council, others as the assembly of rulers. The idea of numinous power is clearly intended in the phrase *le-el yadi* or *le-el yadam*: the power of the hand (Gen. 31.29; Prov. 3.27; Neh. 5.5) which signifies an aura of authority as well as mere physical strength.

2. Rex Warner, *The Greek Philosophers*, Mentor Books 1959, p. 19.

3. Edward Robinson, *Living the Questions*, pp. 29–46.
4. Martin Buber, *Between Man and Man*, Collins Fontana 1961, pp. 41f.
5. J. A. T. Robinson, unpublished dissertation for PhD, quoted by Eric James, *A Life of Bishop John A. T. Robinson*, Collins 1987, p. 17.
6. See p. 28.
7. Brihad-aranyaka Upanishad 1.3.28, tr. Juan Mascaró, *The Upanishads*, Penguin 1965, p. 127.
8. Katha Upanishad 2.10, Mascaró, op. cit., p. 58.
9. Katha Upanishad 4.11, ibid., p. 63.
10. Quoted by Mary Lutyens, *Krisnamurti: The Years of Awakening*, John Murray 1975, p. 158.
11. Katha Upanishad 2.20, 22, Mascaró, op. cit., p. 59.
12. Brihad-aranyaka Upanishad 3.8.11, tr. R. C. Zaehner, *Hindu Scriptures*, Everyman Classics, Dent 1966, p. 57.
13. S. Radakrishnan, *The Bhagavadgita with an Introductory Essay*, Sanskrit text, English translation and Notes, George Allen and Unwin 1948, p. 77.
14. Dudley Fitts, *From the Greek Anthology – poems in English paraphrase*, Faber 1957, p. 70.
15. C. M. Bowra, *The Greek Experience*, Weidenfeld and Nicolson 1937, pp. 160f.
16. John Burnet, *Early Greek Philosophy*, 4th edition, Macmillan 1945, pp. 321ff.
17. Aristotle, *Metaphysics* XI.5.
18. James P. Mackey, *The Christian Experience of God as Trinity*, SCM Press and Crossroad Publishing Co., New York 1983, p. 120.
19. Elmer O'Brien, *The Essential Plotinus*, Mentor Books 1964, p. 41.

4. God With Us

1. C. M. Bowra, *The Greek Experience*, p. 147.
2. Jer. 2.6; 7.22; 11.3, 4; 16.14, 15; 31.31–34; 32.20–23; 34.13, 14.
3. Isa. 11.15, 16; 35.6–8; 40.3; 43.2–4; 52.4.
4. This shift of emphasis from the memory of God's action to the necessity for human action can be discerned also in the strands of narrative of different date that have been knitted together to make up the rescue story as we have it in the Book of Exodus. The earliest strand, called the Yahwist's account, which may have been written in the time of Elisha, presents the whole event as the direct action of God alone. Moses merely announces each forthcoming natural disaster to Pharoah and the next day Yahweh brings it to pass (Ex. 7.14, 15a, 16, 17a, 18, 21; 8.1–4, 8–15; 9.1–7, 18–21, 23b, 25b–34). The second strand, the Elohist's, written perhaps a century later, heightens the miraculous aspect

of the plagues and shifts more of the action to Moses with his rod (7.15b, 17b, 20b; 9.22, 23a, 24, 25). The latest strand in this part of the story, a version produced by a priestly school some time after the Jews had returned from the Exile, makes Aaron the active agent of God in a contest of power with Egyptian magicians (7.19–20a, 21b, 22; 8.5–7, 16–19; 9, 8–11). See also in chapter 8 of this work, pp. 210f.

5. Sec p. 47.

6. Terence E. Fretheim, *The Suffering of God: An Old Testament Perspective*, Fortress Press, Philadelphia 1984, p. 25.

7. B. S. Childs, *Exodus*, SCM Press and Westminster Press, Philadelphia 1974, p. 69.

8. 'Ich werde da sein, als der ich da sein werde.' Martin Buber quoted in Edmond Jacob, *The Theology of the Old Testament*, Hodder and Stoughton 1974, p. 53n.

9. Edmond Jacob, op. cit., p. 273.

10. Gen. 3.22; Ex. 22.29; Deut. 10.17; 33.2; I Kings 22.19; Job 2.6; 38.7; Pss 86.8; 95.3; 96.4; 138.1; and in this general context read Ps. 82 in full.

11. Hans Küng, *Does God Exist?* Collins and Doubleday, New York 1980; reissued SCM Press 1991, pp. 617f.

12. Typical examples from the Old Testament are Isa. 13.6–16; Zeph. 1; Hab. 3; and from later Jewish apocalyptic writing, Wisd. 3.6–8; Enoch 1–36.

13. All the biblical references bracketed a few lines above with reference to the dynasty of David look forward to a warrior Messiah. So also, much later, does the 17th of the Psalms of Solomon which was probably composed by members of the Pharisee party for use in the synagogue after Pompey's invasion of Palestine in 63 BC. The well-known vision of the Son of Man and the holy ones of the Most High in Daniel 7 would have symbolized a historical person or persons, just as did the monstrous beasts that are described first, and may have pointed to the victorious heroes of the Maccabean revolt in the mid-second century BC. Hopes of a warrior Messiah persisted through the first century BC, e.g. IV Ezra 10.60–12.35 and the Apoc. of Baruch 27–29; 36–40; 53–74.

14. The prophecy in Ezek. 34.24, 25 and 37.24–26 fastens on the image of David as shepherd rather than war-lord. Zech. 1–6 clearly points to Jeshua the Levitical priest (either singly or jointly with Zerubbabel of the tribe of Judah, the secular governor) as the promised Messiah, the branch of David's stem. The familiar passage about the king riding on an ass (Zech. 9.9–14) stresses the humility of the priest-king (vv. 6–13), even though it goes on to threaten the Greeks of the later period with slaughter. The commentary on Habakkuk among the Dead Sea Scrolls shows that the Qumran community believed that God would send them two Messiahs, one priestly and one a warrior.

15. The last chapter of the apocryphal book of Tobit prophesies the building

of a greater temple and the voluntary conversion of the Gentiles, but 'not until the times of the age are completed' (Tob. 14.5, 6). No messianic figure is mentioned here, nor in the visions of the end of all things in the last section of the Book of Enoch (chs 91–104).

16. Gershom Scholem, *The Messianic Idea in Judaism and other essays in Jewish spirituality*, George Allen and Unwin 1976, p. 6.

17. The section of the Book of Enoch, known as the Similitudes (chs 37–71), was at one time thought to have been the main source from which Jesus himself and the earliest Christians drew their imagery of the heavenly Son of Man who was to come on the clouds of heaven. Rudolph Otto based his book *The Kingdom of God and the Son of Man* upon that surmise. But now many scholars believe that the Similitudes were written after the time of Jesus. Whereas the other sections of the Book of Enoch have been found among the Dead Sea scrolls, those chapters 37–71 have not. It seems more likely that their author was influenced by early Christian teaching than the other way round. (See R. N. Longenecker, *The Christology of Early Jewish Christianity*, SCM Press 1970, pp. 82–93.) The same must be said of the book called II Esdras in the Apocrypha, which also speaks of the Messiah as a supernatural being 'whom the Most High has held in readiness during many ages' and who 'flew with the clouds of heaven' (II Esd. 13). The only extant apocryphal writing portraying a heavenly Messiah that may have been in circulation at the time of Jesus is an earlier section of the Book of Enoch, chapters 83–90. It begins to look as if the image of the heavenly Messiah awaiting his moment to appear as judge and king, which St Paul depicts in the earliest of his epistles (I Thess. 4.16, 17), was the product of Jesus' own adoption of the role of the Son of Man from Daniel 7, reinterpreted by his disciples on the strength of his resurrection and exaltation, though there must have been some supporting notion of heavenly messiahship already in circulation to make it plausible.

18. J. A. T. Robinson, *The Priority of John*, SCM Press 1985; J. B. Lightfoot, *Biblical Essays*, London and New York 1893, pp. 1–198; C. H. Dodd, *Historical Tradition in the Fourth Gospel*, CUP 1963; A. M. Hunter, *According to John*, SCM Press and Westminster Press, Philadelphia 1968; T. W. Manson, *Studies in the Gospels and Epistles* ed. M. Black, Manchester University Press and Philadelphia 1962, pp. 105–122; R. E. Brown, *The Gospel according to John*, Geoffrey Chapman 1971, Vol. 1 pp. xxiv-xxix, xcviii-cii.

19. Leslie Houlden, 'The Creed of Experience' in *The Myth of God Incarnate* ed. John Hick, SCM Press and Westminster Press, Philadelphia 1977, p. 130.

20. Flavius Josephus, *Antiquities of the Jews*, x. 267f.

21. See C. F. D. Moule, *The Origin of Christology*, CUP 1977, pp. 13–17.

22. Some scholars have regarded this incident as a post-resurrection appearance rather than something that occurred during the period of Jesus' ministry,

and have suggested that it became displaced as the stories were passed on orally. The weakness of this theory lies in the fact that none of the resurrection appearances are marked by unearthly radiance, as might have been expected; on the contrary it is the normality of the risen Jesus that is stressed. On the other hand, the accounts of the Transfiguration belong to the same category as other numinous experiences.

23. Thomas Blackburn, 'A Broken Image', from *Selected Poems*, Hutchinson 1975, p. 84.

24. The only real exception is the exclamation of Thomas, 'My Lord and my God' (John 20.28) which, as an impulsive avowal of personal adoration rather than a theological statement, exactly reproduces the position of the disciples. Other instances all fall short of the simple identification, Jesus is God. John 1.1 speaks of the eternal Word, while II Thess. 1.12, Titus 2.13, and II Peter 1.1 should probably be read as naming God and Jesus as separate entities.

25. A. M. Ramsey, *God, Christ and the World*, SCM Press 1969, p. 98.

5. How Shall This Be?

1. Plato, *Timaeus* 41 C.

2. Id., *Phaedrus* 2470 E.

3. Id., *Timaeus* 28 C.

4. Id., *Sophist* 249 A.

5. Justin, *Apology I* 61.11.

6. Clement of Alexandria, *Stromateis* V.12.

7. Gregory of Nyssa, *Sixth Homily on the Beautitudes*.

8. Werner Heisenberg, *Physics and Beyond*, George Allen and Unwin 1971, p. 41.

9. John of Damascus, *The Fount of Knowledge*, Pt III. Ch. iv., PG 94, col. 800.

10. John Eriugena, *Periphyseon* 680 D.

11. Nicholas Lash, *Easter in Ordinary*, SCM Press and University of Virginia Press 1988, p. 232.

12. Abraham J. Heschel, *The Prophets*, Harper and Row, New York 1962, p. 227.

13. Justin, *Dialogue with Trypho* 61.1.

14. Id., *Apology I* 32.4.

15. Origen, *On First Principles* 1.2.8.

16. Henry Chadwick, *Early Christian Thought and the Classical Tradition*, OUP 1966; paperback edn 1984, p. 16.

17. See also Justin, *Apology I* 13.3 and *Apology II* 6.2.

18. Tertullian, *Against Praxeas* 7.

19. Origen, *On First Principles* 4.1.2.

20. Id., *Commentary on the Gospel of St John* 13.25.

21. Athanasius, *Orations against the Arians* 2.25.

22. Didymus the Blind, *On the Trinity* 2.6.4.

23. Gregory of Nyssa, *Treatise to Ablabius – 'That there are not three Gods'.*

24. Gregory of Nazianzus, *Oration 34* MG 36, 352A.

25. Origen, *On Prayer* 1.1.

26. Athanasius, *On the Incarnation of the Word* 3.

27. Id., *Treatise against the heathen* 2.

28. Gregory of Nyssa, *Sixth Homily on the Beatitudes.*

29. Aquinas, *Summa Theologica* 1a., Q.12, art. 1. Here and elsewhere I have used the concise translation ed. Timothy McDermott, Methuen 1989, for greater clarity.

30. Gregory of Nyssa, *Catechetical Oration* 5.

31. Augustine, *On the Trinity* 14.6.

32. Aquinas, op. cit., 1a, Q.12, art. 4.

33. Augustine, *Confessions* X, paras 12–25.

34. Aquinas, op. cit., 1a, Q.85, arts 1–2; Q.87, art. 1.

35. Karl Rahner, *Hearers of the Word*, Seabury Press, New York 1969.

36. Abhishiktananda, *Saccidananda*, ISPCK, Delhi 1974, p. 4.

37. Karl Rahner, *Foundations of Christian Faith*, tr. W. V. Dych, Darton, Longman and Todd 1978, p. 217.

38. Ibid., p. 222.

39. Irenaeus, *Against the Heretics*, iv. 20.7.

40. Austin Farrer in *A Celebration of Faith*, Hodder and Stoughton 1970, p. 61.

41. Karl Rahner, *Theological Investigations*, Vol. 5, Darton, Longman and Todd and Crossroad Publishing Co., New York 1966, p. 467.

42. Arthur Peacocke, *God and the New Biology*, Dent 1986, p. 11.

43. Gregory of Nyssa, *Catechetical Oration* 25.

44. Aquinas, op. cit., 1a, Q.8, art. 2.

45. John Macquarrie, the supreme exponent of this insight, is careful to avoid the static character of the analogy of God as holy Being by insisting that 'any adequate notion of being includes becoming' (*Principles of Christian Theology*, SCM Press and Macmillan Co., New York, revd edn 1977, p. 196 and n. 13.

46. L. Charles Birch, *Nature and God*, SCM Press 1965, p. 94.

47. St Symeon the New Theologian (tenth century), *Hymn XIII*, 11.71–74, 78–80, Sources Chrétiennes No. 156, p. 262, tr. Kallistos Ware.

48. Dietrich Bonhoeffer, *Akt und Sein – Transzentalphilosophie und Ontologie in der systematischen Theologie*, 2nd edn Münich 1956, p. 94.

49. Karl Rahner, *Foundations of Christian Faith*, p. 63.

50. *We Believe in God – A report by the Doctrine Commission of the Church of England*, Church House Publishing 1987, pp. 108f.

51. Irenaeus, *Against the Heretics* iv. 20.4.

52. Origen, *On Prayer* X.2; cf. Athanasius, *Against the Arians* 3.24: 'Our being in the Father is not ours but is the Spirit's who is in us and dwells in us.'

53. Athanasius, *First Letter to Serapion* 6, 9, 12, 14, 20, 24, 28, 30, 31.

54. Ludwig Wittgenstein, *Tractatus Logico – Philosophicus* 7.

55. Basil, Letter ccxxxvi.10.

56. 'Identity', of course, may be no less ambiguous since it can also mean 'being the same', but I think the context would always make the sense clear. If, as it seems, the verbal adventure is fated, this only increases one's esteem for those who first made the attempt.

57. Basil, Letter CCX.5.

58. Augustine, *On the Trinity* VIII.12.14.

59. See p. 71 above.

60. Augustine, *On the Trinity* 5.3.

61. Aquinas, op. cit. 1a, Q.9, art.1; 3a, Q.2, art.1.

62. Gregory of Nyssa, *Funeral Oration for Placilla* PG 46.888D; *Life of Moses* PG 44.405 C-D; *Song of Songs, Sermon 5* 865A – 868A and 873C–876C.

63. John Eriugena, *Periphyseon* 453A.

64. Ibid., 432D.

65. Irenaeus, *Against the Heretics* III.18.3, 4, 6.

66. Athanasius, *Tome to the People of Antioch* 7; *Against the Arians* 3.30.

67. Tertullian, *Against Praxeas* 27.5.

68. T. Schleiermacher, *Dogmatics* 96.1.

69. Tertullian, op. cit. 27.7 and Athanasius, *Against the Arians* 2.53f; 3.20, 30, 34.

70. Athanasius, ibid. 3.34.

71. Gregory of Nyssa, *Against Eunomius* 5.5.

72. Aquinas, op. cit., 3a, Q.21, art. 1.

73. Athanasius, *Epistle to Epictetus* 5/6; Cyril of Alexandria, *Epistle to Nestorius* III; Aquinas, op. cit., 2a 2ae, Q.112, art. 1; 3a, Q.19, art. 1.

74. Cyril of Alexandria, *Epistle* 17.8.

75. Aquinas, op. cit., 3a, Q.4, art. 1.

76. J. H. Newman, *Select Treatises on St Athanasius*, Vol. 2, 2nd edn Pickering 1881, p. 293.

77. Abraham Heschel, op. cit., p. 257.

78. Wolfhart Pannenberg, *Jesus – God and Man*, SCM Press and Westminster Press, Philadelphia 1968, p. 339.

79. See above, p. 104.

80. Tertullian, *On the Flesh of Christ* 3.5.

81. Hilary, *On the Trinity* 9.3, 4.

82. T. S. Eliot, 'Seneca in Elizabethan translation' (1927) in *Selected Essays*, Faber 1932, p. 104.

83. See above, pp. 116f.

84. Athanasius, *On the Incarnation* 41.

85. Gregory of Nyssa, *Catechetical Oration* 25.

86. Herbert McCabe OP, 'The Involvement of God', article in *New Blackfriars*, Vol. 66, No. 785, November 1985, p. 469.

87. Wolfhart Pannenberg, *Basic Questions in Theology* Vol. 2, SCM Press and Fortress Press, Philadelphia 1971, pp. 161f.

88. Karl Rahner, *Foundations of Christian Faith*, p. 224.

89. Aquinas, op. cit, 1a, Q.23, art. 2.

90. Ibid., 1a, Q.13, art. 7.; 1a, Q.45, art. 3.

91. Abraham Heschel, op. cit., p. 224 (italics mine).

92. Aquinas, op. cit., 1a, Q.21, art. 3.

93. J. Maritain, article in *Revue thomiste* 1969.

94. Origen, *Homily on Numbers* xxiii.2.

95. Hilary, *On the Trinity* 10.23.

96. Aquinas, op. cit. 3a, Q.47, art. 1.

97. Augustine, *On Marriage and Concupiscence* i.28; *Confessions* x.43–56.

98. Baron Friedrich von Hügel, *Essays and Addresses on the Philosophy of Religion*, Dent 1926, p. 200.

99. Melito, *Homily on the Passover* 69–71.

100. Origen, *Homily on Ezekiel* 6.6.

101. Aquinas, op. cit., 1a, Q.25, art. 2.

102. John Macquarrie, *The Humility of God*, SCM Press and Westminster Press, Philadelphia 1978, p. 65.

103. Austin Farrer, *Said or Sung*, Faith Press 1960, pp. 34f.

104. François Varillon, *La souffrance de Dieu*, Editions du Centurion, Lyon 1975, pp. 16f.

6. And All the Prophets

1. Gershom Scholem, *The Messianic Idea in Judaism and other essays in Jewish spirituality*, George Allen and Unwin 1976, p. 19.

2. Edmond Jacob, *Theology of the Old Testament*, Hodder and Stoughton 1958, p. 38.

3. G. Scholem, op. cit. p. 1.

4. It appears from I Chron. 8.33f. that the true names of Jonathan's son and stepbrother respectively were Merib-baal and Ish-baal, reflecting the syncretism of a period when the name *baal*, lord, was applied to Yahweh. The compilers of

the books of Samuel and Kings expressed their disapproval by replacing *baal* with *bosheth*, 'a thing of shame'.

5. Abraham Heschel, *The Prophets*, Harper and Row, New York 1962, pp. 57–59.

6. Terence E. Fretheim, *The Suffering of God: An Old Testament Perspective*, Fortress Press, Philadelphia 1984, pp. 47 and 49–51.

7. Abraham Heschel, op. cit., pp. 188f.

8. Ibid., p. 198.

9. Ibid., p. 285.

10. Ibid., p. 280.

11. See above p. 80.

12. Heschel, op. cit., p. 308.

13. Fretheim, op. cit., pp. 130–137.

14. Phyllis Trible, *God and the Rhetoric of Sexuality*, Fortress Press, Philadelphia 1978 and SCM Press, London 1992, pp. 40–50.

15. Extract from 'Dialogue of a man weary of life with his soul', *The Literature of Ancient Egypt* ed. W. K. Simpson, Yale University Press 1972, pp. 270f.

16. Sophocles, *Philoctetes*, from *Electra and other plays*, tr. E. F. Watling, Penguin Classics 1953, p. 208.

17. Euripides, *The Trojan Women*, tr. F. Kinchin Smith, Sidgwick and Jackson 1951, p. 47.

18. Luke 13.34–35, cf. 19.42–44 AV.

19. From 'The Ruins of Lo-Yang' by Ts'ao Chieh (AD 192–232) in *Chinese Poems*, tr. Arthur Waley, George Allen and Unwin 1946, pp. 79f.

20. Shakespeare, *King Lear*, V.iii.259–263.

21. Alan Paton, *Cry, the Beloved Country*, Jonathan Cape 1948, p. 76.

22. Fretheim, op. cit., p. 55 and see p. 131.

23. E. L. Mascall, *The Openness of Being*, Darton, Longman and Todd 1971, p. 162.

24. Heschel, op. cit., p. 307.

25. Ibid., pp. 57–59.

26. W. Macneile Dixon, *Tragedy*, Edward Arnold 1924, p. 220.

27. Jean Anouilh, *Antigone* tr. Lewis Gelantière, Methuen 1960, pp. 58f.

28. Kazoh Kitamori, *Theology of the Pain of God*, SCM Press 1966, pp. 135f.

29. Fretheim, op. cit., p. 150.

30. See above, p. 123.

7. God Saw that it was Good

1. *Mister God, This is Anna*, © Fynn 1974, published by Fount, an imprint of HarperCollins Publishers Ltd, p. 41.

2. Ibid.

3. Laurens van der Post, *The Heart of the Hunter*, Hogarth Press 1961, p. 152.

4. Austin Farrer, *A Science of God?*, Bles 1966, p. 74.

5. Wordsworth, *Poems of the Imagination* xi, 'A slumber did my spirit seal'.

6. Arthur Peacocke, *God and the New Biology*, Dent 1986, p. 120.

7. I. Prigogine and I. Stengers, *Order out of Chaos*, Heinemann 1984, pp. 156, 159.

8. R. Riedl, *Die Strategie der Genesis: Naturgeschichte der realen Welt*, Münich-Zürich 1976, p. 122, quoted by Hans Küng, *Does God Exist?* Collins 1980; SCM Press 1991, p. 645. See also Peacocke, op. cit., pp. 62f. and 97–100.

9. Farrer, op. cit., p. 76.

10. Austin Farrer, *Saving Belief*, Hodder and Stoughton 1964, pp. 52f.

11. C. Day Lewis, 'Walking Away', *The Complete Poems of C. Day Lewis*, Sinclair-Stevenson 1992, p. 546.

12. Jürgen Moltmann, *The Trinity and the Kingdom of God*, SCM Press 1981, pp. 109f.

13. Simone Weil, *Intimations of Immortality among the Ancient Greeks*, Routledge and Kegan Paul 1957, p. 192.

14. Simone Weil, *First and Last Notebooks*, OUP 1970, p. 120.

15. Rev. 13.8. In this verse the phrase 'from the foundation of the world', with which the verse ends, can be applied either to 'the Lamb that was slain' as the older English versions have done, or to 'whose names have not been written' as the more recent versions have done. The first is the more straightforward rendering, the second is idiomatically quite possible. I prefer to believe that the divine self-sacrifice was pre-determined rather than the exclusion of particular human beings.

16. Gershom G. Scholem, *Major Trends in Jewish Mysticism*, Schoken, Jerusalem 1941, p. 261.

17. Ibid., p. 258.

18. Miracles, so far from evoking faith as they once did, have become a serious obstacle to faith in our time, and 'walking on water' has become a classic caricature of all pretensions to supernatural power. Rather than dismissing the story as a stumbling block, it is possible to read it as a quite natural event. The Fourth Gospel says, 'They saw Jesus walking on the sea (*epi tes thalasses*) and nearing the ship.' The same Gospel uses the same phrase in John 21.1 to mean 'beside the sea'. According to Mark Jesus had ordered the disciples to make for Bethsaida some three miles up the coast from the probable site of the feeding of the multitude, and this accords with the fact that he could keep them in sight from the hills even under the fitful moon of a stormy night (Mark 6.45, 49). It could be that Jesus set out in the small hours along the water's edge intending to meet the ship at the pre-arranged landfall which would make sense of the

perplexing statement, also in Mark, that 'he was going to pass by them'. In the heavy seas they may have been nearer to the shore than they thought, and the sudden glimpse of a man standing so close over the waves could well terrify them. Peter, realizing that the figure who seemed to be striding the water was none other than Jesus wading through the shallows, might characteristically have plunged from the ship, only to be overwhelmed in the undertow until Jesus dragged him to safety. And, as John adds, no sooner were they ready to take Jesus aboard than the ship was at the place they were making for. That, of course, is not how the evangelists came to tell the story, and, if we choose, we can accept it, as C. S. Lewis did, as a miracle of the new creation, a momentary foretaste of that new Nature that the resurrection of Jesus inaugurated. Either way, the incident presents a striking picture of real danger, helplessness and triumphant power.

19. Karl Rahner, *Theological Investigations* tr. David Bourke, Vol. 10, Darton, Longman and Todd 1973, p. 250.

20. Moltmann, op. cit., p. 108.

21. Andrew Elphinstone, *Freedom, Suffering and Love*, SCM Press 1976, p. 106.

22. Khalil Gibran, *The Prophet*, Heinemann 1926, pp. 36f.

23. Baron Friedrich von Hügel, *Essays and Addresses on the Philosophy of Religion*, Second Series, Dent 1926, pp. 198f.

24. Nicolas Berdyaev, *Freedom and the Spirit*, Bles 1935, pp. 161f.

25. Elphinstone, op. cit., p. 135.

26. Ibid., p. 127.

27. Ibid., p. 140.

28. Ibid., p. 147.

29. Oh thou, who Man of baser Earth didst make
And who with Eden didst devise the Snake;
For all the sin wherewith the Face of Man
Is blackened, Man's forgiveness give – and take!
from *The Ruba'iyat* tr. Edward Fitzgerald

8. Where is Now Thy God?

1. Hans Küng, *Does God Exist?* Collins and Doubleday 1980; SCM Press 1991, p. 654.

2. Aquinas, *Summa Theologica* 1a.Q 105 art. 5.

3. See above, pp. 158f.

4. Ex. 19; 20; 24; 32.1–34.9.

5. John Wain, *Weep before God*, Macmillan 1961, p. 5.

6. Austin Farrer, *A Science of God?*, Bles 1966, pp. 77f.

7. Arthur Peacocke, *Creation and the World of Science*, OUP 1979, pp. 105f.

8. *The Collected Poems of Wilfred Owen* ed. C. Day Lewis, Chatto and Windus 1964, pp. 44f. and 185–188.

9. T. J. Gorringe, *God's Theatre. A Theology of Providence*, SCM Press 1991, p. 86.

10. Thomas F. Tracy, 'Narrative Theology and the acts of God' in *Divine Action – studies in the philosophical theology of Austin Farrer* ed. Brian Hebblethwaite and Edward Henderson, T. & T. Clark 1990, p. 192. For this section I am indebted also to Rodger Forsman's chapter, ' "Double Agency" and identifying reference to God' in the same book.

11. Peter Brook, *The Empty Space*, McGibbon and Kee 1968; Penguin edn 1972, p. 43; quoted in T. J. Gorringe, op. cit. p. 79.

12. Dorothy L. Sayers, *The Mind of the Maker*, Methuen 1941, p. 104.

13. Ibid., pp. 62f.

14. Francis Bacon, *The Essays*, 16 'Of Atheism', ed. John Pitcher, Penguin 1985, p. 108.

15. Sayers, op. cit., p. 67.

16. Elie Wiesel, *Night*, Penguin 1981, pp. 75f.

17. Narrated by her mother, Margaret Spufford, in the last of the series of articles in the 'Faith and Reason' column of *The Independent*, 18.11.89, arising from the publication of her book *Celebration*, Collins 1989.

18. In spite of the truth and beauty of the King James version of this passage which in Handel's setting can never be forgotten, the Hebrew text does not justify it. In fact the text of Job here and at other important points is very corrupt and the original sense has to guessed.

9. Dwell in Me, I in You

1. For the ideas in this paragraph and much else in this chapter I am indebted to Rosemary Haughton, *The Passionate God*, Darton Longman and Todd 1981.

2. Austin Farrer, *A Celebration of Faith*, Hodder and Stoughton 1970, p. 89.

3. Ibid., pp. 89f.

4. Martin Buber, *I and Thou*, T. & T. Clark 1937; paperback edn 1966, pp. 55f. See also Nicholas Lash, *Easter in Ordinary*, SCM Press and University of Virginia Press 1988, p. 186.

5. Lash, op. cit., p. 192.

6. 'Bors to Elayne: On the King's Coins' (from *Taliessin through Logres*), *The Arthurian Poems of Charles Williams*, Boydell and Brewer 1982, pp. 44f.

7. Charles Williams, 'The Way of Exchange' (originally James Clarke 1941), reprinted in *The Image of the City and other essays*, selected and introd. Anne Ridler, OUP 1958, p. 153.

8. Ibid., p. 149.

9. First published in *Time and Tide*, December 1940; reprinted in ibid. pp. 166ff.

10. Buber, op. cit., pp. 53, 112.

11. Buber, *Between Man and Man*, Collins 1961, pp. 241ff.

12. Ibid., p. 244.

13. Dante, *Il Paradiso*, lx.73–82.

14. Williams, *The Figure of Beatrice*, Faber and Faber Ltd 1943, p. 204.

15. Williams, *Descent into Hell*, Faber and Faber Ltd 1937, pp. 98ff.

16. Williams, *The Descent of the Dove*, Longmans Green 1939, p. 217.

17. Williams, *The Image of the City*, pp. 151f.

18. Ibid., p. 152.

19. Williams, *The Descent of the Dove*, p. 69.

20. Ibid., p. 28.

21. 'The Founding of the Company' (from *The Region of the Summer Stars*), *The Arthurian Poems of Charles Williams*, pp. 36ff.

22. Ibid., p. 38.

23. Ibid., p. 41.

24. Rosemary Haughton, op. cit., p. 249.

25. Ibid. p. 245.

10. Whose I Am, Whom I Serve

1. David Nicholls, 'The Invisible Hand: providence and the market', *The Values of the Enterprise Culture* ed. P. Heelas and P. Morris, Routledge 1992, p. 218. I am also indebted for what follows to Nicholls, *Deity and Domination*, Routledge 1989, pp. 80–84.

2. Dietrich Bonhoeffer, *Ethics*, SCM Press and the Macmillan Co., New York 1955, pp. 197f.

3. Ibid., p. 198.

4. Ibid., p. 200.

5. J. H. Yoder in an unpublished study prospectus, *Power and Powerlessness*, prepared for the World Council of Churches and the International Review of Mission in 1985.

6. Ibid.

7. Nicholls, *Deity and Domination*, p. 82.

8. Dietrich Bonhoeffer, *Letters and Papers from Prison*, The Enlarged Edition, SCM Press and the Macmillan Co., New York 1971, pp. 348f.

Index of Subjects

Index of Names